new orleans griot
the tom dent reader

University of New Orleans Press
Manufactured in the United States of America
All rights reserved
ISBN: 978-1-60801-149-0

Cover design: Kevin Stone
Interior design: Alex Dimeff

All photos courtesy of Amistad Research Center

This project is made possible by the generous support of
the New Orleans Jazz & Heritage Foundation

UNIVERSITY OF NEW ORLEANS PRESS
unopress.org

new orleans griot
the tom dent reader

by Tom Dent

edited by Kalamu ya Salaam
afterword by Jerry W. Ward, Jr.

PUBLISHER'S NOTE

The previous printing of this book contained an essay that was misattributed to Tom Dent. The essay, "In Search of Black Indians," was actually written by Jason Berry as a chapter draft he asked Tom to critique. The completed chapter, substantially longer and entitled "In Search of the Mardi Gras Indians," appears in the book Jason coauthored with Jonathan Foose and Tad Jones, *Up from the Cradle of Jazz: New Orleans Music Since World War II*. We deeply regret this error. A draft of the essay was among Tom's papers collected after his death, and it was mistaken for original work by Tom Dent. We have corrected the error in this edition.

A NOTE ON CAPITALIZATION

Over the course of his career, Dent vacillated in his capitalization of "[B/b]lack," whether as a noun or descriptor, sometimes even within the same piece of writing. While Dent does not comment directly on this stylistic choice, its political implications are complex. For clarity, we've standardized the dominant mode of capitalization within each of the individual works, but have left the overall inconsistency intact in order to let this suggestion of Dent's ideological grappling stand.

THE TOM DENT PAPERS

The Amistad Research Center is proud to house Tom Dent's personal papers and library as part of the Center's extensive literary collections. Tom's association with the Center dates back to the 1970s when he first donated a small number of his writings—poems and articles—to Amistad while it was housed on the campus of Dillard University. Additional correspondence, writings, and over 150 oral histories conducted by Tom were donated in 1991, with the remaining portion of his papers donated to Amistad from his estate following Tom's passing.

Tom's papers are like those of many writers—rich in correspondence with fellow authors, editors, and publishers, and contained poems, articles, and assorted writings in various draft forms. Adding to the scope of Tom's papers are his detailed journals and notebooks, files on various community projects he was involved with, photographs, and collected ephemera and publications, totaling close to 150 linear feet of material and over 1300 books and periodicals. The complexity of a collection like the Tom Dent Papers requires time and financial resources in order to organize and describe the materials according to professional archival standards. It was through the generous financial support of Tom's brothers, Walter and Benjamin, that the organization of Tom's papers was completed and made available to researchers around the world. Amistad staff who aided in the organization of Tom's papers include Laura Thomson, Florence Borders, and Laura Chilton. Today, the Tom Dent Papers are one of the most consulted collections at the Amistad Research Center.

contents

free southern theater/BLKARTSOUTH

new orleans

griot work

interviews

INTRODUCTION
from writer to Griot

Tom Dent was the first writer I ever consciously met.

The initial contact was in the Free Southern Theater's all-purpose auditorium, located in a concrete building on the corner of Louisa and Lauset in the Upper Ninth Ward, across the tracks from the infamous Desire Housing Projects. My girlfriend at the time had recommended the Free Southern Theater to me in early 1968, as I prepared to leave the army and return to civilian life in New Orleans. My re-entry was tumultuous. The young civil rights activist and college drop-out who had enlisted in 1965 under draft board duress was not the same as the young man returning, seasoned in both positive and negative ways by his military stint. But it was in this liminal time that I fell in love with Tom, who he was as a person as well as his day-to-day example of what it meant to be a writer and arts activist.

Undoubtedly because he had been reared in an upper-class home and educated at Morehouse College, one of the better institutions of higher education available to our people, Tom was easily able to follow mainstream manners and mores. But seeking to be what he wanted to be meant moving far away from the shelter, and shadow, of his father, who served as the president of Dillard University from 1941 to 1969. The rub, of course, was that regardless of what Tom wanted or willed himself to be, part of him was, and unavoidably remained, his father's child. As an example: all of his life, Tom owned and used a finely crafted ink pen, even though pencils and ballpoint pens were cheaply and readily available.

Given his upbringing, which emphasized propriety and responsibility, throughout his lifetime Tom grappled with the dueling
imperatives of what he deeply wanted to do and what he deeply
felt he *ought* to do. While these two motivations weren't always divergent, there were times when Tom was torn in two both personally and socially. He would ultimately refuse to choose one side
over the other, but this stance was achieved at a very high cost: his
marriage did not work out and, unlike his father and brothers, he
was never financially secure or celebrated by mainstream society.

But then Tom was never satisfied with simply knowing, doing,
and being known—he wanted to document and evaluate. With
the critical eye of a Frantz Fanon, he unsparingly inspected and
dissected himself along with the communities of which he was
part. This was no easy or conflict-free aspiration.

Although philosophically closer to King's non-violence and social reform than to Malcolm's militancy and revolutionary ardor,
Tom was nevertheless a staunch supporter of the black power philosophy: self-determination and self-respect for our people. As for
self-defense, the third element in the black power philosophical
triad, Tom, like his friend Ishmael Reed, advocated writing as
his chosen weapon for fighting. I never knew Tom to own a gun,
whereas when Tom and I initially hooked up, I owned a semi-au-
tomatic carbine that I often carried in the trunk of my car.

When I first met Tom, I had not published anything since high
school newspapers. I'd tell my mother I wanted to be a writer, but
I had no clue what a writer did besides literally write. Tom showed
me. By the end of 1968, I was Tom's eager apprentice, co-edit-
ing *Nkombo*, the literary magazine of our writing workshop. By
the summer of 1969, we had published five small poetry chap-
books. Tom threw himself headlong into all of these endeavors,
modeling a style of leadership that eschewed self-aggrandizement
and self-promotion.

Some may have seen in Tom's genteel bearing a Ghandi-like selflessness, a noble self-effacement rarely coupled with the vocation of writing. Especially within the bohemian atmosphere of the sixties, narcissism and the writer's life too often seemed to go hand-in-hand. Even those artists who avoided the vice of hogging the spotlight generally did not avoid the hubris of thinking themselves superior to the hoi polloi.

Tom's pedigree and education certainly seemed to set him apart from, if not socially above, the average black New Orleanian—but, much like Langston Hughes, Tom made the ordinary Joes and Jackies the focus of his life's work, in terms of both recruiting Free Southern Theater members and addressing his primary audience. Tom would wrestle to produce texts that were elegant as well as meaningful, for and about working-class black New Orleanians—not to the exclusion of anyone else, but certainly always keeping his folk at the conscious center of his work.

Tom taught me to love Black New Orleans—not simply to immerse myself in our dearly beloved culture, but to actually investigate and study the origins of it, including individual contributors. In a period when being loud and brash was de rigueur, through his quiet but unrelenting commitment, Tom modeled the fact that true love requires honest and serious intimacy, not just public displays of affection. I learned that relevance as a writer extended far beyond intellectual curiosity and perceptiveness. Our real work required actual contact with people.

For example, we believed that really embracing and writing about music—which we both regarded as a major, if not indeed the major, form of black cultural expression—required far more than just going to gigs or buying records. To fully know the music, we had to get to know the musicians, which in turn necessitated not just spending time in joints, bar rooms, and restaurants, but also going into their homes, into their front rooms, and eventually sitting at the kitchen table, regaling each other with tales of the good times and commiserating with each other through the ubiquitous not-so-good times.

This intimacy meant non-judgmentally consoling each other through the inevitable truly tough moments, such as when a parent died, a lover left, an illness or addiction incapacitated, an accident or robbery impoverished, debilitated, threatened or actually brought about death. In our work and ethos, Tom and I exemplified the inside secret to the clichéd, albeit accurate, "Big Easy attitude": that is, the classic stoic acceptance of life's disappointments through a sharing and celebration of what's good and beautiful about each other, and our relationships to one another.

Certainly I had decided to be a writer before I met Tom; certainly I was my own man. But Tom became more than a mentor, more than a friend. Tom became my father. Before Tom, I never consciously thought about what it meant to be a black New Orleanian. Since Tom, I've never stopped contemplating what has become a life-long commitment: learning from, propagating, documenting, and loving black New Orleans. Ultimately, our second line culture enables us to elegantly deal and dance even with death. Individually, each of us will sooner or later expire; collectively, we will never die.

Since Tom's death in 1998, I began to think I was moving on and beyond where he had gone. I got heavy into computers, developed a deep online presence. I became a radio personality. I also used video to document and express myself, eventually developing into what I called a neo-Griot. I wrote with text, sound, and light. As is often the case with generational developments, I thought of myself as building something new on an old foundation.

When Abram Himelstein, director of the University of New Orleans Press, presented me the opportunity to edit a collection of Tom's writings from my progressed perspective, I agreed without hesitation. I felt both honored and obliged, anticipating what I assumed would be an enjoyable and easily managed task. After all, I had been a confidant to Tom as well as a colleague. We had loaned each other money during rough periods, asked each other's advice as we went about engaging or declining various writing projects. I'd been entrusted with a key to Tom's apartment, and after his death set up an office in Tom's last domicile on Treme Street. When I travel north during the wintertime, I wear Tom's leather gloves. Figuratively, Tom is still holding my hand.

So I proudly and confidently undertook that task of editing what would become a Tom Dent reader. The first thing I learned was how much I didn't know. Tom's papers are archived at the Amistad Research Center on the campus of Tulane University. In the winter of 2013, I walked into Tilton Hall expecting to spend a couple of days going through ten, maybe fifteen boxes of Tom's writings. Earlier in the year, Amistad had mounted an exhibit of Tom Dent memorabilia to celebrate the fiftieth anniversary of the Free Southern Theater. From that program, I thought I had a sense of Amistad's collection.

Yet I was stunned both by the collection's breadth and depth, and by the breadth and depth of own my ignorance about Tom's work. There were more than five six-foot steel archive cabinets of writings, journals, notebooks, and letters, plus a healthy cache of photographs, tape recordings, books and other possessions housed in storage. The collection of Tom's work amounted to over 149 linear feet of material. The work published during his lifetime is dwarfed by the thousands and thousands of archived pages—he probably published only one page for every couple of hundred that he wrote.

Tom kept everything. He was an indefatigable letter writer to a wide range of people. Some of the letters are professional business documents, but the overwhelming bulk of the missives are in-depth musings and reflections addressed to friends and close colleagues. These writings are often embarrassingly candid about Tom's thoughts and feelings. I was reading words that, out of respect for his privacy, I never would have asked Tom to read while he was alive. I'm sure that, because he consciously and conscientiously preserved thousands of documents, Tom was aware that in some not too distant future his private thoughts and feelings could become public. Nevertheless, knowing that everything he wrote might eventually be revealed did not seem to inhibit Tom— that's how frankly and freely he wrote.

While I admire Tom's willingness to forego secrecy and even privacy, this nevertheless creates conundrums for researchers, especially those of us who were his friends: Are there aspects of a person's life that are best left undisturbed? Do the dead have a right to the dignity of privacy? Fortunately, the focus of this collection is on writings that were obviously meant to be public. The sheer volume of both typed and handwritten letters, journals, and diaries made it easy for me to leave that material for other researchers and biographers to explore and perhaps publish. Realistically, it could easily take another three or four hundred pages to adequately represent this literal library of material. Perhaps in the future there will be a second volume to *The Tom Dent Reader*.

Most of us who considered ourselves writers and worked with Tom thought of writing mainly in the creative sense of poetry, plays, and fiction. Yet without fanfare, Tom Dent had undertaken the additional and far more arduous—indeed daunting—task of documenting and analyzing his culture, his people, and himself. In short, Tom decided to be more than a writer: Tom Dent became a griot. In his case, this meant combining the acuity of a ethno-cultural anthropologist facing his past with the critique of a public intellectual and cultural activist confronting his present. Moreover, the dimensionality of Tom's work was consciously aimed at audiences of the future.

New Orleans Griot: The Tom Dent Reader is an introduction to the single most important New Orleans writer of all time. No other native New Orleanian has documented the cultural life of this city as extensively, and with as much personal and social insight, as has Tom Dent. Tom was a social auditor, assaying and triaging into specific categories what was distinctive, what was valuable, and what needed changing in our collective reality. Social and political issues I had thought about a thousand times before, as well as ideas and situations I'd never considered, were fodder for Tom's investigation and documentation. But more than simply "what," Tom aimed to determine how come and to what end we do the things we do in the Big Easy, and beyond.

After returning to New Orleans in 1964, Tom willingly made the immense personal sacrifices required of a true griot. Yet his valuable and complex work is undervalued, as far as society at large is concerned. If you ask most New Orleanians if they know who Tom Dent is, they will say no. Yet, if you want to know who black New Orleans once was, you would do well to ask Tom Dent. "New Orleans Griot" is no honorary title, nor a glib marketing phrase: it is a life-long commitment to documenting and passing on the unique vibrancy of black New Orleans culture. Tom Dent is a learning tree rooted in his people. By his fruit, we know and are nourished by him.

Tom's example fuels my work still, and hopefully my example will encourage others to carry on this invaluable griot tradition. From the beginning of human life among our people, and on and on for as long as we exist, thus it has been, thus the griot will always be: working, bearing witness, and testifying to the specifics and to the miracle of human existence.

KALAMU YA SALAAM

new york years/
umbra days

like a rumbling underneath...

Tom Dent the Griot grew out of the complicated young man who went home to New Orleans for a brief visit and ended up staying for the rest of his life. That young man lives on in Tom's early work, along with his personal conundrums of social status and self-expression. The New York years offered Tom a distance from his upbringing that, on his eventual return to New Orleans, allowed him to embrace his own blackness as never before. In Tom's words: "It was as if I was coming to an acceptance of myself that was not possible before, [not] a part of my reality." But first, New York became the place where Tom "raged" over the conflict of self-acceptance.

Facing the reality of all that we are as individuals can be both frightening and liberating: frightening because much of our inner reality is pure fantasy, unreal, and even unrealizable, and we know it; liberating because once we wrap our psychic arms around ourselves, once we embrace ourselves, we no longer have to expend energy running away from being as we are. Tom's long letter to Dr. Brayboy (yes, that's a real person, a real name) exemplifies how well Tom knew himself and how adept he was at literally writing out the labyrinth that is the individual personality.

In this section we can discern the three seeds that eventually grew into the major pillars of Tom Dent's lifelong work, including his efforts to honestly reflect on who he was as an individual; to act on his responsibility as a member of a society that he thought needed to be changed in fundamental ways; and to compose a body of writing that combined his individual explorations with his social commitment.

Included here are two pre-New Orleans pieces on the early sixties, New York-based, black writers collective known as Umbra, within which Tom established lifelong friendships and professional connections. Tom wrote with warm compassion an overview of Umbra that reflects his sense of responsibility to document the facts and meaning of his cultural milieu. He also wrote a scathing satire that reflects his self-conscious, analytical bent, a characteristic that enabled him to dispassionately inspect the blemishes on personalities (including his own) and events that he loved.

Tom's piece on Dave Brubeck reflects a number of issues, one of which is not obvious. In grad school at Syracuse University, Tom studied international relations and focused on Poland; Dave Brubeck was of Polish heritage. Can a Pole play the blues? Is race an essentialist quality? Is culture learnable? Tom explores these questions. Tom had white friends throughout his lifetime, even though he chose to live most of his post-New York years securely embedded within the black community. While acknowledging the immensity of the political implications and realities at play in any social scenario, Tom was of the mind that race did not necessarily have to be a barrier to relationships. "Dave Brubeck" plays with this complex social give-and-take.

This first section also includes a short story, "Legacy of the Scottish Owner's Will." Prior to the Black Arts Movement, most aspirant black writers chose either journalism or fiction as their focus. Even Langston Hughes made his mark as a journalist while producing fiction. Once he returned to New Orleans and took up working with Free Southern Theater, Tom soon moved away from fiction and focused on non-fiction and poetry, both genres that emphasized the topical issues of the times.

KALAMU YA SALAAM

YOUNGER GENERATION SAD REPRESENTATIVE OF AMERICAN YOUTH

Tom thought he wanted to be a writer, and in the beginning he thought writing was about ideas rather than about life. The editorial in The Maroon Tiger *talks in very general terms about a new generation, but you will notice it does not talk about his father and breaking away from the mores of the black professional class in New Orleans. Tom does not write about the problems of being a professor, a city administrator, or a high level corporate executive, although he certainly could have. He chose instead to write about musicians, laborers, and people of no particular professional persuasion.*

Of recent magazine articles none has impressed me more deeply than "The Younger Generation," which appeared in the November 5, 1951 issue of *Time*. This article was written by the editors of *Time* from information gathered by their different offices throughout the nation. It presents the youth of the nation as a poor lot. In short, it says the younger generation (18-28) lacks drive, lacks a belief in something, and just lacks—period. To me, this conclusion is without a doubt justified, and I'll tell you why.

I think there is plenty wrong with our generation for several reasons. For one, we are confused. And rightly so. We came up in what was and still is, to say the least, a confused world. We don't know what's right because nobody knows what's right. We don't know which way to look, how to act. So, there seems to be little to expect from life but confusion and disappointment. It isn't hard to reason, "why go to school?" "Either the Army will get me while I'm there, or, if I'm lucky enough to finish, right after I finish." Or, "why prepare for life?" "If I ever get set, Uncle Sam'll grab me before I can do anything." We seem to be disappointed, for there isn't much else to look forward to. We are a confused, puzzled generation.

But even the stigma of confusion doesn't characterize our generation properly. Many generations have been confused, but it seems to me that the outstanding characteristic of our generation is an apathy and general attitude of nonchalance. We lack zip, fire, and spirit. We aren't for anything, and we aren't against anything. We just let things rest if they'll let us rest. This, to me, seems to be very bad because it means that we are making no attempt to get out of the confusion. We don't want to fight it; we're too tired. We've had too much fighting, and there is no desire to do any more of it.

Why is this so? I think it is because the younger generation has already become old in every way except age. We have fought a war and are depended upon to fight another one. We had zip, but it's gone now—lost on foreign battlefields. We have experienced too much in too short a time; we want to get away now and have some peace, some security. Nothing is more desired by the younger generation than these two factors. Most of us don't even know what security is. Born in a depression, raised during a war and being drafted to fight a new one if we didn't fight the last one, we have experienced nothing but insecurity.

Consequently, a listless race has developed. We are children of insecurity, worry and tension, and we would wish nothing better than to get away from it all.

This is the younger generation of America today. It is sadly lacking. Maybe someday we will wake up and lead the world. But now
there is hardly a chance of that happening. We are too tired.

[WHEN THEY FINISHED]

Typical of many educated people, Tom thought he had to learn how to do something before doing it. So Tom dropped out of college, and spent a couple of years in the military. He took correspondence courses to formally learn how to write.

The correspondence courses had exercises that Tom was required to complete. Tom's initial (and short-lived) formal training stands in contrast to the literary heritage he soon joined and extended: the oral story-telling tradition of the West African Griot. Up through the 20th century, almost every major African American Writer had not been formally taught writing.

(Unpublished, circa the late 1950's)

When they had finished the boy did not leave. He lay on the bed, smoking silently, watching the way she dressed—no deliberation, no method.

She could have been thirty-five, he thought, maybe even forty. Through the haze of his liquor he could see that she was hefty, short, moon-faced, and wore a red blouse that hardly fitted in the drabness of the room. He watched her nervously combing her hair, studied her while she peered into the mirror as if she were looking for her face.

When she began doctoring herself with the eyebrow pencil he knew then it was time to leave. It was a dark night, humid the way New York can be in August. He rolled out of the bed, slipped on his trousers, and looked absent-mindedly out of the window at the next building.

"What's your name again?" he asked.

"I told you it was Dinny."

"What?"

"Dinny."

She said no more. He turned, looking about the room, and noticed a picture of a man who looked like Jesus Christ in a full dress suit.

"Who's the picture on the wall?" he asked with a smile.

"My husband."

"You married?"

"I was."

"Well," the boy said, lighting himself a cigarette, "he sure don't know what he's missing."

She turned from the mirror and looked squarely at him. He smiled, but did not quite understand her stare.

"What's it to you, buster," she said acidly. "I don't need no pity from guys like you."

"Don't get excited," he said, with even a broader smile. He was a handsome youth.

"I'm *not* excited." She turned back to the mirror and began fumbling with her hair. Then she went into the small bathroom.

When she returned he was fully dressed, with even his jacket on. He had placed a ten-dollar bill on the bed, and he pointed to it winking significantly. When she saw it her face twisted into a rage.

"I know God," she screamed. "I know religion! I got no love. I got no life. I'm nothing. It don't *matter* that I'm nothing, but don't try to rub it in, buddy, don't try to get smart. Don't get smart with me, you hear!"

He started to leave, but she grabbed his arm. He stood impassively while she faced him, nervously stroking her hair. "I'm leaving soon," she said softly, as if it were confidential information. "I'm leaving this dirty, filthy, shitty city. I'll tell you, boy, this city is for shitty people and dead cats."

He leaned back against the door, and looked blankly past her to the window. "You don't believe me," she bellowed, pushing him back against the door. "You don't believe I will! Just mark my words, buster. I'm going back to Iowa where I came from. I was *made* to come here, thinking there was easy jobs. I was *made* to do it."

Then, as if a strange vision had come over her, she said, laying her head on the chest of the boy, "I'm going where I can find the fresh air and the fresh people. I'm going back where the blue skies is."

The two of them stood there for a silent moment, she throbbing against the youth, holding him as if he were life itself, he limp, looking blankly across the room at the colorless flowered wallpaper.

She began to sob uncontrollably, released the boy, and ran to her bed, moaning a low cry as she rolled from side to side.

The youth descended the steps of the apartment building quickly. When he was far enough away to be sure she could not possibly hear him, he said aloud, "That's the queerest whore I ever seen."

He was glad to get out into the misty, damp night of the street.

LEGACY OF THE SCOTTISH OWNER'S WILL

"The Scottish Owner's Will" references John McDonogh, who was the largest slave and land owner in America. His will stipulated that half of his estate be used to educated whites and free people of color in New Orleans. In order to prevent free people of color from receiving education, the state of Louisiana sued all the way to the US Supreme Court. The funds from this estate were used (and misused) in building the segregated public school system of New Orleans.

Tom entered writing with an interest in fiction, but the times demanded action. As a poet and dramatist, you could be a part of the community's forward motion. If there was a rally, a poet was invited to be on the program. Drama and orated poetry take place in the here and how, with an audience. Most fiction is not read with the author present. Fiction, which is contemplative, was not in the moment, and not what Tom was interested in writing. For Tom, storytelling replaced fiction. Whenever movement people got together they would tell stories. And the stories, with so much at stake, felt stronger than fiction. That said, this story is one of the few extant examples of the kind of fiction of which Tom was capable.

Robert could not sleep. It was mid-Louisiana summer, so hot, so muggy in his cabin. Besides, the disappointment of the meeting was worrying him, and something Bessie'd said. What she said, "you can't depend on niggers for nothing, you just a fool Robert for workin for nothing," ached in his brain, wouldn't go away—it hurt because there was so much truth in it. Now he wondered if he hadn't been a fool all his days; hadn't every opportunity, every potential good fortune evaded him, escaped him just when it seemed within grasp?

He was seventy-three now, and he hadn't come as close to crying in a long time as he had tonight. He felt foolish, he swelled up with rage at his own emotions. He thought they would at least have brought in something. True, he hadn't spoken to old man LeBlanc, as he was assigned, and he felt terrible about it; he had let the committee down. But he knew. He knew they knew old man LeBlanc wasn't going to give them any money to build a school. Why play games.

It was too hot to sleep. He had tried, but he couldn't do it. All his tossing and turning was only disturbing Bessie. He got up from the bed and shuffled to the front room of his cabin.

It was an unusually dark night, he noticed, heavy clouds hiding the moon; possibly there would be rain. Why make him play games? Seeing Mr. LeBlanc was a pain in the ass; yet he might have seen him—what was so difficult in that? Had he injected his personal feelings too deeply into community business? Yet, he didn't want to see LeBlanc. He knew deep in his heart LeBlanc's attitude toward blacks; he knew LeBlanc had said "a nigger will never walk in the front door of my house" to one of his friends; he figured if LeBlanc said it he meant it. No matter how friendly he acted in the presence of his blacks. Really, Robert thought the committee would raise some money from the community, not depend so much on his seeing LeBlanc.

He went outside as silently as he could and sat on the porch.

*   *   *

Robert could smell the heaviness of the night, the sweet, sometimes sickening odor of the canefield. The buzz of insects and
birds was intense, it seemed they were engaged in an argument
that went on incessantly, never to be resolved; "just like people,"
he thought.

He felt like walking. He decided to walk to the levee. The road
was dustier than usual; it hadn't rained in a long time. He was
happy no one was out; he didn't want to have to speak to anyone,
to explain why he was out this time of night.

When he reached the levee the surface of the river was dark but
not really still. Small ripples washed ashore, as if an unseen boat
had recently passed. Toward the middle of the river, the moon,
playing games with clouds, cast a reflection that spotlighted the
rough, uneven surface of the water. The surface seemed like liquid
stone, as if carved out of the earth from tremendous stress over a
period of time longer than Robert could possibly imagine.

Yes, he could sense it, yes there was something, there was something strange about this place, the levee landing at the river. He let
his body relax, still, as if letting the river's muddy water float into
him, inundate him, flow into the dreamlike essence of his being.

There was another time, another place, just like this one, but
when, where? Yes, yes, it's coming—of course, the night of the
news of the Scottish owner's will, slipping away from his cabin
deep in the fields, stealing to the levee, to the river to ponder the
enormity of that news. "That news", he sighed deeply, his knees
wobbly; he laughed, he laughed for the first time tonight, for the
first time in a long while; he relaxed...yes, that was it...and like
now, the river revealed no secrets. He felt so relieved. The Scot's
will, how long had it been since he had even thought about all
that? He had put that out of his mind. Even Jason knocking on

his cabin door that morning, bursting in with the news almost before dawn.

Yes, it was true; as he sat down carefully, it was as if it had never happened, and he wondered if he wanted to endure the pain of thinking about it even now, if he wanted to tear open the wound again. So much hope. They were breathing a special air then, and that air brought so much pain. Even though they kept working, as the overseer said, "just keep on working," they were smelling the gas and it smelled sweet, like the wonderful fragrance of spring flowers. No, he wasn't even worryin' bout no work. Not then.

He felt so foolish, even now. Why hadn't they at least asked about the will? Niggers never ask; it seemed impossible to him now. He wondered what was going through the minds of the whites then.

Yes, the will had grown to be a new, massive, untalked-about fence separating the whites and the slaves, a fence never crossed though everyone knew it was there. Really, as he recalled now, the will was never mentioned by the whites, only among the slaves; it was "secret news." Robert laughed to himself; he had supposed that suddenly one morning, as with the news of the will itself, the overseer would appear muttering "well, according to the owner's will youalls free. He left land too; the crazy bastard given all you niggers some of his land, damn his soul in hell." Then he would show Robert the arpents he had inherited, part of the fields he had worked for the last eighteen years as if they were his. Fields he had worked since he was sold to the Scottish owner from the ricelands of South Carolina, where he was told he was born, where he supposed his mother still was, if she was alive.

The sweating work in the canefields had continued as usual; the masts of river boats passing slowly by, belonging always to another world, teasing him simply because they were there, then not there. He had foolishly let himself dream he would soon be working his own land, purchasing his wife, Bessie, from Mr. Richard's plantations downriver, selling his own cane, possibly even finding the where-abouts of his son, Louis, who Bessie believed was in Louisiana on a Red River plantation. Ah, those were the days of hope. He felt so foolish, so sad, his body sagged, as if wanting to melt into the levee. Yes, all of it...dreaming he would build his own cabin from strong river cypress logs. Seeing he and the others of the Scottish owner becoming a marvelous curiosity along the river. When river road carriages passed their cabins they would be pointed out as "those free niggers"—he had let himself dream all that.

In "litigation," that's how he heard it, yes that was the word they wondered so much about, their lives, their hopes held in tenuous balance by the word "litigation." Then they heard the will had been contested by the owner's relatives in Scotland. He had no family, no wife, no children in Louisiana; only land and sugarcane and slaves and money, and strangeness. He was a mystery then and now, in death. News came to them like bits and pieces of driftwood, floating in from patches of white folks' gossip. "No one tole us nothing," Robert recalled. They heard the Scottish relatives claimed the owner was insane when he wrote the will.

And then there was the waiting, waiting, and singing. The long church meetings in the fields, singing, singing, singing "Be Not Dismayed", and the hoping, hoping, hoping through long nights of anticipation. Whispering, whispering, trying to believe, trying to believe; yes he too had believed, he too, he could not lie.

And he had watched sun-filled hopes turn to dust; watched heads held higher than he had ever seen begin to droop. It was the waiting, the waiting—that is what he remembered the most, no one ever really speaking about the hurt. Finally, no one spoke about it at all, not even in whispers. They only said about anything they couldn't understand, for years afterwards, "he was insane, he was insane when he did it." The saying always brought on great, unrestrained laughter. In time they forgot where it came from.

*   *   *

He was sold to Richard's plantation downriver, where Bessie worked in the big house. She all the time then overhearing talk of problems between what they called "the accursed North" and Louisiana; the problems were them, what to do about them; there were people in the North who thought maybe they should be free; Robert remembered how the idea that all of them everywhere would be freed moved through his body like a cold chill; it was too enormous, too much. The excitement then, Bessie rushing back to the cabin repeating white folks' angry talk of their niggers, their land, their Louisiana. Robert remembered that the days got more interesting then, the hushed, anticipatory conversations between the slaves more excited. Bessie said to hell with it all; she could care less; she didn't trust *no* white folks.

*   *   *

During those days the will was forgotten...almost. Bessie over-heard that the state of Louisiana had appointed a lawyer to repre-sent the slaves, though no one ever told the slaves that. Once, he asked Bessie whether she thought they could ask Richard about it. He remembered that she said "no, if we's free, when they get ready to free us they will, according to God's plan. Til then they ain't nuthin we can do."

He grew silent about the will for a long time after that, though it weighed on his mind, grated on his mind. When he tried to bring it up among his friends they would laugh him off, saying, "you still worried about that. That's dead and gone now. No use even talkin bout it." And Robert remembered he would smile and agree. But it wouldn't go away. Not that he ever hoped for anything anymore.

*   *   *

Now the river was still. Whatever movement there had been had stilled. Even the birds, the field animals seemed still, the insects silent. The threat of rain had passed. He could see the moon, stars. It had been a long time. A long time. Yes, it was painful. Here in 1870, all those memories, those hopes drowned in burning tears.

Robert turned his gaze from the river, turned to face the sprawling fields. And here we is, ain't no damn progress, same river, same land, same us. He looked at the rolling plantations. In the black-greenness of night they seemed almost too certain, too unyielding, as if they had been there always, always had been there, and would be there. But when he looked again, the fields seemed to waver in liquid mist. *I could be anywhere, anywhere—it's only fate that brought me here. And I ain't got the power to move, the power to go. When I first heard about the emancipation I thought Bessie and me could go anywhere; we would go far, far away from here—from Louisiana—but this river, these canefields cast a spell on us.*

He wondered if he, they, could change anything. Just like they were singing "Be Not Dismayed" tonight they were singing it twenty years ago, twenty years ago—how long would it be before they did something besides "Be Not Dismayed"? They were waiting, waiting—he looked at the cane plantations, at the sweep of the road until it disappeared from view, at the river and all he could see of it, all he could not see, but he knew it must contain all those memories, those sufferings they never talked about, those deaths, those wills, those promises, those lies, those tears floating deep beneath the surface, and those waits, weighing the river down, making it heavy, dark, black, murky; the river was heavy water, dirty with the dirt of unmentionables. And their waiting was unmentionable.

Robert laughed to himself. "Be Not Dismayed," well shit yeah, but they had to go further than that...Or they'll be like this waiting forever and ever.

And him? What about him. He felt himself suddenly shivering. What was he ready to do? What had he done? Except wait? Yes, he had been waiting too, like all the others. Though some, he knew, looked to him as leader, said he was "more intelligent," he had led them nowhere, nowhere at all. He was a victim too.

And he knew it was easy enough to say he was a victim, that at seventy-three he couldn't do anything, but then he hadn't done anything at fifty-three, or thirty-three, or thirteen but survive— live through it, and now looking back on it he wondered what that was worth, mere living through it.

So whether they could change anything came down to him. Didn't it? And he couldn't do much.

But he knew there would be no change unless they did *something*, put one foot in front of the other to walk in the direction of their own freedom and independence. No one was going to give it to them. They thought they would give them freedom just because he put it in the will. As if their being there was a mistake that could be that easily erased. Well, it wasn't a mistake, he knew that now. Their being here certainly was no accident, no mistake: someone brought them here, and not by accident.

*   *   *

Then, as he was walking back, back to the shack they lived in, walking with the heaviness of seventy-three years, he thought they *could* create small currents in the river, even if they were only small circles made from a small stone's throw, and the stone could be him, Robert, seventy-three years him, and why not? What else was there to live for now?

Why had he ever thought it would be different? He was walking faster now, almost running, why had he thought it would be any different from before? The river over there, it knows the answer to what makes things move, what creates movement. Hell, he had been looking, I been looking but I never seen, never seen.

I'm blind. We blind.

*   *   *

His heart was beating too fast, too fast, blood seemed to be leaping up through him to his brain. He hadn't been excited like this in a long time—'taint no *we*, he thought, it's *me*, I'm gonna go back and hustle, beg, borrow from *us*, us—it's *for* us, *we* should pay for it—build the school. Any damn thing we want, we got to have. Whatever made us think LeBlanc or anyone else would give us money?

And yes, it would be dangerous, there were some whites milling around tonight near the church, what were they doing there? Maybe building a school was innocent, but this was Louisiana, built on free toil like mine, not on niggers going to school learning to read and write and count. That was dangerous. People might learn to think. They might ask questions. They might be begin to read what the white folks thought about them. There would be burnings and shootings and jailings, he knew that, all that flashed across his mind in an instant, he just *knew* it, and he knew also he would never see it, not *all* of it, but he wanted to, he wanted to be part of all of it, a hundred years of it, two hundred years of it, he wanted to be part of them learning to read, then the young ones wanting *everything*, even the foolish things, the things it made no sense to get, he could endure that too. If he had endured his past, he could endure that future.

When he reached the cabin he tried to slow down, slow down the rush of his thoughts. He sat on the stoop. He head was spinning as night was just beginning to break, ah, how he loved the night. He hoped the vision, the clarity of that night would never fade under the hot scorch of the day's blistering sun, the day's twists and turns.

Yes, he would wake up Bessie. What was she sleeping for anyway—there was no time to sleep—there would be plenty time to sleep, in due course.

*   *   *

When Bessie finally awoke she looked at Robert like he was a fool. "We're gonna do it ourselves" was all Robert could say. She thought he was in a spell.

"Do *what* ourselves?" she demanded.

"The school, everything. We gonna do it ourselves, taint no other way."

"Man, you crazy," Bessie said. She rolled over. Robert went to make some coffee. A few minutes later Bessie half-stumbled into the rear of the cabin where the stove was.

"You ain't been here," she snapped. "Where you been?"

"To the river," Robert answered evenly.

"To the *river*?"

"Yea."

"For what? This time a night?"

"To think about things. All that's happened to us. To prepare to leave this confounded world. To remember things. That's all."

There was a long pause. "I suppose you mean givin money for the school," Bessie finally said. "That's one way of doin it. We could give the little money we been savin for Christmas. You ready to do that?" She looked at him hard.

"Yes," he ventured. He was afraid to look at her.

"You serious?" she finally asked, getting up to pour herself some coffee. "*If* you serious I'm serious. Seen too many Christmases anyway. Gettin tired of it."

Robert rose and went to the bed, lay down. He fell asleep almost instantly, fully clothed. When he awoke a few hours later, it was the storm, the thunder that awoke him, and the patter of the rain leaking through the roof into the tin pans they had placed on the floor. Bessie had been after him to fix the roof; he tensed, fearing she would be angry now.

But she didn't say anything. He felt relaxed, at first he wasn't sure why. Then the thoughts of the just passed night came back slowly, in pieces. He had to fix the roof. He looked—Bessie was sitting in the kitchen. He arose, stumbled into the room.

"I been thinking about what you said last night," Bessie began. "You know we need things. Things we ain't never had."

"We never will, I guess," Robert said. It made him feel better to say that. "I want to give the money. Both of us to do that. I don't care if the others don't," Robert added quickly, looking squarely at Bessie now. "That's the main thing. You understand?"

"I reckon so," Bessie answered. "I reckon so."

Then Robert went over to one of the tin cans on the floor, moved it so it caught more rain. He felt good, he really felt good. He sat down beside Bessie and listened to the rain, letting the sound flow into him.

EMOTIONAL AUTOBIOGRAPHY

This is a personal inventory Tom did on himself once he decided that writing was what he was going to do in life. (Unpublished)

I am introverted, ambitious, envious, egotistical, cautious, methodical and dreamy. If I am introverted it is because I was always considered different as a child, set apart because of my family, and also because my father is introverted. We have never talked about anything in depth which is personal or emotional. My father is a killer of emotion. This is the trademark of his personality: "killer of emotion."

I am truly ambitious, in that success was always expected of me and I want desperately to achieve it. My father was successful, mother well known and successful in the brief pursuit of her art, grandfather a successful doctor—ambition comes naturally for there is no family tradition of do-nothing, lazy, ineffective people. I am ambitious to make my own mark in the world by becoming a writer. By becoming a writer who is good, writes something of value, I not only match or excel the success of my forbears, but become important in my own way by achieving in an area where my father is sterile.

I am envious. I am envious because I have never been aggressive to assert my own desires, wishes, ambitions—therefore I envy those about me, especially of my own age, color, race, who assert themselves. As I become more aggressive, I will become less envious.

I am egotistical. I am egotistical because I am continually involved with myself, my own desires, problems and frustrations. I
am also egotistical because I was looked upon as something special as a child, and allowed to exist in this state for a long time. My
ambition to be someone special, to be equal or greater than my
father, to be extremely important to people leads to an egotism.
I believe that by satisfying myself I can satisfy others in a concrete, wholesome way, and that my own viewpoint of life—and
my expression of it—is valuable and important. I am really more
properly egocentric than egotistical.

I am extremely cautious. I am cautious in that I like to shield
myself from revelation, for fear that others will see me as I really
am, i.e. my inadequacies. I procrastinate to an unjustified extent
before acting for fear of what others will say which may challenge
me and for fear that others will look upon what I do unfavorably.
I do not like to plunge myself into any activity of which I cannot
anticipate the result. I have an innate love for the act of self-revela-
tion, but it is deeply repressed and blocked in by inhibition. I feel
that this trait of over-caution is to some extent inherited from my
father, who is also extremely cautious, and also comes from the
social conditions of my youth, where my every act was watched,
evaluated, and where I was expected to play a certain role without
deviation. I am speaking here of New Orleans, and the awareness
people had of my name in that town. The shield constructed to
protect my real self from the arrows of a society and parentage
that expected me to play a role I did not desire. To reveal myself at
a tender age was to expose myself to continual pain and criticism.
Therefore the shield was constructed. But the crust and extreme
caution still exist.

I am methodical. I am methodical in that I like to have something concrete like an intellectual system to hold to, in the absence
of emotional revelation. Because I am extremely cautious I only

proceed by steps, slowly and surely, seeking to make sure that my footing is safe. For me, intellectual method has become a substitute for emotional security. I also inherit this trait from my father, who admires systems, and approves in me anything I might want to do as long as I can show it is logical, concrete, and planned. I am methodical because I do not trust my impulsiveness. In the absence of emotional knowledge of myself, method becomes something concrete, tangible and material that I can hold on to.

I am dreamy in that I have always indulged in fantasies of success that replace my feelings of inadequacy in real life. Being lonely often as a child, creating my own games, having little deep communication with my parents, I learned to communicate and act out my life through fantasies, dreams and imaginary people. As a youth, it was difficult for me to build transitions between my fantasies and the reality of my life. Now I seek to use the capacity for sustained imaginary concentration to act out on paper the lessons of reality in characters who are projections of my insecurities.

UMBRA DAYS

Umbra represents Tom's conscious decision to be a black writer in the context of community, and not just as an individual. Umbra was a collective of aspiring black writers in New York City, most of whom were not from NY, but had gone to there to make their mark. Umbra is the major precursor of the BLACK Arts Movement.

There are two pieces here by Tom about Umbra, one a memoir, and the other a satirical piece. Taken together they represent the amazing ability Tom had to be socially committed, and at the same time, to have the emotional distance to laugh at oneself. This was reflective of the two side of his personality, the professional and the personal. The professional and the proletariat. There is also an interview at the end of the book that discusses this time period.

"Memorandum" is a perfect example of Tom's wry and often sardonic sense of humor, in which he chuckles knowingly rather than guffaws.

(Unpublished)

I would characterize the essential quality of Umbra as search, quest, many individual quests woven together. Actually, for me the search began in 1959. I had just completed two years in that desert called the US Army, and I came to New York wanting, rather vaguely but still wanting, to be a writer. But what does that mean, 'to be a writer'?

Certainly I had no concept of what it meant to be a black writer. I was brought up under an educational system (in the South) that not only ignored black literature but lacked a concept of blackness period. I took a literature course at Morehouse College in Atlanta, which was enthusiastically taught but included no writers of our race, as if they did not exist. In none of my courses can I remember reading books by black writers, or hearing a consciously black line of thought, of comment, of reality. We were taught and prepared to 'belong,' i.e. to become whites in brown skins by mastering white standards. Literature meant the world of Shakespeare, Hemingway, Faulkner.

So coming to New York in 1959 I knew I wanted to be a writer, but I didn't really know what that meant. We had been taught that race as subject matter was limiting, something to escape from if possible, and the further one escaped the more successful one became. The idea of 'universality' had been drummed into our subconscious until it became a foreboding drone; if we wrote about race at all we were told to somehow make it 'universal.' What was meant but not said was it had to be acceptable to white people or it was worthless.

My first job in New York was in Harlem with the now defunct NEW YORK AGE, one of the oldest black weeklies. Also on the staff at that time were activist/nationalist Calvin Hicks and artist Tom Feelings. Journalists Al Duckett and Chuck Stone were editors. We all wanted to do more creative work than a newspaper would allow. Langston Hughes lived around the corner from the AGE office, and I sent him some of my poems. He was as generous and encouraging to me as he was to many other young writers, though when I touched on the feasibility of a new black literary journal I remember him saying, "Those things never work."

Also, around that time, Raoul Abdul, who was Hughes' secretary, organized a series of readings by young black poets at an art gallery on Seventh Avenue and 135th Street. There I met poets Phil Petrie, Raymond Patterson, Lloyd Addison and heard the work of Calvin Hernton (read by Roscoe Lee Browne). To me all this was a revelation because none of these people had been extensively published, if at all, and I didn't know they existed.

Something else was happening. Calvin Hicks, who had moved to the Lower East Side in 1960, was instrumental in organizing ON GUARD FOR FREEDOM. ON GUARD was one of the first sixties creative, multidirectional groups composed of young black intellectuals. An important part of the ON GUARD idea was a newspaper to attack racism in American society and American international policy. ON GUARD was also strongly black nationalist and pan-Africanist. I found the radicalism, projection of pan-Africanism, and comradeship with writers and other artists in ON GUARD invigorating and became deeply involved.

Actually in the more or less two years ON GUARD existed we only published two issues of the newspaper, though the group did provide an important forum for idea interchange. At one time or another ON GUARD included Hicks, his wife Nora, authors Sarah Wright and Rosa Guy, critic Harold Cruse, musicians Archie Shepp and Walter Bowe, his activist wife Nanny Bowe, poets Imamu Baraka, Joe Johnson, Bobb Hamilton, Alvin Simon, Virginia Hughes, and musicians Max Roach and Abbey Lincoln. Though ON GUARD was transitory, it was an important factor in establishing the Lower East Side (despite a temporary office in Harlem) as the place where young black radical artists were living and working.

Before hippies, and before the mafia moved in, the Lower East Side was an interesting place. It was the home of many ethnic groups, especially Eastern European and Jewish, but by the sixties it had become substantially Puerto Rican with an increasing population of blacks. It was one of the few sections where people could live cheaply, and where racial hostility wasn't *too* oppressive if you knew how to protect yourself and traveled in groups. Such cultural heterogeneity attracted many artists and gave the LES a truly bohemian quality, very unlike the better-known West Side (Greenwich Village), which was extremely racist and housed few artists.

Most of the black artists who migrated to the LES were not native New Yorkers. We had come to New York to try to escape our parochial beginnings, our hometowns and neighborhoods, to find ourselves and to find each other. We hung out primarily at Stanley Tolkin's bar on 12th & Avenue B, a place we transformed overnight. It was an empty Polish cafe that soon became a busy communications center for artists, writers, actors and the people who hung out with them. If you wanted to see somebody, or find out what was happening, you would check out Stanley's.

Another meeting place was coffee shops, many of which held open poetry readings. Open readings meant just that: everyone could come and read. Through these readings issues, styles, personal followings were created. Because the idea of oral poetry was novel, they [the readings] drew a large audience, and many writers who had no national or formal literary reputation became well known on the LES scene.

The early sixties was also the time when the civil rights movement in the South was the major national news (it hadn't yet reached the North in any organized form). We, as black artists, related to the Movement in one form or another and shared many friends who had gone south to work. It should be emphasized that in terms of our concerns, the world of the black man's struggle for not just existence but *identity*, the world of rapidly growing disenchantment with America and the so-called American dream, the world of new-found interest in Africa: this was our world, the intense and rapidly changing world we lived in.

It was not a world of trying to 'make it' in the formal literary sense. The 'literary' world, the world of the white literary establishment, was more distant from us than a nine-to-five. Baldwin was becoming the rage of the bigtime, and Ellison was fully accepted (though largely silent at that time). Still, we were acutely conscious of the fact that we had no means, no road to traditional literary success even if that had really been what we wanted.

I remember a long taped discussion several of us participated in with Seymour Krim, the poor man's Norman Mailer, at Alvin Simon's house in 1961 or 1962. For some reason, Krim decided to play devil's advocate, with us desperately trying to explain that the black man wasn't fairly represented on the American art scene, not even in jazz. No matter how much talent we had the white man controlled the economics. Krim seemed to have a hard time seeing the point, and I remember him saying, "I don't understand why any black writer can't publish. There's nothing more fashionable today than a black writer." (Probably he had a fixation on Baldwin). The discussion ended on this note: Krim told Archie Shepp that if he wrote an article it would be published in CAVALIER, the magazine Krim edited.

The Krim discussion and the little we knew of the publishing scene made us, either consciously or subconsciously, aware of the reality that if we wanted to publish we had to publish ourselves. The surfacing of one black writer at a time in the white literary world, like a long chain of single black voices, was not an acceptable situation.

*   *   *

When I moved to the LES in January 1962, I lived on Second Street, between Avenues B & C. It was a typical East Side block: many Puerto Ricans, several blacks, a few artists, Mobilization for Youth offices, etc. Aldo Tambellini, a painter-sculptor I had known at Syracuse University, lived on the block. Aldo was interested in getting the artists and writers on the Lower East Side together in some kind of avant-garde movement to protest the policies of the artistic establishment (and, incidentally, to demand that his junk sculpture be accepted at the Museum of Modern Art).

Aldo sponsored several meetings. But from my point of view, the first really getting together of what became Umbra was when I located Calvin Hernton, who to my surprise was back in New York (remember I had heard his poetry but never met him) and living on the LES. I discovered that Calvin hung out and read poetry at a coffee house on 6th St. I left a note for him and my telephone number. He called the next night. I told him I wanted to meet him, that I was a writer too and had heard his poems read in Harlem. He said something like, "I don't know if you want to meet me. I'm a very unsavory character." Calvin had his poems on him when I got to the coffeehouse, and we came back to my place where I read his stuff and he read mine. My work was elementary compared to his, with his metaphysical, sea-loving self, but that was the beginning of something. Calvin said he was staying temporarily with a young poet, David Henderson, and it wasn't long before the three of us got to know each other and became friends.

By this time, the summer of 1962, ON GUARD had pretty much dissolved and those of us who wanted to write began to look toward something else. Those black writers who had been in on the meetings at Aldo's house were not satisfied with Tambellini's direction. His objectives were too broad and vague, and we (Joe Johnson, Roland Snellings, Charles Patterson, Hernton, Henderson and myself) were interested in a group that could meet our needs as black writers. We felt it imperative that we have a device that could deal with race, that could serve to bring us together, that could be a vehicle for the expression of the bitternesses and beauties of being Afro-American (as we called ourselves at the time) in this plastic land.

We called an organizing meeting and sent out a call to all the black writers in the area we knew. Our first workshops, on Friday nights at my apartment, were a way of becoming familiar with each other's work, of airing obsessions, fears, and plodding, jerking toward some concept of what we were by measuring our concepts against the beliefs/experiences of brother writers. We usually adjourned to Stanley's around two o'clock in the morning.

Calvin Hernton, David Henderson, Joe Johnson, Roland Snellings (now Askia Muhammed Touré), Alvin Haynes, Lloyd Addison, Charles Patterson, Lorenzo Thomas, Leroy McLucas and Archie Shepp were regulars at those first sessions.

It didn't take us more than a couple of meetings to decide the workshop should publish a magazine, and to name it "Umbra" after a line in one of Lloyd Addison's poems. We threw two sensational parties to raise funds for the first issue, and those parties helped probably more than anything else to spread the word and put us on the LES map. Specific details about how the magazine was created, expressions of support, etc. are included in an addendum to this article.

The Umbra workshop had an immediate and far-reaching impact. With the exception of John Killens' Harlem Writers Guild, it was the first regular gathering of black writers in a long time. Since the workshop was open to just about anyone, the sessions sometimes took on a carnival atmosphere, with so many people trying to crowd in to hear what was being read. As a form of immediate exposure to sometimes hostile ears, the workshop could at times be volatile. Most of us were beginning writers in the stage where we were coming out of our own private bags, cautiously trying out our ideas like a man dipping his toes in the water. The criticism was often harsh, sometimes too personal, but as I guess anyone will tell you who went through it, after going through that, there's nothing much anyone else can say that will offend you.

During fall 1962 and early 1963 several new writers joined the group. Among these were Norman Pritchard, Ishmael Reed, Lennox Ralphael, James Thompson, Oliver Pitcher, Art Berger and Steve Cannon. Each of these writers were extremely important in the development of both the workshop and the magazine.

Our strongest and most mature voice was, in my opinion, Hernton. Calvin produced a lot of material, and dominated just about everything we did with the salt of his personality. Dig Calvin stretching out, exploring the limits of language, sweating all the time, virtually inundating himself, spinning a long metaphysical combination of multisyllables, chasing that down with down-home blues—E. Franklin Frazier and Memphis Slim cavorting together in an unlikely synthesis. He is a writer whose work deserves far more attention than he has received.

It was not long before we began to read as a group in public. Some of the readings were sensations, like the one at a friend's house in the Bronx who, unfortunately, didn't know what she was in for when she invited us. But just the idea of black poets reading, and using the language black people speak, was unique—no other group had done that. In a sense it was a beginning of the black poetry movement as we know it today.

Whenever the Umbra poets read it sounded like a well-orchestrated chorus of deeply intimate revelations: Calvin into his sea images and metaphysical questions; Roland into his soul chants; David into his narratives; Norman into his sketches; Joe into his lyrics of the urban ghetto; Charmy (Charles Patterson) into his cries of hurt; Ish into outrageous satire...the rich and varied impact of verbal black music. Therefore "Umbra" began to take on a meaning not limited to the magazine or the workshop—it meant the soul, the *spirit* of what we were into, a kind of presence—at the workshop, at readings, at Stanley's, anywhere we were.

Umbra was my introduction to the black arts movement; it tuned me into viewing reality through a black lens. Not that I didn't already know I was black, but the way a *writer* perceives reality is a trained response and carries with it a certain degree of consciousness and self-recognition. The same might be said for other writers in the group, some to a greater, some to a lesser extent than myself. It should be pointed out, however, that the concerns of Umbra were not those of the black arts movement as it later became. Umbra was a predecessor, a progenitor. We might say that Umbra, and a few other writers at that time, anticipated the black arts movement, in fact anticipated all of the black cultural directions that were to develop a few years later. Really, we went through every crisis, every form of confrontation over direction, every emotional attitude that black cultural groups went through during the sixties and seventies.

Philosophically, Umbra offered no basic direction or tenet because it contained so many directions. But we did share several fundamental feelings, leanings. For one thing, a deep cynicism not only toward white America, but toward its potential for redemption as a nation of justice for black people and others who were not white. It was a cynicism particularly northern and urban in the early sixties that set us apart from much civil rights movement thinking, for instance the philosophies of Martin Luther King. It's just that seeing NY in the fifties and having some sense of what America would be like, even with wide-scale desegregation of public facilities, left one jaundiced and pretty despondent about the possibilities of a fundamental redistribution of power. We sensed that we needed to know exactly what kinds of compromises we would and would not be able to make to be able to live here, if any.

We also developed a growing sense of alienation from the white literary world. The reader may think this a negative development born of rejection by the white literary establishment, but it wasn't. It was a healthy development in the sense that the only way we could say certain things as black artists—the things we should be saying—was to recognize that we constituted a separate world, and this world, propelling itself on the cultural integrity of black people in America, is as distinct with its own value system from the main body of American literature as black culture is distinct from whatever mishmash of advertisement majority American culture represents. We discovered that to survive we *had* to protect and in fact advocate and encourage our distinctiveness. How else could we possibly know who we were? Thus the importance of emphasizing African heritage, our music, our church, our talk, our walk—all those things that make us us.

If we accept this assessment of where we were then, we can see Umbra and other NY black writers (like LeRoi Jones) representing an intermediary, transitory stage between the naturalistic protest writing of Richard Wright and what was in a few years to become a separatist, community-oriented, African-flavored black arts Movement (of which Imamu Baraka became a dominant voice).

But Umbra contained within it several artists working on different wavelengths. As people began to crystalize in the direction they were moving it became increasingly difficult to resolve internal conflicts. By late 1963, it was relatively impossible. From the hindsight of today, we can see that no one group could successfully impose its direction on others. Though David Henderson has published several issues of the journal since 1966, the fall of 1963 marks the end of the zenith of Umbra as an integral group—a period of little over a year.

I see nothing wrong with the fact that members of the group have moved in directions as distinctly different as that represented by, say, Muhammed Touré and Ishmael Reed. In fact, the wide spectrum of black literary thrust represented in former Umbra writers is a distinct strength, much healthier than the constrictions in many of the journals of the black arts movement of the late sixties and early seventies.

After all, we have to realize that black life in America is rich and varied and must be rendered specific to be real, to make us feel it—as specific and varied as our music. There's too much imitation in our writing—not only of theme, but style, right down to spelling. A couple of poets set the style and that's it; everyone wants to play it safe. More variety needed *and* more self-criticism. One thing about Umbra: at least you didn't feel like you had to write like someone else to get over.

Finally, if Umbra has any lingering meaning/importance for younger black writers it is in the example of black artists working together to produce something. How important this is, because if we don't turn to and develop our own cultural institutions we'll have nowhere to go but the white establishment—and we'll be wiped out in a hurry. This doesn't mean all black artists, even within a group, have to agree—that's a mistaken notion. But it does mean that we have to have a sense of our role beyond our individual visions—and the importance of that role to the black community. Which is historical.

Umbra: beautiful and tumultuous. A time of discovery, of seeking. And now for the fulfillment of multi/blk vision.

Tom Dent Summer, 1971
Fall, 1979
Copyright Tom Dent, November, 1979
TOM DENT
Box 50584
New Orleans, La. 70150

Addenda

THE NAME "UMBRA"

We took "Umbra" as the title of the magazine & group from a poem by Lloyd Addison, "The Poet Talks to A Face and the Face Talks Back," which used the term "penumbra." From that fertile suggestion we settled on *Umbra*. A sort of poetic core black.

HOW THE FUNDS FOR UMBRA WERE RAISED

Most of the money for the two issues was raised at fundraising parties at Advance, the Communist Youth Org., 80 Clinton St. The parties were widely attended and helped popularize us through the LES. Archie Shepp and Bill Dixon performed. We sold beer, wine and David Henderson's blk-eyed peas.

Many people contributed to the making of the magazine. Artist Bill Day laid out the issues. Tom Feelings artwork; Leroy McLucas, Alvin Simon, Don Charles, and Henri de Chatillon, photographs.

Submissions were selected by majority vote of the three editors, Henderson, Hernton & myself. Hernton was mostly responsible for arrangement of material and section titles.

One thousand copies of both issues were printed by Bill Day.

REACTION AND HELPERS

The reaction to the first issue, published in March, 1963, was extremely enthusiastic. Among those people who were particularly encouraging I would like to especially mention Langston Hughes, John A. Williams, John Henrik Clarke and the entire staff of *Freedomways*, Don Watts of *Liberator*, Hoyt Fuller of *Negro Digest*, and John Killens and members of the Harlem Writers Guild.

Most of the typing was done by Mildred Hernton. Nora Hicks and Jane Logan Poindexter also played important roles as secretaries and attending members of the workshop. The late Margie

Doswell, treasurer of the Legal Defense Fund, supervised our extremely amateurish bookkeeping.

WRITERS WHO SHOULD BE BETTER KNOWN

Several of the writers in the Umbra group have become important figures in black literature. The reader will also find a wealth of valuable material in the works of poets James Thompson, play-wright-poet Oliver Pitcher, poet Joe Johnson, poet/painter Albert Haynes, poets Ray Patterson and Lorenzo Thomas, and prose writer Steve Cannon.

MATERIAL ON UMBRA

Art Berger published an early essay on Umbra in *Mainstream* in 1963, which I believe is generally accurate in describing our activities.

In 1966 David Henderson, Len Chandler and myself taped a lengthy discussion on Umbra that I believe is remarkable for the intensity of its recollections. Other members of the group may also have tapes.

Ishmael Reed discussed Umbra in his introduction to *19 Necromancers From Now*, but his explanation of the crisis that disintegrated the group in November 1963 should be read against the background of my analysis of what we were into in this article.

Lorenzo Thomas' essay, on the literary underpinnings of Umbra and the New York black arts scene in the early sixties in Callaloo #4, "The Shadow World: New York's Umbra Workshop and Origins of the Black Arts Movement," is superb.

MEMORANDUM

FROM: James Bonded, Special Reporter and Trouble Shooter
TO: Jack Getajumponem, Magazine Editor, Herald-Tribune
SUBJECT: Possible Material for a Sensational New Article

Jack, I think I hit on something tremendous. I've been doing reconnaissance down here in the jungle of the East Village at a bar called the Adjunct, you know, for the last four weeks. I've been hearing rumors floating through the peanut shells of an incredibly bitter and violent *new* group of Black poets called the Hombre... Oumbrea... Sumbra...or something like that; anyway they are supposed to be very, very African, native-like, primitive (and of course quite brilliant). It seems as if news of them has not traveled into the civilized world, and I thus followed up my initial discoveries, only to discover that these writers exist in an impenetrably closed tribal-like state, and that they come to-gether once a week in the as yet unchartered and extremely un-der-developed area known on our map uptown as Second Street, between Avenues B & C. That is, they were at one time meeting in this area, no one knows now whether they still conduct their weekly ritual, and no one at the Adjunct bar has ventured to ascertain the present condition of this tribe, because of its repu-tation for secrecy and violence.

One of the knowledgeable whites I was able to interview about this group is Arthur Berger, beat poet, printer, yachtsman and man-about-town in the outer perimeters. His quote follows: "This group is the new generation of black poets, the writers people everywhere will be talking about 30 years from now. They are so bitter against white people and Western society that they make LeRoi Jones seem like a faggoty esthete, and compared to them James Baldwin is only a white liberal." What about that, chief!

I thought this was pretty good stuff, so I decided to see what else I could dig up. I had long planned to cut through the jungle south to another bar called the Unreliable, which is very near the alleged territory of the Hombre tribe, in the hopes of divulging more information. Boss, this bar is wild! Hip spade cats weaving in the smoke near the jukebox to the tom-toms of Thelonious Monk and Miles Davis. White chicks in blue jeans sitting at beat-up tables in a room in the back with their legs open, longingly looking at the spades! Then they dance together! Police cars cruising outside. I made sure I would be unnoticed by wearing the beret my cousin brought me from Paris, some old worn out jeans, and a black leather jacket. Maybe one of the Hombre poets would come into this bar and, un-announced, begin reading some flaming, exciting, licentious poetry, so I sat at the bar near the door to be on the lookout.

This is what I found out about the Hombres at the Unreliable:

1) The Sumbra tribe put out a magazine a year or two ago of unmentionable and heretofore unheard of poetry. Lines that in-voked brimstone and the wrath of Attila the Hun against white people and American culture; words that suggested whites think all Negroes have huge phallic equipment, and that whites only go to Harlem for lascivious excitement; verse that implies a white girlfriend of one of the poets does not know how to use her box.

2) White women attend the weekly rituals! They, of course, are allowed to say nothing, but must sit quietly with appreciative and admiring smiles on their faces. White women sleeping with black poets of the tribe is considered a grievous sin, punishable by threat of death, or by threat of having 'sold out.' They consider that LeRoi

Jones sold out long ago, as he is married to a white woman. One or two white poets belong to this group, but they are required to take a lesser role, though they are allowed to arrange readings for the tribe.

3) The weekly ritual consists of members of the group reading their poetry, followed by long and vociferous criticism by other members, then usually an impassioned defense by the author. The usual procedure, however, is for the author, in the end, to confess that he really didn't know what he was doing, under threat of a knifing. One of the habitués of the Unreliable has said, "Maaan, these cats really *believe* in what they write. Their poetry is *part* of them. They're the most uncommercial artists in history."

4) Apparently, before this territory was chartered and invaded by reporters from the civilized countries, the Hombre tribe actually gave public readings, though it seems as if internal dissension has brought to an end these legendary appearances. There is a wholly unsubstantiated rumor these poets read at Vassar, most unlikely, but I am sure we can use it in our magazine article. The college administration, it is said, would never have allowed them on the campus, but they arrived completely undetected and unheralded because the campus policeman thought they were members of the Saturday night Sweetheart Ball dance band. The rumor has it they read in roundtable fashion for an hour, then one of the poets lectured for two hours on the subject "What Is Wrong With America" in answer to a question by one of the innocent Vassar girls: "What can *we* do to help?" There was another legendary reading, it seems, at a Missionary Association in Brooklyn, during which the just-mentioned poet is reported to have read one of his longest poems while marching between the rows of the audience drunk. The other tribal authors took this as a cue to give inspired readings of *their* works, completely demolishing the program planned by the Missionaries.

But the most famous appearance of the Sumbra poets was at a lovely, lighted back-garden, artiste, cocktail party in the Bronx at the home of a woman who has not yet recovered from the event. Eight poets read to an audience of two enlightened Negro Intellectuals and three White Liberals. Cocktails were served, shrimp salad to follow. The reading descended on the summer evening like a heavy snow. The mistress of ceremonies called it a night and the entire group descended to the basement for refreshments. Exactly what happened then is such a confusion of myth, legend, distortion and excited whisper that no one, not even I, could possibly distill the truth. It seems as if this *same* aforementioned poet (boss, I'll discover his name if it's the last thing I do) somehow did not read in the garden, and therefore undertook a lecture to the guests.on the inadequacies, peculiarities, and perversions of their sexual lives, in language that would make LeRoi Jones' the Toilet sound like Bach's Mass in B Minor. Great consternation on the part of the hostess followed, and the husband of the hostess is reported to have threatened to call the police. It was not long after that that the Hombre poets were asked to leave the Bronx and take their poetry with them. One version of the legend has it that one of the poets stole a bottle of champagne out of the hostess' icebox on the way out.

I have heard comments, however, that the Hombre poets are really just like us. Imagine that they have read in a church on semi-civilized Second Avenue, that they play ping-pong and basketball together just like we do, and on many Sunday afternoons may be found in front of the television sets of their non-tribal friends looking at football games, or baseball games, depending on the season! Once, they even went to the Polo Grounds in the old country to see a baseball game. There is a rumor that the Hombre poets smoked marijuana in the bleachers in center field, and even offered visiting centerfielder Willie Mays a stick, but this is entirely unsubstantiated, and sounds too far-fetched for us to print.

5) There is another story about parties given by this tribe. They are reputed to have given certain wild, bacchanal parties to raise money for their magazine at the headquarters of one of the Chinese Communist units down here. These parties, I am told, displayed great racial solidarity. No records by white musicians were played. Lights were non-existent. Only 'soul food' (a hit Black term meaning southern fried chicken and related African delicacies. P.S. - I've had some, boss; quite tasty) was served, and, I might add, a white friend of the tribe called, unexplainably, Superspade, cooked this 'soul food,' the only instance in the entire world where a Black group has a white cook.

All of this has now settled into vague, nebulous legend, but as it would be easy to dig up more facts, I suggest that we unearth this story, this *scoop*, and do a smash lead article in our New Year's Magazine on the Hombre, or whatever their name, group. There is still another story circulating on the cause and circumstances of the dissolution of the group, something about a weekly ritual meeting ending up with knives flashing, but no one, simply no one down here will tell me what it was all about. I'm sure, however, that the *Herald-Tribune* can come up with the *real* story, and it should make a fitting climax to our article.

Suggested title: BLACK KNIGHTS OF THE NEW BOHEMIA.

I think it would be terriff! Rush instructions by telegram, then runner to me at the Unreliable Bar. If I am not at the Unreliable, send runner forward to a place called Muggings, another bar near the Unreliable, as I am pushing deeper and deeper into the bush.

Yours, as always,

J. B.

DAVE BRUBECK

Can a Pole play the blues? Tom became friends with Dave Brubeck and they entered into interesting discussions about what would today be called "cultural appropriation." To whom does jazz belong, and can an "outsider" play the music? These questions are deepened by the fact that Tom's academic concentration in International Studies was on Poland.

(Unpublished)

No matter what anyone says, Dave Brubeck thinks he can play the blues, and no one can tell him he can't. He'll try rinky-dink blues, Negro spirituals, down home stuff, anything, and he'll do it on record too. And if you say, "Dave, why don't you study the blues, or play something you understand?" he'll tell you, "Man, I been playing the blues before you were born," and mean it too.

Brubeck and I are old friends, of a sort. I first met him as a fan, before he made the money he's making now, and Dave takes to his fans. Gradually, through my persistence and through mutual acquaintances, we actually became friends. I mean I began to spend time with him, got hustled into the back door of his concerts, and we discussed the "race problem," usually between sets or over meals. Now I don't know if all this is friendship, but it is more than a hero-fan relationship.

So it was natural that we should talk about the blues.

"Dave," I would tell him, as he attacked a fat-trimmed steak, "this 'I'm in a Dancing Mood' stuff is nice, but it's not really jazz, man, it's pop stuff."

He would look up, for just a moment, not eager to answer, his face, dominated by its hawk-like nose, unsmiling and intense.

A surprisingly athletic man, Dave's family were Polish immigrants who emigrated to the West, and became cowboys—rich ones.

"But people like it," he would say, in a thin, squeaky, earnest voice. "Everywhere we go, we play it, and everywhere we play it, people like it."

He is, offstage, one of those perennially industrious, busy people who must always be doing something, making contacts, cooking something up, checking dates, purposely not relaxing.

He is the patriarch of his Quartet, and the patriarch of everyone who will accept him, for he loves to wear the robe of benevolent fatherhood, to offer advice to friends and others, in or his out of his profession.

As his nose protrudes defiantly from a rocky face, Dave is defiantly certain of his convictions.

"Listen," I'll never forget him telling me when I had offered that jazz is basically an Afro-American music, "jazz is an assimilation of African rhythms and European harmonics. So how can jazz be all African?"

He told me that when he was in the army he began to take lesson from Arnold Schoenberg, the great modern classical composer. One day, Dave brought in his lesson, and when he had finished, Schoenberg said, "That's good; now why you did that?"

"What you mean, 'why?'" Dave asked.

"Everything you do," Schoenberg explained, "you must know the reason why—*everything.*"

"Why do I have to know *why* I do something?" Dave exclaimed, getting hot. "If I do it, it's valid on the face of it. I *feel* it. That justifies it."

Schoenberg didn't give. Brubeck didn't give. That was Dave's last lesson with Schoenberg.

Brubeck works now in a swanky East Side club that is far too expensive for most jazz fans. He competes with clinking glasses and the incessant chatter of Madison Avenue "expense accounters" (as Miles Davis calls them), old grey-haired men out for a nightcap with music before bed and enterprising young prostitutes surveying the scene for the evening's trade. As he cruises through "Gone With the Wind," dropping other familiar tunes into his solo, alto saxophonist Paul Desmond wanders off the stage and out into the street for clearer air and a smoke. At the set's end, the spotlight shifts to drummer Joe Morello, who bangs away like a many-armed machine, while Dave sits thinking, probably about the home he would like to build for his wife and five children in the Rocky Mountains, where, if the bomb falls, he is least likely to be affected by radioactive fallout.

Recently, Dave made a record with staunch old blues singer, Jimmy Rushing. I happened to be in the dressing room when the first pressed copy was played by a Columbia A & R man for all parties concerned. Rushing was there, for one of the star attractions at the club, Sarah Vaughn, had had an accident, and was not appearing that night.

In that small dressing room, Rushing's hugeness of sound was his tradition, but it wasn't a bad record. "Man, I think we wailed," Dave said, looking at Rushing, and Rushing nodded his assent.

They were going to do a few things together that night, Rushing to come on later. As the Quartet went to the stage to begin its set, I remained in the back with the blues singer.

"This is a filthy business," he said. "I been taken advantage of for a long time before I made two cents I could afford to lose." He told me about a man who filmed one of his appearances at a Boston club, sold prints without him knowing it, and never gave him a cent in royalties.

When it was time for Jimmy Rushing to join the Dave Brubeck Quartet on stage, Dave pulled over the microphone and announced, "Now ladies and gentlemen, the Father of the Blues, Jimmy Rushing," and a murmur of disappointment swept through the audience, for they had expected someone important, like Bobby Darin.

Rushing sang a few numbers, and then, together they swung into "Going to Chicago."

Suddenly the Quartet began to come to life. Rustling's powerful voice brought the old blues home, and the club grew quiet. Even the busy waiters stopped to watch what was happening on the stand.

"Going to Chacaagooo," bellowed Jimmy, laughing and making even Dave believe what he was playing. Desmond slipped in with a cool, drifting, satirical solo, awake for once.

They brought the house down.

Dave came off the stage excited and laughing. He spotted me and shouted, "This child tells me I can't play the blues. Man, I was playing the blues before you were born."

Jimmy Rushing sauntered by, his night's work done. He was still singing "Going to Chicago," as if he were really going.

I laughed at them both—especially at Dave, for I realized then that East is East and West is West, and seldom shall the twain meet. If Brubeck thinks he can play the blues, you can't tell him he can't. All you can do is hope that when the blue mood hits him, Jimmy Rushing is pretty close by.

DEAR DR. BRAYBOY

Tom is writing a letter to a psychologist about himself as the subject of psychoanalysis. (Unpublished)

May 28, 1968

Dear Dr. Brayboy,

I have been wanting to write you for about a week now. Last week I plunged into one of my sustained attempts to solve my long-standing personal riddle: how to accept my parents and at the same time retain some sureness of my own identity, without guilt. Even though these three years I have been here since the Spring of 1965 have been the busiest and most involved of my life, I have never really been able to solve the riddle. It has always been present like a rumbling underneath, sometimes boiling over to completely disrupt my surface activity, most times if I look to activity hard enough I hardly hear it. I believe this riddle is the key to all my internal problems, certainly those that revolve around creativity and those that revolve around sex.

In a way, one might say the FST has presented me with a theoretical meaning for my life that I am not personally ready for. All I need to give my life meaning is inherent in the theater's promise. As far as my writing is concerned the theater provides a ready outlet, a method of establishing contact with audience in a way I found most difficult when I began to write seriously in New York. When I came to the FST in 1965 the audience already existed and was expanding. The theater also provided, still provides, an image for me, or a method by which I can project myself as a distinct person from my father. It has been true that most people in New Orleans who know my father still think of me as "Dent's son" but by now they probably have come to feel that "Dent's son" is not like Dent. Thirdly, the FST, particularly at first, provided a ready source of friends who shared my interests, of the type I left in New York and missed so much. In 1966 we were a small insular group, working, talking, eating, and, for the most part, sleeping together. We ran with a few other expatriates from the Movement, we always ran together. Such a small inbred group was destructive to us as persons and to the theater, but at least in the beginning it let me live in the South. I was not thrown back with people who I had absolutely nothing in common with.

I also found that I rather enjoyed being in New Orleans, there was something about the climate, the sunlight, the greenness of the place, the sense of space and natural physical beauty that I had always missed in New York. I was also intrigued by the mystery of the Mississippi River, a mystery that always appealed to me as a youth. I made up my mind early after I returned that since I had a car I would travel as much as I could, to really see Louisiana and the South, to get first-hand impressions of places I was near but had always only read about. My favorite release is to drive up the river from New Orleans, or down the river, to follow its many curves, to get some sense of its history. I felt a sense of belonging to the South, to its Black people who I was from, but never really knew. This is what appealed to me so strongly about the theater; we played to these people, in small towns in Mississippi and Louisiana that I had never been to, and all over New Orleans in communities I had only passed through as a boy. It was as if I was putting back a piece in the puzzle of my personality that had been missing for a long time. I also perceived that part of my value to the FST was that I *was* from the South and New Orleans, whereas they weren't. I could share their artistic sophistication and interests because I had been in New York and part of that world, but I was also a product of this world, which gave me inherent advantages. And as most of them became disenchanted with New Orleans and the South and drifted away to pursue their careers in New York I somehow developed a stronger commitment to staying here, believing with a kind of mysticism that this is where I belonged, this is where my work was to be done.

Also, possibly mystically, I developed a stronger affinity for black people, I found myself believing and accepting ideas I had merely mouthed before. I say mystically because it was not an ideological development, it happened apart from that without the dedication or resolve of reason. Of course being in New Orleans helped. That is what I could *see* again how I had developed, how my esteem for things white, for non-African hair, for non-Negro culture had developed so firmly in New Orleans, for these were, and to a great extent still are, the values of New Orleans. It was as if I was coming to an acceptance of myself that was not possible before, a part of my reality. Certainly such acceptance was not possible at Morehouse and Syracuse, where I longed to be white, or so light that my Negroidness would not be visible. Or in New York when my being raged over this conflict. By identifying with blackness I could achieve a new freedom: I was a part of something larger than myself or my family. True my own *personal* role as a Black person might be vague or undefined, but unless I was too sharply attacked by doubts I could achieve a feeling of togetherness and homeness which I could also relate to the work of the FST.

Loving black people does not mean that I hate white people. I hate white oppression but not white people. To be sure of ourselves and our strengths excludes the necessity to put whites down simply because they are white. I hate white assumptions of superiority but I hate our assumptions of inferiority just as much. Both assumptions are very strong in American society. I love Steve Scott who is 20 and lives in Sunflower, Mississippi, because he can talk very coolly and purposefully about becoming mayor of Sunflower. There is no inferiority there, and the fact is he *can* become the mayor of Sunflower. Not that becoming mayor of Sunflower or anything is a big thing, but the hope is in his belief in himself and his people, and he meets all the standards of the poorly educated, poverty-stricken, "culturally deprived" black youth. In him and those like him I feel something worth being a part of, and worth championing. It is this that has glued me fast to the South.

*   *   *

Back to the letter, which I had to leave Wednesday. I hope this isn't an imposition; "why is this cat telling me all this stuff *now*?" I was going to write you earlier, back in 1965, to try to sum up what those three years meant, but I couldn't do it then. Besides, you shouldn't indulge yourself to feel a good three years, then forgotten. It was always, I thought, for a lifetime. So much for apologies, etc.

I am reading Fanon's *Black Skin, White Masks*. He talks about the need of blacks from Martinique to assimilate French culture, and how this gave them status. It made me reflect on my own desire for anonymity, with respect to both family and race. Once again I am trying to define what must be a vague feeling, but my earliest desires after leaving home, well even before leaving home, were to free myself completely from my background, from history. This was the compelling fantasy, or one of its main themes. I was not acceptable to myself because my history was not acceptable?

It probably began with the fantasy of the Indian-Negro Dent who was born in Gary, Indiana, of undetermined parentage (the child of a prostitute and unknown customer), a fantasy which began in high school in idle hours, which continued with great intensity through Morehouse, gradually declined at Syracuse and stuttered to a halt in the early 1960s. My alter-hero was fantastic athlete, absolutely poverty stricken, literally raising himself from bootstraps, attending Dartmouth, becoming a great athletic star there, marrying a white woman (of whom I had no sharp image), going on to pursue a career in professional football while at the same time pursuing a doctorate in sociology, finally near the end of the fantasy beginning to speak out on social issues, beginning to identify as a Negro. I always kept the alter-hero two years older than myself. As I filled in the details of the fantasy, or as I filled out the hours the details were always very realistic, as if this one person were operating against a background of extremely real events. Of course there were many other fantasies, particularly athletic, identification with stars, teams, etc. Always there was the feeling of enormous general acclaim, but not at the complete cost of identity, for I would always retain some aspect of racial identity, though usually I would discard my family altogether, or effect a complete separation from them and their influence at a very young age.

During the last few days I have been looking through the notebooks I made in 1963 and 1964, about my days at Morehouse and Syracuse. At Morehouse I certainly had no clear concept of what I wanted to do. We were all taught, vaguely, that we were to "make it," which always remained for me very vague because I wanted a kind of success that would be acceptable to everyone. I had, as far as I can remember, no clear concept of what it would be. Even though my major was political science and I was the best student I could not envision myself as either a politician or teacher. I liked writing and was editor of the student paper but considered literature as beyond my reach, and at any rate, totally unacceptable. I didn't know anyone, no one at Morehouse knew anyone, and my parents didn't know anyone who had made a "career" of literature. It wasn't so much that it was opposed, it was simply unthinkable. I hated people who called me "Dent," wanted everyone to call me by my first name.

At Syracuse I found myself continuing, with a heavy workload and good grades, in a direction which was not the product of any choice. My strongest emotion on leaving Morehouse was a tremendous fear of the future because I wanted to stay; at least in the *Maroon Tiger* I had found a way to express myself and something of a home. This only happened in the last year. Now, it was torn from me. There was no question that I was expected to go to graduate school. Since I was a political science major I applied and was accepted in that field. I was only twenty and needed desperately time to breathe and live, but I never had that time. I was always younger than my classmates, my assumption was always that of a luxury of time to make decisions. The reason why I left Syracuse was not because of overt rebellion or concrete vision of what lay ahead for me; I simply ran out of gas.

It was impossible for me to exist not knowing what I wanted to do, not really wanting anything. By the fourth year I was so confused that I couldn't complete anything I began, and I did not complete my master's thesis. Because I realized that Syracuse was not a step toward anything for me, I have never regretted leaving. I should have left sooner. During this time my fantasy was a vague dream of going to Europe, living in Europe for many, many years. Physical separation seemed the only way I could deal with the imposing image of my parents; maybe if I put myself three thousand miles away I could forget them and vice-versa. Other psychological motions formed. The strongest was an idolatry of Dave Brubeck. It was during this time, 1952-56, that Brubeck came to prominence in jazz. Don't forget that I knew nothing of jazz before Syracuse; the music was introduced to me by a Jewish friend there, and introduced through Brubeck, who had enough classical remnants to appeal to those who were only familiar with classical music. Brubeck symbolized, and I hit on it very quickly, a kind of freedom for me through identification; he was rebelling against middle class American antipathy to jazz, but not completely. He was middle class himself, his appeal to college students and the young whites of that day who could not understand Parker and what the black jazz revolutionaries were doing. But he appealed to many college blacks too, products of the black middle class who were taught that jazz was the devil's music, but how could that be when Brubeck did not drink, was not a dope addict, was a college graduate who studied classical music, yet called himself a jazz musician? When Brubeck played a concert at Cornell, all the black students (only ten of us in 7,000) went to Ithaca to hear him, including Jim Brown.

I not only identified with Brubeck, I *was* him. I mean the fantasy of being Brubeck was so real that I lived through it day by day, expending more emotional energy in dreaming it than in real life. I also attempted to make it real by seeking out Brubeck in New York, hanging around him, making a nuisance of myself talking to him, and trying to arrange a concert for the quartet in Syracuse. He was probably overwhelmed by all this attention from a black youth and he never discouraged me. I was always able to go to concerts or clubs with the band, never had to pay. Advocacy of Brubeck also became an excellent device to use against my parents, who were not sympathetic to his music, particularly my mother. Somehow I was able to try to define myself as distinct from them, not directly, but through the conflict over Brubeck. This was an important point, because my mother was a classical pianist herself and extremely knowledgable; any disagreement with her views in our family was considered sacrilegious. She would say Brubeck was simply "a conservatory boy gone wrong."

I don't know what made me realize that Syracuse was taking me nowhere, that it wasn't going to work out, that I would never be able to merge my dreams with reality. I know that I went to a white psychiatrist at Syracuse for four months, it was there that I had to ask myself what I was doing there, and I couldn't give an answer. I did not want to work for the American government. I had no great desire to teach. I didn't want to go to law school. I knew nothing of wanting to be a Negro, wanted to be white, yet the Negro world was my world, it was what I knew and came from, it existed like a former world in my past that I might wish to eradicate, to forget, but it wouldn't go away. I was living in too many worlds and I couldn't marry them, couldn't put it all together with any meaning. One world is enough, but I was trying to deal with four or five.

I was trying to find a connecting link that would give my life meaning. This was the search that led me to writing, to New York, to you, to many other directions. Of course I quickly found that I could not find the connecting link *through* writing; it must already be there. To write and have something to say, one must already know who he is; this enables him to interpret life. I think it was my failure to…or rather the collapse of my efforts to know what I wanted to say on paper that led me to analysis, to a deeper look into myself. My notebooks are filled with repetitions of an attempt to interpret my life, to give it a clarity other people and artists had. There is one note from May 6, 1963: "Like Genet, Rimbaud's development as a poet comes from a mythological interpretation of his life, a philosophical acceptance of some arrested development which he can see, understand, accept and interpret. One's power comes from some rocky, hard-rock interpretation of one's reality?" There are many comments like this, for I knew this is what I lacked. "Arrested" is interesting because one does not usually think of an artist in that sense, but I think all the great ones are. It has to do with what one accepts about himself that will not change, can never change as long as he lives, which makes it possible to look at one's life from present back to the beginning as if through a long funnel of predictable developments. In this way one never loses touch with his origins, with the basic terms of his existence. I believe this sense of self is the precondition of vision. In reading writers, in particular Black writers, there is this. In Douglas there is no debate about the basic motion of his life, from slavery to freedom to advocacy of freedom for his people. How clear things must have been to him! Notice how those writers who followed (the great ones) DuBois, Hughes, Wright, Baldwin, Malcolm, all of them could interpret their lives with a connecting link, a single theme which was broad enough and strong enough to carry the weight of all their experiences. Notice also, that with Black writers, our strongest tradition is autobiography; their lives had such meaning as they lived them, that it was unnecessary to invent story, fancy or plot. I also could not help noticing that each of those writers gained strength by paralleling his experience with the experience of Black people, so that their stories became both personal and mythological, they were able to see themselves mirrored in life around them.

I observed my friends who were psychologically strong, creative, productive. (I have always been attracted to strong people, possibly in my quest for strength.) Many of them had the same problems I did, or worse. Somehow, however, they were able to keep driving, keeping producing despite everything. There was a kind of pride, a sense of wholeness, a confidence in these people. They were not destroyed by guilt. At the base of all their self-questioning they believed what they were doing was right, had a value they would die behind. The talented writers from the Umbra group had that, David and Calvin, particularly David. David was proud of the fact that he *could* write, of the power it gave him. Whereas everytime

I prepared to write I would have to go into a long analysis which always led me back to the first principles because I wasn't sure, they seemed somehow to *know* what they wanted to say without asking themselves. Whereas my work was much too conscious, what Baldwin calls "attitudes," theirs was usually unconscious.

*   *   *

News came last night of the shooting of Bobby Kennedy. Here we go again. Rap Brown's best statement was "violence is as American as cherry pie." I think it's just a reaping of what has been sown with Negroes all along. Black people have been eliminated traditionally by violence without serious repercussions from the power structure with such monotonous and predictable repetition that when it happens all we can say is "there we go again." Certainly black people were not too surprised when King was shot, many of us had been expecting it as a foregone conclusion. As far as violence against black people is concerned, I think it will increase as we become more potent and the old means of keeping us in check break down. But the spread of this into the political situation at large has some of that chickens coming home to roost quality when one considers that the CIA has adopted political assassination as a legitimate means of maintaining American imperialism in South and Central America, and all of what we have done in Asia & Vietnam smacks of this kind of thing. If this legitimization of violence by the power structure is acceptable for their own ends, they shouldn't be surprised when it is turned against them. As for us, I think if we continue to do aggressive material in small towns in Mississippi, etc., and if we are clearly and publicly singled out as a danger to the white power structure there is a good chance some violent act will be attempted against us. It's amazing this hasn't happened already. We have had, of course, police harassment both here and on the road.

So much for the Kennedy matter, which now (night of June 5) looks as if it will conclude fatally for him. From all the medical reports he hasn't responded to treatment. I just walked out on Bourbon St., which beats with the same tasteless pseudo-excitement for many, many tourists who seem not the least concerned with Kennedy, if they even know what happened. Bourbon Street is going to go on, no matter what. If against the reality of Bourbon St. Kennedy's life doesn't mean anything, with all his power and money, you can imagine what the life of a black man means. It is a cruel observation that the only thing we can do that could slow down a Bourbon St. oriented culture would be to riot, or to threaten to riot. Dig all those stories coming out of Washington about the effect of the King aftermath—riots and poor people's camping on the Cherry Tree Week Festival and the normal spring tourist trade. And Johnson is going on TV tonight, who has perpetuated more crimes and masterminded more assassinations than any president in memory, talking about the need for law and order. These people want everything as it used to be, as it was when white was white and black was black and they could paint themselves white. I remember when JFK was shot and we had a session the next day and you said "they weren't all that disturbed when Medgar Evers was shot." I believe all those little things catch up with you, but not in the way you expect it, or when you expect it. That's what's happening to American society.

*   *   *

Let me try to bring to a close this painfully long and I'm afraid turgid letter. I didn't mean to get into a history of my life, and all that stuff, which I'm sure after three years of, you could certainly do without now. I have been trying to approach...trying to say that in the last few weeks I have a new way of looking at my life; it has to do with history, my history, some omitted facts that I now think are important, but which I had never accorded importance before. Understand that it is difficult to write about myself, particularly now in the throes of the Kennedy tragedy which, like all these kinds of things, give me a sort of perverted pleasure. Because everything seems more important, my senses sharpen, somehow the sorrow which drenches people as in this and the King thing makes me a little happier to be alive than I usually am, and I function better. Except in the Medgar Evers one, where I knew him personally and it cracked me up. But I have noticed that in what we used to call the Movement, and in most black people that are really involved in something and have ability, they don't think about themselves much. Of course this is a blessing; I can be accused of thinking about myself too much with such little reward. But sometimes the emphasis on *doing*, on image, becomes a substitute for really understanding what we are doing. And I believe this is what I, certainly as a writer, must try to do, or at least understand what I want to do, but I am simply making the point that the nature of life as I find it here now is so fast, so mercurial, so subject to abrupt changes that trying to understand in some methodical, disciplined, time-consuming fashion is not possible; black writers have to play too many roles. And most of those roles or at least many of them have to do with nowness, with image, with surface, not analysis and unemotional objectivity. This is the problem I must solve if I am to produce good new material for the FST: how do you make it meet the demands of now, or at least some of them, and still have substance. I feel like the man who is faced with a huge piece of beef but can only get a skinny hamburger here and there. Life is too big and too fast and too slippery to get hold of by traditional methods.

Always my search for identity goes on, like a bubbling organism just below the surface, occasionally bubbling over. This theater has done wonderful things for me and I know why: it gives me an audience. You've got to have an audience, or believe you have one. I have never believed it. Who would listen to *me*? I remember once you said "there's too much shadow-boxing with you," and it hurt. Of course it was true. You just can't work hard at it, really refine it and prepare it, the "it" being something that must come so much from yourself, from your senses, from your capacity to live with and accept your sense, unless you really believe someone will receive it. If not now, someday. The theater can give me this, but as I said I am not ready for it. I have not been ready for it. I began to be fascinated by history, details. I found great joy in searching the bones of West Point, Miss., for its black heroes, but its black heroes take meaning against the details of the white tapestry that surrounds and envelops them, and the history that gave the tapestry its colors. West Point was Indian country. When I see the Indian burial mounds, the Indian-named streams and ledges and ridges and rivers, that means something to me when I look at it through the lens of the violence of the area's current rules against black men. Somehow it has its own cruel, irrational yet sure explanation. For a while there, just a few months ago, I said I know what I'm going to do. Everytime I try a poem I'm going to preface it: TO THE GREAT BLACK PEOPLE OF THE FUTURE. But that didn't work. I was trying to find that audience. I even had a thing where I saw myself as a latter day descendant of the Mali Republic, with all its power, glory and culture. Life is too fast; I couldn't keep up. I'm the father of the FST writer's workshop but workshops won't cure that problem. You can have a hundred people there listening to you but unless I believe it, believe what I am saying and know who I'm saying it to, physical presence won't do the trick. So often I could see myself drifting into the image of me New Orleans negroes see: "he's Al Dent's son, rebelling, but that's all he'll ever be." Then the sexual troubles start. West Point was so invigorating because they didn't know I was Al Dent's son; if they did they didn't care. They thought I had something on my own and it made a difference in me. I was freer, and not guilty about it. Sometime the attacks go like this: "who are you to presume to have anything to say? You who have been given everything." Sometimes like this: "you can never be a black writer like the great black writers because they came from nothing into something, their life had a consistent arch upward, you came from money and not poverty, you can never be part of the 'folk,' only a fakir." Another variation: "you can depart from the values of your parents if you want. But blood will be on your hands if you go too far. Don't you love your parents? And how can you claim you arrived at your newfound position on your own when your parents helped you financially. If you burn your bridge to them you'll be doomed to a life of bitterness and unhappiness. Is ideology and self-assertion worth this?" This kind of stuff brings on sexual and every other kind of trouble. Of course I can never win over my parents. We're lightyears apart in more ways than I can name. My father doesn't bother me, but my mother still seeks some magical resolution, out of the empty dreams of her stagnant garden; it is all too depressing for words. I really believe I would be married ten years by now if my mother would stop telling me she thinks I should get a "help-mate." Out of these little despairs I continue to search. And I want, and have planned, and it is possible, to change my role in the FST from that of administrator to creator. That is possible now.

Then it hit me to search my own history. To search it again, to go back so far so I could and examine, not the enigmas and vacuous emotions, but the facts. To find something to hold on to, something to tie my image, my identity to, something factual and personal, something I considered positive.

*   *   *

It's kind of hard trying to finish this. The entire Kennedy thing presses in on my consciousness. One can't help but hope that assassination doesn't become contagious, because there is really no defense. It means we will be right back on the wild west, on the plains, because even if there is a gun registration law everyone will have one if they feel it necessary. Too many people already have weapons and all these people in Vietnam are being trained to use them. It could be that America will break out into a series of small wars over the next few years, and if they are race wars it will be suicide for us. Did you see LeRoi's recent statement in Newark that his group was suppressing violence because when they analyzed the political situation they discovered they could control the city anyway by ballot in 1970? Very interesting. I would not be surprised to see Stokely Carmichael & Rap Brown develop similar positions, especially now that Stokely & Miriam Makeba are trying to purchase a $70,000 home in Washington. You don't burn down a town where you have a $70,000 home.

Continuing to read Fanon's *Black Skin, White Masks*, which is excellent. His analysis of the man of color and the white woman, chapter three, is very apropos to the creole problem in New Orleans, and I believe Jean Venuse has many traits similar to the ones I'm trying to defeat. Fanon calls him an "abandonment-neurotic." Black man in Bordeaux can't decide whether he is white or black, so he asks his friends to tell him. Naturally he doesn't believe anything they say. It's a very sad case, but Fanon believes his problem is personal, not racial. Watching the funeral yesterday reminded me so much of the Kennedy & King funerals that one begins to wonder if we aren't developing a new theater form: the national funeral. It seems fitting that public figures should have public funerals, but the conscious selection of images and rituals,

the organization and money required to pull it off, the crowds &
spectators who are the key to the whole thing; it really is too much.
But aside from the morbidity of it, I prefer the funerals to political campaigning and our other national rituals; even Johnson
and others who run this inhuman government seem humanized.
That it takes a funeral to do it is a comment on the nature of our
government.

Back to what I was driving at. I began searching for the positive image in my own family history. Something actually there,
that I could believe. I didn't see any possibilities in my father. If
anything is true it is that my ideas have developed differently
from his, not only because of different experience, but different
temperaments. I could find something in my mother's artistic inclination and accomplishments, but my mother, unlike most Negro
women, is too insulated from life to really be a strong image. On
my mother's side her father had a lot of traits I like: independence,
iconoclasm, folksiness; but he also was a strong conservative. His
wife had the same quality of independence and drive that he had,
they were both country people who came to the city and made a
slight fortune, but she had a streak of religious fundamentalism
and a domineering tendency that was unbearable. My grandfather
was a pioneer Texas physician and his wife active in civic work,
but they were both straight out of the middle class bag, Western
Americana. My father's sister and her husband are straight out of
the middle bag, Atlanta black Americana. You know what that
means. Except that my "uncle" is a social climber.

*   *   *

Another long break. Believe it or not I am in New York, been here
about a week. We are trying to finish a book on the FST for Babbs-
Merrill, very behind on deadline. I think it will be a good book,

a compendium of all our work: articles, letters, journals, memos, poetry, plays. Should be out Feb. 15. Also working on structure of FST, fundraising. We hired a lovely and very bright girl, Bobbi Jones, who will work for us in NY fundraising, publicity, etc. I see the basic organization as set for the next years, with John O'Neal as administrator, but we must still find our theater person. It has to be a black person who wants to work in the south, wants to play to black audiences, wants to do experimental things, who has a feeling for our popular music and knows how to use it on the stage. And who will stay two years. That's going to be hard to find, but each of those qualities is very important. As I believe I said earlier in the letter (when I began years ago) I will move into an artistic role as writer, with a voice in selection of plays, etc. But mostly I want to write, believe I can, especially if this statement I am making now is a kind of watermark. It would be too much to tell you about Gil Moses, who is one of the founders of the theater along with O'Neal. And who left in 1966 about the time I took over. But he is a fine writer with quite a theater background, and really gave the FST its first artistic thrust. Very young at the time (now 25) he became enmeshed in his own personal problems and just tired, and left to sort out the FST behind him and find himself as a musician. Now Gil has come in at the last stage to work on the book with me, and he is becoming excited again about FST, about writing for us. Collaborating with him on the book is so rewarding (we always got along well in NO though he is an abrasive person) that I hope we can collaborate on some shows for FST this fall. Our hope is to begin playing in the South around February after organizing a rehearsal company here in November.

All that to say I believe things are looking up for us, and I feel I can really, actually limit myself to the role I hope to play.

*　　　*　　　*

I was leading up to something about my family. Family history. It is my paternal grandmother that I hit on and thought so much about. Because she was very poor, unlearned, born around the end of slavery, lived in Georgia all her life, but with an extremely acute, perceptive, see-through-the-holes-in-people mind. I called her "Grand." She died while I was at Morehouse of cancer, at about 85. Now, here is the thing. It was Grand who raised me in my earliest years. Not my mother. My mother was still in school, at Oberlin, and Grand was brought from Atlanta to raise me. She left an indelible impression on me, because despite her age I believe she really understood me, understood my nature. Understood and was tolerant of my fantasies. Despite the gush of love and possessiveness that issued from my mother toward me it was really Grand to whom I owed my allegiance in my earliest (until 5) years. I now think this is very important. And it has quite a lot to do with my difficulties with my mother. Because Grand had nothing, had never anything, but my mother was the daughter of quite a well-off family, the only daughter. Unconsciously, they expressed quite different outlooks toward life. They must have. And it was Grand's that I adopted, not my mother's. And I help allegiance to her because it was she that I was very close to when I went away to college. To Morehouse. How interesting that she lived until one month after I graduated, then passed away from cancer. Also, Grand did not raise my father. Or I might have been more like my father. I don't know who my father's father was, and it has never been discussed in our family, but he was "adopted" (not legally) by friends of Grand's, the Thomases, after whom I am named.

So I see some interesting facts, the details of which I have never really given significance before. There is no clear line of descendence from my grandmother through my father to me. It is rather a jagged line. My grandmother raised me, but did not raise my father. My grandmother raised me, not my mother. In the case of my younger brothers, they were more directly influenced by my mother and father. Thus a reason for my personality as different from theirs in certain respects.

I can identify with my grandmother. With her poverty, but mostly I would say her attitude toward life. She was submissive and idolized my father *but* I'm not so sure she didn't see through him. She once said of her son-in-law (the uncle I talked about who is now a real estate man in Atlanta) when she was ironing shirts for him for a "vacation," "he wants to be a big man, but he'll never be it." I loved her ungrammaticalisms, but she read the newspaper and kept her mind alert until the day she died. She read everything I wrote. Her mind never died. In other words, in using Grand as an image in my own family and history to identify with, I have someone who I really liked, who shaped part of my personality I think my parents have often tried to subdue, or just didn't understand, and who is consistent with the majority of black people in this country, with their condition. In rediscovering Grand I rediscover something in my own past and in myself which I have never given proper significance. It thus becomes possible to deal with my mother without guilt because I was free from my mother from the beginning, since she did not shape my earliest feelings. I don't owe her anything but the love of being my mother. But no more. I'm not saying it very clearly, but if I look at the true history of it I can see how I am free in ways I had never thought possible before. People who want to tie me too closely to my direct parents can't do it, because father wasn't there either.

One more key thing. Dad can't face the fact of his own heritage, the fact that is almost surely illegitimate. I can. I don't care. To be able to accept the history of our family, with love (because of my love to Grand), gives me a power of clarity and emotional freedom which my parents don't have. I sense a jealousy on my mother's part to my allegiance to Grand. Way back, a thing sensed, never proved.

These are the facts, and they give me other ideas. I love history, I love the historical method. I want to use it in my work, to use it more, consciously applied to prose poems, and in whatever I do toward theater. As an artistic method I have to refine it, but if I ask myself, as I so often have, what is the "stuff" of my work, where other writers use psychology, mysticism, philosophy, documentation, then I know it is the history, the story of what happened, that feeling of putting in all the facts. Because when we rewrite our lives, we have a way of leaving out the unpleasant facts. I want to put them back in.

I'm going to stop now. I hope it hasn't been too much, but I would be very happy to hear from you at some time, to know what you think about the viability of this solution. I don't want to get too mystical, but I have to have a way of looking at my life. That I can accept. Then I think some of those other problems will fall into place.

Best wishes,
Tom

Free Southern Theater & BLKARTSOUTH

Here we are dreaming while thinking we are wide-awake

Malcolm X warned us to be careful when we wake someone who is sleeping, especially if they are dreaming. When we are dreaming, we are invariably convinced that what is happening is real. Our task, the task of the Griot, is waking people up; it is delicate and often misunderstood. Tom Dent understood that socially conscious writing was an arduous, sometimes painful, and often thankless undertaking. Few sleepers appreciate being woken.

When I met Tom, the Free Southern Theater [FST] was his tool for waking up our people. Tom believed that theater provided an important way to publicly deal with the complexities faced by blacks. Many of us in the FST volunteered to go South (or to stay South) and shoulder the task of waking up our people. And that vision led to massive internal struggle.

FST had been founded by three SNCC activists: Doris Derby, Gilbert Moses, and John O'Neal. Within two years of its founding in Jackson, Mississippi, the Theater relocated to New Orleans. Doris disagreed with pursuing the bright lights of the big city and remained in Jackson. Shortly after FST settled into the Big Easy, funding ran dry. John was sentenced to community service in New York when he refused induction into the military, and Gilbert went off to pursue his interests in music. Tom, who had joined the Theater in New Orleans and become its manager shortly thereafter, was left with little more than an empty building.

When I met Tom in June of 1968, on Louisa Street in the Upper Ninth Ward, I was searching for a place where I could develop as a writer who was actively interested in the black movement. Tom shared that interest but, and I realize the weighty implications of this only in hindsight, he was also vested with the near impossible mission of building a revolutionary theater in the urban bush of late sixties New Orleans—a task which carried its own set of conundrums and contradictions.

Theaters are like circuses without the animals. The stage attracts freaks, eccentrics, runaways, and especially people who are talented but troubled, and FST cast an especially wide net. Not all of us were thespians or even cultural workers. FST was an initiative of civil rights workers, and as such always had a political vector that attracted non-artist activists who were interested in the arts as a tool of struggle, rather than art for art's sake. Tom understood the potential of a theater that made room for those who were interested in drama only to the degree that it served an overtly political purpose.

Perhaps because he was an administrator and not solely a playwright or actor, Tom's thinking on theater was, to use the Crescent City patois, "beaucoup" complex, as exemplified by his long letter to Robert "Big Daddy" Costley and Leroy Giles. Big Daddy, who was our resident director, was a holdover from the mid-sixties generation of FST staffers. Leroy came down in 1969 with the newly hired professional company of actors, joining after I did.

One bit of context illustrates the complexity of the decisions FST faced, reflected in Tom's letter and in his rigorously critical essay "Beyond Rhetoric." Gilbert had directed FST's touring version of Baraka's play *Slaveship*. In the late sixties, it was a startling production that moved audiences to deep, visceral responses sometimes verging on what might be called literal civil disobedience. Gilbert's FST production led directly to a New York Broadway run, which in turn raised the questions: Was Broadway the goal of the production, and what did Broadway offer that performances in small towns in Mississippi, Alabama, and Louisiana did not offer?

Many years later, while addressing an Urban Bush Women program, I brought up this issue. John O'Neal pointed out that the difference between the FST and the Broadway production was not in the productions themselves, but rather in the audiences. The meaning and impact of the play was precisely located in the consciousness and conditions of the audience. The audience was an essential element in determining the significance of the theater.

Generally, professional theater is like Catholic mass: the actors provide the pomp and glitz, with the audience as the onlooking congregation. Our community was more Baptist in orientation. Scratch that—we were like Holy Rollers. We wanted our audiences to scream and shout, swoon and fall out in enraptured revolutionary seizures. As far as we were concerned, Broadway was just a street in the university district of uptown New Orleans. When we moved from our Ninth Ward home in the early seventies, it was not to Hollywood but rather to Central City. We were a "black" theater.

Tom constantly reminded us to be mindful not just of the craft and content of our work, but also to be conscious of our audiences, and indeed to accept the necessity of audience development among our people. By "audience development," Tom didn't mean accruing paying box office customers; he meant raising the consciousness of both those who attended the theater as well as those who created it. As Tom expressed it in a journal entry: "In the south, after all the trials, the tribulations, and demonstrations of the sixties, we have learned that there can't be meaningful change until black people, the ones in the streets, not the leaders, have consciousness." There was no wall separating thespians from audience, or in capitalist terms, no essential gap dividing producers from customers and patrons. The theater had the task of changing all of us.

Harriet Tubman said she could have freed a thousand more people if only she could have convinced them that they were enslaved. In the USA, slavery was perfected in ways unmatched anywhere else in the western hemisphere. The psychological process of turning former slaves into mind-bent/mind-broken doppelgängers of their masters was almost alchemical. Somehow we blacks were taught and eventually believed, at least reductively, that "free" meant free to vainly try to become white—as though being white was some magical and desirable transformation. Yet in actuality, "becoming white" invariably requires cultural and ethnic erasure, even as it requires us to forget that we are anything other than a color. Whiteness subsumes, covering and smothering the multitudinous cultural identities of the United States beneath an alabaster blanket.

Through his ability to move comfortably in mainstream society and his deep commitment to black culture, Tom saw that progressing along the prescribed American way was actually suicidal for a black identity. He also recognized the double-bind of racial consciousness. To him, focusing mainly on race was as dangerous and debilitating as being racially blind. We shouldn't try to become white, but neither should we try to ignore being black. Tom taught me to walk the tightrope: celebrating the beauty of our skin did not mean that other skins were ugly. The world is not binary, he suggested: life is dialectic, dynamic, both/and. Yes, we were beautiful, but we also could be ugly as any other.

Tom delved deeply into what some would consider our dark side as a people. His play *Ritual Murder* did not spring from imagination only, but primarily from Tom's willful immersion into the life, and death, of everyday black people, as he describes in "The Task of Building Black Consciousness." The play deals with the confounding complexity of black-on-black homicide that not only frequently happens, but also not infrequently involves friends killing friends. Such incidents, he wrote, "occur as part of our daily lives[;] they are not only the result of a history of physical oppression, but of a deep-seated psychological oppression. And it is a valid function of the black arts to deal with this psychological oppression, this self-hate. No people with a strong, viable culture can ever be a psychologically destructive people."

Tom and I both strived to contribute to that viability. We were friends, and he was my mentor, but Tom and I were also competing—for ears and eyeballs, for audience, for acclaim. On one level I out-wrote Tom as a playwright. But though I won numerous awards and had a play produced internationally, it is Tom's *Ritual Murder* that remains forty years later a timely and topical play.

During the seventies, when we were aggressively pursuing our respective ways ahead, Tom would quietly remind me that the world was round, that there were others here, and that none of us were superior to any of the others of us—that indeed our birth identities were accidents, not choices: our fates, yes, but not our destinies.

Tom worked hard at capturing such dialectic complexities. There were always more questions than answers in his writings, along with a healthy skepticism that allowed him to pledge allegiance to the totality of life rather than the simplicity of one way. This may seem obvious to us today, but back during the heyday of awakening black consciousness, waving the flag of blackness while at the same time embracing the rainbow of diversity was no simple task.

As something of a reprieve, Tom and I would often go listen to music in the small joints that dotted the neighborhood landscapes of New Orleans. We would hear the Dirty Dozen Brass Band revitalizing the old street music tradition, or especially revel in the deeptitude of Walter Washington, who'd invoke the folk wisdom with Willie Dixon's lyric about the world being round, but crooked just the same.

Yes, that was it: our understanding that everything could also be its opposite. And we would jump up and shout *hell yeah* because we understood how profoundly fucked up beautiful life was. "Everything is everything" was as small as we could boil it down.

KALAMU YA SALAAM

DEAR LEROY & BIG DADDY

Tom was the on-the-ground-administrator during major transitional years, as Free Southern Theater [FST] moved from an integrated theater company to an all black theater company and from a subsidized theater company to a flat broke theater company. Tom had to implement changes for FST. When most people write about the history of the FST, Tom's name is seldom mentioned as a theoretician, but he became the major theoretician of FST as a community based organization. This letter is a profound meditation not so much on how to do theater, but on why we do theater and to what end. (Unpublished)

January, 1970

Dear Leroy & Big Daddy,

This is an effort to try & pull together what we went through in 1969 as an organization, an effort I am undertaking after probably too much thought & self-deliberation…I don't even know if I can get out what has been going through my mind.

I'm doing this because I feel one of our greatest mistakes as we undertook the events of last yr was to proceed without not only agreeing on anything, but without even understanding our different approaches or different assumptions about what the FST should be doing. My hope is that those of us who have an investment in the artistic work of the theater can at the very least arrive at a talking point, a beginning point for understanding what we are doing, and that we can do this very soon. This letter is an effort toward that end.

Never before had we begun a season with more hopes than we had for 1969. Not only did we have money for the first time, both Gilbert & John were returning for the first time since 1965…so that the key people in the FST's planning from inception to now would all be in New Orleans, or within telephone reach in New York.

But despite this atmosphere of excitement & hope there were some deep, underlying problems. For one thing, despite several attempts to meet & discuss fully the direction of the theater, there was little agreement between John & myself (the two producing directors entrusted with developing direction in the Nov. 1967 board meeting) about what kind of theater we wanted, and in the hustle & bustle of Dec. 1968 & January and the desire to 'see some results' the potential for such frank & open discussion about direction rapidly went down the drain.

This was a bad omen, because if anything was true about the FST [it was that] we had always had considerable disagreement about the direction the theater should take. The growth of community programs such as the acting-writing workshop & the development of enough people in New Orleans in 1968 to do community productions without the aid of new personnel from New York was happening at the same time that we were beginning massive preparations for a New York organized touring company to begin rehearsals at Riverside.

Nor was it this simple. The decision to organize a company from New York seemed a return to the ideas of 1964-65 when few if any performers could be found among blk people in the South whereas what was happening here with the acting-writing workshop was the most artistically developed project yet since we began the effort to develop something in the New Orleans community in

1966. I remember John saying to me, after we had come from a workshop last February: "why, these people think *they're* the Free Southern Theater" in a surprise of recognition, and indeed they did. They had never seen a touring company & didn't know about Gil & John & the glories of 1964 & 65 so since they were doing the artistic work why shouldn't they think of themselves as the FST. Meanwhile we had a company rehearsing at Riverside that thought of itself as the FST, though most of them had never been South.

So much of our theory, or at least mine, had dealt with the need to develop a theater *of* the South, as well as for the South, yet this theory was not the basis on which we organized the 1969 company (possibly, because it was assumed it was too early to organize from the South).

Out of this conflict came most of our problems last yr, and I see it as only a natural culmination of a conflict that had been present for a long time, and had to come to a head. I want to try to go into some of this.

The Touring Concept – began in 1964 when there was quite a bit of integrated Movement activity in Mississippi. The idea was to hit small towns in Mississippi were COFO had projects, and since John & Gil had begun in Jackson and since the first company in the summer of 1964 included volunteers who were already in Miss. working for the Movement (white & blk), this was a logical and not very costly thing to do. Schechner and at times Gil & John were in NY working on funds to support the theater through the organization of a NY committee & several benefits. When the group moved to New Orleans in the fall of 1964 this remained its rationale. The second tour consisted almost entirely of Mississippi towns, though there was an opening in New Orleans of Godot & Purlie. This was also an integrated company, with only one Southerner, Stanley Taylor, who played a small role.

After this tour culminated in NY in Feb. 1965, a showing organized for fundraising & publicity; in the spring of that yr our largest company was organized (including, as Big D will remember, many volunteers) with only one southerner, Joe Perry. New Orleans was played several 'rehearsal performances' that summer, but the theory was still the same: to hit Movement centers, mostly in Mississippi. Though people were being paid only $35 a week (and didn't get that much of the time) the money didn't hold up, and John's four month tour with rumors of a nation-wide ACLU-sponsored tour had to be abandoned.

Late in 1965 John's draft troubles began to drag him out of the picture; it became evident that he would have to move to New York. But it was during this period (fall, 1965, Jan. & Feb., 1966), when the handful of regulars were trying to hit Los Angeles, Chicago, San Francisco & New York to raise money, that Gilbert led a re-evaluation of the theater's concepts. Gil thought that since the idea was basically his & John's that the FST should be a blk company, in fact only a blk company *could* relate to the blk community. Though Murray & Erik were here, most of the whites who came down in 1965 as an extension of their 'Movement' adventures were not invited back. After many meetings we developed a program where the emphasis would be less on touring, at least 50% of the time would be spent playing in New Orleans. We would begin acting & writing workshops in New Orleans in an effort to develop talent here. Two or three youngsters were hired from here as apprentices. Stanley Taylor was hired as general manager. Whites who were on the board mostly because they were Schechner's friends dropped off like flies. Schechner himself resigned as chairman, and I took his place. We rented and built Louisa as a home for the theater, all part of a drive to become a part of the blk community here, for the first time. Upton & Oretha Haley were added to the now small board of directors toward this end.

Then Gil left, leaving us with an excellent play. Roscoe & Denise & Big Daddy developed a blk poetry show, and two other short scripts were readied. But 1966 was undertaken only with great difficulty & stress. Salaries were raised to $65; money was always low. Though the movement toward a blk-oriented theater was paralleling a similar development in the Movement most of us here did not understand what it meant, or whether it could or should apply to theater. Murray and Erik had deep emotional commitments to the FST and somehow they never were asked, and never felt it necessary, to leave. The pressure of rehearsals made it necessary to give up the drama workshops. Scattered performances were given in New Orleans and two short Mississippi tours were undertaken. The New York fundraising committee was "befuddled" by the blk orientation (being almost entirely white) and stopped working.

The shows had been good and aggressive, but when we quit in October 1966 the entire company, including myself, went to New York, leaving no program, no activity here in New Orleans.

Let me try to summarize. Up until this point, the two axes of the FST were Mississippi & New York. New Orleans was where the office was and where people lived, but it was never really an important part of our thinking. The members of the company did not come from New Orleans or the South, but from New York or the New York art world. The money for the theater was not raised in New Orleans or the South, but from New York with its Movement-oriented committee. I don't have the figures, but I would guess between 1964 & 1966 the company played ten times as many dates in Mississippi as it had in New Orleans. The appeal of the company to the fundraising sources & the publicity sources was the Mississippi Movement. At this point, both John & Gil were pretty much out of the picture. Roscoe & Denise indicated they would not return in 1967.

We faced a grim prospect for 1967. Had we not had a small grant from Rockefeller I believe the theater would have stopped at this point. But in January those of us who were in New York met with the NY committee to discuss our situation frankly. We told the committee that though Murray might return for 1967 we were moving toward an all-black theater, controlled by blk people and designed specifically & probably exclusively for blk people. We asked the committee if they could support that. With Ben & Carol leading the way, they said they could. We then asked them to do an affair in the spring for fundraising & for further enlargement of the NY committee. Out of this grew the Limelight benefit.

The company we organized in 1967 had only Bob & Murray returning as veterans. It seemed liked every problem hit us. We had no director outside of Bob. We couldn't settle on the shows. We couldn't find a black technician. We had new people who had no idea what the theater was about. Yet we went ahead valiantly in an effort to make the tour and at the same time do some playing in New O.

The Limelight affair was a success in NY, & out of it came a larger, expanded committee with Brock as chairman and with John playing a larger role. The Board here was still small & meeting, but problems of lack of communication began to settle in, with the Board here moving in certain directions & the committee in NY & John moving in a different direction.

The end of the 1967 season left us in a dismal position. No money, a short, difficult season with many obstacles. It was then that I began to question the idea of trying to hire actors from New York, at least an entire company. For the sake of consistency I felt we had to begin to build something in New Orleans. 1967 represented the company's fifth season, and we had still hardly played or established our identity in New O. It made no sense to me to gear everything toward a tour before we had something here, a home base, a home audience, a home body of supporters, no matter how small. Another factor was the obvious difficulty of hiring blk actors from New York. New York is not only the center of the white theatrical world, but of the blk theatrical world. Good people with some experience were hardly interested in coming to the South, which they knew nothing about, even if they weren't working in NY. And we could not pay equivalent salaries. Even the most dedicated blk actors spend a lot of time in training, and when the opportunity comes they want to make some money. Movement-oriented people were willing to work for little or nothing for a while, but now they wanted to make some money. We might have been able to get white actors, who would be willing to partially subsidize themselves in exchange for an opportunity to work, but we weren't looking for white actors. My feeling was that the best we could hope to do for the next season was hire a few people from New York, and supplement with talent from New O or the South.

Accordingly, in September 1967 we began our most ambitious workshop program to date, with emphasis on writing & community drama. Out of this workshop came Self's play, *The Smokers*.

Meanwhile, in NY, John & the committee continued to move in what I can only characterize as a counter direction. John had not been in New Orleans for the 1966 or 1967 season, nor had any member of the largely new NY committee. To try to summarize what I think John's position was, he felt that: (1) NY was the key to the financial future of the theater, and the only way to hold them was to give them more say about what the theater did. He thus proposed that seven members of the NY committee come on to the Board in Nov. 1967, with Brock becoming chairman. Since the NY committee was not familiar with any of our problems in 1966-67, their interest was in the kind of tour first proposed & sold by John & Gil in 1964. They assumed that whatever problems we had with the tour could be solved by more money. (2) That the problem of finding adequate administrative & financial personnel in New O could be solved by moving those activities to NY (we were having problems straightening out the financial mess of previous yrs & it was necessary to have an audit to secure our NY fundraising permit) where he could use his & the committee's contacts. A NY office would be opened. But this took almost all of the administrative & budgetary powers away from the New O board & staff. In hindsight I do not necessarily disagree with this decision, but the point is it set the stage for problems that cropped up later. (3) John was ending his alternative service term, · and he wanted to play a larger part in the operation, with a view to playing the dominant or a dominant role when he returned to the staff fulltime. We were continuing to have conflicting actions & statements by the NO board on one hand and John & the New Y committee on the other. John at that time wanted to propose to the Board that he become chief administrative officer, a proposal which I opposed because I could not see how we could have an organization in New O with its chief administrative officer in New Y.

It was hoped that we could resolve these growing conflicts in the Board meeting held here in Nov. 1967. John & I could not agree on a proposal so we presented separate proposals. I asked that we guarantee a sum for community workshops so that we could continue this program year-round. Brock said that he was not primarily interested in supporting a New Orleans company; the New Y committee was interested in reinstituting the 1964-style southern tour. The meeting solved nothing. John & I were appointed joint producers, John to work in New Y, me in New O, and told to resolve conflicts, hire an artistic director, and get a company in the field. Milton became Chairman, Brock vice-chairman for NY.

Into the beginning of 1968 we continued a small-scale community program here, but a program destined to have many stops and starts because of the lack of steady funds. We were still operating primarily on the Rockefeller grant of 1966. In a Jan. 1968 meeting in NY, Milton & I asked the NY committee to do an emergency drive so that a full-time fundraiser could be hired to work in NY by at least that spring. This drive raised approximately $10,000 by April 1, and Bobbi was hired to work on resources full time. What little funds were left in the New O budget were lent to NY to get the fundraising effort launched, and the program here was abandoned in April.

Bobbi's effort bore fruit with the announcement of the Ford grant in August, our first substantial foundation money. Meanwhile the community program was resumed here on Sept. 1, with emphasis now on a concentrated acting-writing workshop. In Sept. John left his church job to come on staff full time in NY. Other NY fundraising programs were undertaken which were bearing fruit.

Everything looked good on the surface, for we now knew we had money to do things in 1969. But the conflict over what kind of company we would have, how we would build a theater and related activities continued unresolved. John and I met, not nearly as much as we should have; there was no meeting of the minds.

I continued to feel at that time that even though we had money, to hire actors & rehearse in NY was fallacious. We might have done as well to move the entire theater office to NY if we were going to do that, and plan a simple two or three month long swing through Mississippi from there. I believed that our theater should not only be for southern blk people, but built largely by those people, and from their artistic knowledge and talent. We hadn't settled on a director, an important question if we were going to begin early in 1969 as we hoped. This task fell largely to John, who was in NY where most blk people with directorial experience were. But John felt there was no one on the horizon after a thorough search. The issue was further complicated by John's desire to become artistic director himself as well as chief administrative officer (Producer-Director). My feeling was that despite John's feeling for the theater & his position as a Founder, one, he did not have the theatrical experience for this job, and two, becoming Producer itself was job enough for any one person. I found it increasingly difficult to talk to him about what kind of theater we would have. John seemed eager to get whatever it would be on the road.

My own feeling during the fall of 1968 was that it was almost hopeless to try to settle the conflict over the direction of the theater. The emphasis and excitement was in NY. That's where the money was. My own desire was not to have an all-out fight anyway, for with John & others taking over the direction of the company I would be free to pursue my own writing and work with the acting-writing workshop, which was becoming increasingly exciting and productive in New O with no large expenditure of funds. It was as if we were developing our first really homegrown valid program here, but no one wanted to look at it, and when they did look at it they didn't know where to place it. All the excitement was over the company to be hired from NY. Since the acting-writing workshop was not recognized as anything but a side, non-legitimate effort, there was no discussion of how the new company would relate to this community effort, if it would relate at all. At the end of the 1967 season I had been convinced & had argued that we could only validly build another company from people in New Orleans *first*, then augment that with people from New York. Somehow, this theory was completely discarded.

At the NY Board meeting in Nov. 1968 John became producing Director, Bobbi (who had taken over more duties than fundraising) Associate Director and myself Associate Director. Brock became chairman. We still had not hired an artistic director, though there were two or three outside possibilities. John still had some hopes of becoming artistic director himself.

At a NY meeting soon after, Bobbi & I told John that we simply could not agree to his becoming artistic director, the Producer job was becoming immense, and that if he persisted in this idea we would resign. John then gave up on the idea of becoming artistic director.

John's thinking then (Dec.) turned to Gil. Gil had indicated he was interested in returning. And would be available in January.

My reaction to the choice of Gil was indeed mixed. On one hand I knew Gil had artistic integrity, was responsible for many of the good ideas that had developed over the years, and the idea of both John & Gil returning to New O to work, adding to what we had been able to develop and hold to, this was exciting. It was a dream we often had in the days when we were struggling along here without any of the old gang who gave the FST its first meaning.

On the other hand I knew that Gil was involved in trying to get his band going and the opportunity for a recording contract was nearing. I didn't know how these two interests could be resolved. What worried me more, however, was something that was extremely difficult to talk about. As founders, Gil & John had always operated in the theater as free forces, and somehow, until 1966 when they both left, final decisions had always rested with them, on their ability to reach agreement. Now Gil would be re-turning as one member of a team, a team whose leaders had been set by the Board, and which would include many more people who had come into the picture in the three years he had been away. Knowing Gil's strength and unwillingness to compromise about things he believed in, I wondered if it would be possible for him to return and work smoothly. For instance, John, who before was always on the same level as a founder and producer would now technically be his boss. I called Gil from here to try to talk to him about this, and to tell him that if he returned as artistic director he could not pull 'founder's rights', and as I understand the conversation, he felt this would be no problem.

John, Bobbi, & myself then arranged a meeting with Gil in NY around Christmas to make a final decision on his appointment. The issue of the conflicting interests over the band was discussed, but not the other thing. Since John's ideas of becoming director had been scuttled, and Gil was the only person then being considered, and if Gil was not acceptable it would cause untold delay in organizing a company, we agreed to hire Gil.

*   *   *

In my opinion when we began 1969 the situation was already doomed. None of the basic conflicts about direction had been resolved or even discussed enough to agree on something. There was no operating budget for the company. Key administrators and community people had not been hired. We knew that we had the funds to do something 'grand', but no one knew just what, or just how grand. The salary scale was ballooned up immediately by the hiring of a technical director who asked for and received considerably more than the job was budgeted. Everyone else's scale went up accordingly.

What I am going to say now has the benefit of hindsight, and I do not mean it to be taken as an out and out condemnation, as if I could have done better. But we should try to run down what happened with as critical an eye as possible, so as to set ourselves off on a sound footing for 1970.

In my opinion Gil cannot be blamed for setting off on the 1964-tour concept when he began to organize the company in January. No one told him any different. And he had a continuously free hand to do pretty much as he pleased, including the hiring of members of his band as acting apprentices. People were hired and rehearsed for a month in NY who had no idea what FST was, or of its history, or what kind of 'tour' they would be going on. No one else does a tour like ours, so if they were not told they had no basis on which to go. We tried to pay an equity scale based on other scales. Not only was this too high for us, the equity contract, particularly as it applies to tours, is hardly designed for our kind of theater. When John drew up his six-month tour, covering some five states, playing five nights a week, we were off on a trip to the stars.

Conceptually, I began to accept that since we had no agreement on what we were doing, we would work on several concepts. I was not about to abandon the concept of community-organized theater, with generative power coming from our writers here, and with the excellent work of Bob & Val as staff we continued to produce. This work was designed to be more than community training, or YMCA-outlet, but of the highest quality we could make, specifically designed for this place & this time. Don was hired as community workshop director and immediately pro-posed a newspaper as his first project, which would be another way of hitting the community with ideas, designed for this place and this time. These were different concepts that could be made to groove together if we tried, if we did a little looking and learning, looking & learning from the community we were working in, but somehow this never happened.

Let me drop back a minute to try to make a point. The key people in the theater had never agreed about what the theater should do. If there was one thing we never lacked, it was rhetoric. In the early days one reason why this was true is that we were the only ones in the South trying to do this kind of thing. Everything was needed. We needed a theater, we needed writers, we needed a newspaper, we needed community training, we needed an audience, we need-ed community financial support. We needed everything. And we often tried to do everything, and nothing really well or with consistency. But what held us together, besides some fascination with being martyrs in the South, was the lack of money. Since we had no money we had the excuse for not doing any one thing well; we didn't have the bread to do anything. Three-fourths of our activity was rhetoric, argument, debate about what *should* be done… if we ever came into any money. It isn't surprising that people felt that money would cure everything, that once we had it we would do all the things we always dreamed about and talked about, and become a 'power'. With money we would radicalize everyone.

Here we were in early 1969 *with* money, at least enough to do *one* thing well. Yet we hadn't agreed what that one thing was. Plus too many of us assumed that the battle for funds was won, whereas we were really just blk people hustling in a very tricky & transient business, and what we had raised for 1969 could go as easily as it had come. Funds for 1970 weren't even committed. Some members of the company seemed to feel that even this wasn't enough, and that at any rate we were fortunate to have them down here at all. This attitude didn't help relations any.

I believe John began to see many of these problems in the late spring (maybe Gil did too), and he says he wanted to stop it and begin all over again, but Gil wouldn't go along. Weighing everything, Gil's argument to try to salvage something, with a much-shortened tour, had weight. Once a motion begins, and fifteen or twenty people are involved, it's not just possible to stop on a dime, and say it was all a mistake. Sorry.

Gilbert also had a point, I think, when he said more was needed to actually *produce* the theater, particularly on the road. No matter how much we depend on sponsoring organizations to do for us, there are certain things you have to do yourself, particularly if the sponsoring organization is not familiar with the special problems and needs of FST. But this would have meant even more personnel at an even greater cost, or the elimination of other projects (community projects) so that those personnel could work on the tour.

I thought *Slaveship* was a good show, possibly the best we've ever done. But when we think of the amount of money it cost to have the touring company doing that kind of tour ($110, 000 from Feb. 1 to Sept. 1, not counting fundraising and support costs), the fact that the company was only out seven weeks during this time, and the immense problems of all sorts involved, I don't think we should ever try that again. Any kind of tour for a theater is difficult. Even when you're traveling first class. Staying in people's homes, a format that had validity and value in the days of the Movement when it was common, was an inconvenience not only to the company but to the communities where we played. For the men, who have easier mobility, it was possible; for the women my impression is that it was often very trying. The tour design was based on 1964.

Also unlike 1964, we were not playing in communities deeply embroiled in civil rights confrontations, thus we were looked on as any other artist making a southern swing. Like a band. Our theory was the same, but consideration of who the audience was and what their concerns were would seem to seriously modify style, approach & deportment.

Finally, what we have learned about the cost of the tour, what it would have cost to do properly, with some convenience, and with that size company at those salaries...what we have learned indicates that to do the four to six month tour John was originally thinking about would have cost a million dollars.

There's no question about where the more than $300,000 we spent in 1969 went. BLKARTS & the Community program together had a budget of $44,000 for the year, but a large portion of this was siphoned off into the company to try and meet its costs. Don's program really ran no more than six months. The cost of

BLKARTS for the entire yr, including salaries, was no more than $15,000.

To me, the tour was like doing 1964 on the grand scale, and that's why they call it the 'grand tour'. It was like an opportunity to act out that dream with real money, at any cost. It related to what the NY supporters (who had never been to New O) imagined the work of the theater to be. I believe it was a mistake. It didn't build anything, it didn't leave us with anything, and it cost more than we had. We should still go out. We should reach out to blk communities who want us, and who feel we can help. But we have to find a better way to do it than 1969.

BEYOND RHETORIC:
Toward a Black
Southern Theater

Continues Tom's questions and meditations on the aesthetics and politics of Black Theater. (Published in Black World *in 1971)*

Larry Neal, in his extremely perceptive article about the Free Southern Theater [FST] in a recent issue of TDR[1] observed that in its earliest days the FST was beset by a basic conflict: a conflict between "the deadwood of American liberal and aesthetic ideas" and a rapidly developing sense of a Black aesthetic.

To understand what is happening now, not only with the FST but in the South generally, we must draw from another conflict which Neal did not discuss, a problem rather unique to the FST among Black theaters. The first conflict has long since been resolved, for the FST could not continue to exist or in any sense

---

1   TDR, Vol. 14, No. 3 (T47), 1970, page 169. A review of THE FREE SOUTHERN THEATER BY THE FREE SOUTHERN THEATER, edited by Dent, Moses & Schechner. Bobbs-Merrill, 1969. Neal's article is the most comprehensive and thorough analysis of the Black cultural movement in the South I have seen. It is hoped that some Black publication will reprint this piece because TDR has a very limited Black readership.—TD

justify its purpose as an expression of a white liberal ideology or aesthetic.

We might say this second conflict developed between people who lived in New Orleans and thought of the FST as a New Orleans Black repertory company which sometimes toured, and people on the other hand who, though they helped build the FST both in New Orleans and in New York, related primarily to the New York theater scene, Black or not, and saw their destiny, their careers in these later terms. The FST for them, then, was a temporary, though deeply-felt commitment, and they saw the FST in terms of its touring purpose first, with no special obligations to New Orleans.

For instance, in 1968-69, we had offices both in New Orleans and New York, funds both in New Orleans and New York, board members both in New Orleans and New York, staff both in New Orleans and New York, supporters both in New Orleans and New York. Some of us would argue, "Listen, this thing can't be in *both* places, it has to be in one or the other. Either it has to be a New York group that tours Mississippi for a few months when it can raise the money, or it has to emanate from New Orleans, stay there, work there, *build* a theater there, and tour only when touring will not conflict with that essential purpose." That was the argument. And we never resolved it.

As a consequence of this disagreement over priority, the BLK-ARTSOUTH Poets and *Nkombo* Magazine, composed of New Orleans workshop members, formally organized themselves as separate organizations in late 1970.[2]

---

2   The FST is still alive under the direction of John O'Neal but not currently programming. O'Neal expects to begin workshops in New Orleans in 1971 and productions late this year or in early 1972.— TD

Other people involved will probably have their own interpretations, but there is no question that I feel the FST should have committed itself primarily to the task of *building* a long-range Black repertory company in New Orleans, and building with the many, many talented Black youth who came into the workshops and staff since 1968.

To do a quick review, those who know something of the FST know it was organized in 1964 by Gilbert Moses and John O'Neal, who had come South to work in the Civil Rights Movement.

The theater was designed, as Larry Neal says, to give the Movement "a cultural dynamic." But not only were the first companies integrated (like the SNCC/Movement), the fund-raising apparatus, legal work, recruiting of the personnel, *etc.* was done, not in the South, but in New York (like the SNCC/Movement). Then as the FST moved its southern base to New Orleans (from Jackson) and continued to survive, most of the original members and organizers returned to New York or left to pursue careers. The majority of the theater members then became native New Orleanians, recruited through workshops and from the audiences. These new people, turned on by the FST's possibilities, which constituted a new and exciting potential for them, knew little of the Movement in its grand days, and since they had never been to New York or even met the New York supporters, had little if any feeling for *them,* and cared less. (Most of the workshop recruits were teenagers.) They conceived of the FST as a perfectly valid New Orleans Black Theater that, if it had sufficient funds, *sometimes* toured Mississippi. I'm talking about 1968. To them, to *be* a New Orleans Black Theater was its logical destiny. They believed: (1) the work of the FST should reflect and speak directly to the needs of New Orleans and the Black South; (2) to do this best southern Black writers should create much of the FST material; (3) New Orleanians, or those committed to stay and work there, should control FST policies and the use of its funds.

These ideas, of course, were in direct conflict with the original concepts and organizational structure of the FST. And deciding who ran the FST was not so easy. In the tradition of SNCC, it seemed as if *everyone* who ever had anything to do with the FST felt he had an obligation to help run it. But the New York fund-raising committee, many of whom by 1968 were on the Board of Directors (with Brock Peters as chairman), had made it clear that they were not interested in raising funds to build a New Orleans theater, but felt the first priority must remain with a touring company and the "missionary" role of such a program. Brock particularly felt such a program was the only key to New York funds.

On the other hand, we argued that it cost a tremendous amount of money to bring actors and technicians down from New York; money could be saved by using available personnel here. For one thing, many of the people who came down needed to make salaries roughly equivalent to the Off-Broadway scale, a scale too high for us. Then, too, many of the imports had never been South before, and it took them time to tune in to that. And we were coming from a movement/political concept of theater, a whole set of ideas developed over the years which differed from what they might be doing Off-Broadway or with NEC (Negro Ensemble Company) or New Lafayette, and it took people time to tune into *that,* if they ever did.

Meanwhile we had instituted an acting-writing workshop in 1968 (eventually BLKARTSOUTH) which had developed some people familiar with the stage (under the direction of Bob Costley), and written almost two dozen plays and enough poetry to get *Nkombo* (a journal) going.

So that in 1969, when the FST had its largest available funds, it tried to do several things, though the most money was spent on the newly organized touring company, under Gil Moses, and in New York and New Orleans administration and fund-raising. We finally ended up with a touring company, a workshop poetry reading and drama group, a literary magazine, a community newspaper, and, thanks to the genius of Don Hubbard and lona Reese, an old-age company, composed of people no younger than 65.

Like it was all beautiful and hectic, but more often than not our projects ran into each other coming around the corner. Naturally, by 1970 the money was gone, and with the abundance of new community projects begun in 1969, what little understanding there was on the part of the New York fund-raising committee was gone too. The FST's counter-directions were on collision course anyway; they were on collision course from the moment the FST took itself seriously as a *southern* theater, but continued to run tours from New York while hooking its fund-raising to the white liberal/New York/benefit complex.

What was happening to those of us who wanted the FST to be a *Southern* theater is not so strange; Black southerners ourselves, we had come to believe that the South is where we wanted to be, and though it had no ongoing theater, it *could* become the seat of a vital and alive Black theater in the same way it had given birth to most of our great musicians.

For one thing, the strong sense of community, which we as Black nationalists give lip-service to, already exists in the South. Black communities in the South are older, more firmly established, and possess a tensile strength that may never break. Despite the fact that whites dominate the economic and political structure, Black people have for more than a hundred years depended on each other for just about everything but jobs and consumer goods. Blacks have always taught each other, formally and informally; Blacks have always come together to worship, have gone to each other for insurance, for funeral services, for entertainment, for music. And it is these very activities that are the sustaining foundations of our culture.

It is the visible, tangible omnipresence of oppression that has forged such community unity; like baby it's an everyday thing, and if you go daydreaming and think you in Sweden you done had it. You might make that kind of mistake for a little while if you were born in New Orleans, but you don't make that kind of mistake and *live* in Mississippi. Of course, the incredible capacity for fantasy in the human being, Black or white, should never be underestimated, and the Canadian border *is* the Mason-Dixon line, but in 'Sippi, Houston, 'Bama, Louisiana you know *who* your enemy is from Year One. You know you're Black, though you may not know all that that entails.

Just as it is visible oppression that forges unity in the Black community, it is the fight against oppression that fuels unity. Now I want to get to something. Because of just this common understanding of where the lines are drawn, of what the Black community must do to achieve power, one grows into maturity without being really consumed with bitterness. That's a weird point, but I think it's true. One is usually taught by Black teachers, who he may learn to respect, love, hate or resent; one gets the feeling of belonging to a community, old, relatively stable, with its own value system; one learns, most importantly, that in that community exist assets and powers that white people don't have and can't have. Like they can steal an imitation of our music; they can steal the money made from it, but they can't really ever *possess* it; it's ours and ours alone. And within all our seeming impotence, the power of that knowledge is wonderful, indestructible.

I have a feeling that many of the Black poets and writers from northern, urban centers have to force upon themselves a sense of community, of Black awareness. By not having around them

a positive sense of the Black community as an old, ongoing, surviving entity, their concept of Black is often filled with a dejection,
not just a bitterness that comes maybe with the discovery of what
being Black entails, but a dejection, a definition of Black life and
Black community by negatives. You know what I mean: Harlem,
Newark, Chicago, Detroit. Of course Black people have lived in
these hellholes for a long time, but many of the communities are
torn by separation of family, destruction of community structure,
and the vicious inhuman pressures of the white technological/
industrial/urban money-making machine, which is not natural to
our people, and from which cultural denial (as well as economic
exploitation) we suffer the most.

In contrast, take a city like New Orleans, a strange old city that
was an important landing point for our imprisoned people. The
New Orleans Black community today possesses many distinctive cultural remnants that can be nothing but African. New
Orleans has a vicious history of oppression, but I want to accent
the advantages we have. We think of the second line (or jazz)
funerals as being direct descendants of African burial rituals,
and if you're fortunate enough to see one, dig the dancing, or
rather series of dances, performed as ritual at the funerals, but
not seen in any other context. Or take the role of the Black musician in New Orleans. I'm not implying that there is anything
going on today that could be considered a revolution in modern
jazz, or that there is even much jazz in the sense that we think
of Coltrane, Pharoah or Monk as jazz. I mean Black musicians
as a living, functional part of the community and culture. To
be a musician here is nothing extraordinary. Musicians play at
church, at school, at dances, at funerals, in the parks, for parades,
as well as for any of the common forms of Black entertainment.
There are many, many young Black musicians. None of the
clubs here are very large, but about 15 to 20 cafes hire bands on

weekends, and some band is working somewhere every night in the week. On Saturday nights some bands work until 8:00 Sunday morning.

We could talk about other indigenous manifestations: voodoo remnants, burial societies, churches, Creole culture, Black Mardi Gras, etc. My point is that New Orleans has a Black lifestyle, and a rather distinct one, within the national Black lifestyle, distinct enough so that whenever Black brothers and sisters from New Orleans get together anywhere in the world they can knock themselves out talking about how weird New Orleans is.

And when we think of Mississippi we think of land, the beauty of the land in its variety of topography, which gives us a feeling of what Africa might be like. We think of land because it is this land that Black people will soon control, politically and economically. Don't let anyone tell you Mississippi isn't a beautiful state, or that we don't have necessary majorities for political control. If there is any place in America where there can actually be a Black nation, it is in Mississippi. Look on your map and draw a triangle between Jackson, Greenville, and Natchez. That's it. Then you can see why Charles Evers thought it important to run for mayor in Fayette.

*   *   *

I remember Richard Schechner once suggesting that we adapt (for the FST) a Brecht play to fit the southern Black situation. "It can be done very simply," he said. So I set out to adapt this play, I forget the name of it…I was trying to make the merchant a white oyster-boat captain in St. Bernard Parish, and the serf a Black oyster-boat worker, and every time I tried it, it came up more unreal; it was ridiculous.

What was becoming obvious as we went through those changes was that we couldn't just change the insides of the white-ori-
ented material to make it Black, we had to invent something
entirely new, our whole concept of Theater had to change. If it
was to reach Black people. It would have to be like someone saying, "If you want to have relevant Black music, take 'Rhapsody
in Blue,' and just change the music to fit in the current hit soul
songs." Like the point is, Black people don't write rhapsodies and
don't need rhapsodies.

We had to learn (and must still learn) to ask, "What do our
people need this play for; how will it be used?"... in the same way
we ask, "What do people need this music for; how is it used?" In
other words, what is its function for our people? And then, when
we answer that, we know what form our plays will take. They may
not even be plays, or be called plays. Who says, for instance, that
Black people have *need* of plays, in the sense that we have learned
what a play is from European drama?

What we needed was a drama that could meet this test: *We
should settle for nothing that Black people didn't feel was natural
to them, that was foreign to our lifestyle, that did not have a use, a
usefulness to our lives.*

*   *   *

So a great deal of stripping had to be done. A destruction. A ripping up of assumptions.

It became necessary to go back to the culture, to build again, to
rebuild from there our ideas of what a Black literature and theater
could do.

It could and should certainly do these things:

(a) Work toward a *positive* consciousness of our culture, as Neal
says, Black theater should "authenticate" the culture;

(b) Reinvigorate and celebrate the rituals and lifestyle of our people;

(c) Provide for our people a form for debate, discussion, and help us define the terms of our existence which involves a knowledge of history and an analysis of where the oppressor is *at,* and how we must counteract this oppression;

(d) Provide love for our people in a realistic, not bullshit, hysterical or jingoistic sense, but real, based on our self-acceptance, our history, vision of the future. Theater, particularly, could provide a place of communion, a meeting place for Black people to come together, much like the church, transcending in importance the desire to see a particular performance.

And as we go back to our culture to learn the things our theater should do, we will discover what *forms* our theater should assume to best accomplish these ends. In my opinion a valid theater in the South should organize itself with the following things in mind:

(a) It must be functional. Take a leaf from the page of our music book; our musicians were always hipper than our poets, anyway. It should play as vital a role in our community as our music.[3]

(b) It should be, makes all kinds of sense to be, a

---

3   Gilbert Moses' FST production of Amiri Baraka's *Slaveship* was a much more effective production in the South than in New York for just this reason. In the South, it was a shorter play that took as its completion (by using the device of unifying cast and audience through group singing at the end) the igniting of the Black community itself. The production I saw at the Brooklyn Academy was longer, did not have as its natural completion an input into the Black community, since it was not played to that community, and in fact took as its completion some kind of artistic self-justification similar to white European theater.—TD

community-staffed and, as much as possible, communi-
ty-funded theater. Aside from the argument already advanced,
this is important if a particular locality expects to hold its Black
talent. And give its theater a long-range thrust. Directors and
stage technicians, because of the shortage of experience in these
areas, will probably have to be imported, but their commitment
should be to teach so that local people can perform these roles
on a long-term basis.

(c) If possible, the new theaters should be related and should
ally themselves with Black community political/economic organizations. There are obvious advantages here. People already
working in community organizations are the ones who most feel
the need for the "cultural dimension" and know best how to use
it. Secondly, this will keep the theaters and artists from becoming
too isolated, from getting off into their own bags and feeling what
they are into is the most important thing in the world. For Black
people, particularly in the South, theater and poetry are *not* the
most important things right now. Even as specialists, we have
to recognize and participate in the battle for Black political and
economic power. Being close to organizations involved in this
struggle will keep our sense of priorities intact (I don't mean an
alliance only with militant or militaristic Black groups. I mean
Black political/economic organizations that may not be as hip, as
avant-garde, as Black as you, but represent where the *people* are.
You know, like when we get too hip and Black to work with our
own people, then we can forget it.)

Thirdly, many of the community organizations have physical facilities adequate for a theater. Very good, it solves that problem and
provides a head start on community participation and attendance.
Even a sharing of staffs might be a good idea, particularly in the
initial stages of a community theater. Why? Because many community organizations have people experienced in administration,

in the handling of monies, the making of budgets, all the little worrisome details that artists hate but must be handled.[4]

Finally, some kind of local fund-raising should be undertaken as an absolute prerequisite for community survival and relevance. To do this in conjunction with an ongoing community group is a valid place to begin for any budding southern theater.

(d) The new southern Black Theaters should be more musical, using musicians as regular, full parts of the company. I say more musical, because I don't believe our existing theaters, though they emphasize music, are musical enough. Music is our greatest strength. Black people can be reached immediately through music with a power, impact and subtlety that rhetoric simply doesn't have. Out of the use of musicians will come new forms, and our use of music should never be patterned on the Broadway musical. Too much of the music we have been using in our plays is "Broadway," anyway. Let's kick that habit, let's use soul music, Black music in the forms our people know it: Brown, Redding, Aretha, Cleveland, Coltrane, John Lee Hooker and BB; let's get them *in* to Black Theater where they belong, and stop going with rhetoric and polemics alone. Too often our plays sound like mere reactions against white theater *in the same forms* in which the man speaks to his money honkies.

---

4   And this takes a long time and much patience to learn. John O'Neal commented on this in reflecting on the problems of the FST: "Perhaps the most dreadful struggle of all (was) the one to keep up that energy required to go on in the drab fashion afforded by the *real* situation, while being tortured by the vast, almost overwhelming, potential implicit in the idea." FST By The FST, p. 173. This kind of torture literally drove impatient, demanding Gilbert Moses out of his mind. —TD

*   *   *

In the last two years there has been a tremendous growth of new Black cultural projects in the South, based generally on the format I have just outlined. The work of the FST[5] and the BLKARTSOUTH Poets (as a part of the FST but on separate tours) has obviously been a great influence, but in my opinion we are in a national boom of Black poetry and theater. I would like to mention a few of these new groups in the deep South:

(a) The Sudan Poets of Houston are just a year in existence, but they work out of a context of active, vital poetry and considerable use of music, particularly the guitar and singing of poet Thomas Meloncon. We should also note the work of HOPE, and their new Blk Arts Center on Lyons Street, which will open this Spring under the direction of poet Connel Linson. The Sudan magazine and the weekly Voice of Hope can be ordered through Bro. Linson (Box 21098, Houston, Tex. 77026).

(b) The Last Messengers of Greenville, Miss., were organized last summer as a Black teenage poetry-performing unit by James Cooper. They adapted some of the BLKARTSOUTH things, but I was more interested in some of their poems and chants, like "Save Me" (Don't know who wrote it). Everything they do has chants involving the entire group. Leader does his thing to group response and backing. Very basic Black stuff. Cooper had to leave (no bread), but he needs to return (For information contact Donald Sutton, 1114 S. Theobald Street, Greenville, Miss.). We will include some of their work in the second issue of *Nkombo*, 1971.

---

5   Whatever its fate, the FST has been a leader in advocating a political, committed theater, and in the important idea that the theater must go to the people, particularly in the first stages, if it expects the community later to come to it. —TD

(c) Dashiki Theater in New Orleans was started by Ted Gilliam (Dillard U. Drama Director) in 1968 as part of a local community organization, operating out of the basement of a Catholic church. Dashiki has concentrated on contemporary Black material, not always relevant or well done. But Gilliam has a brilliant resident playwright in Norbert (N. R.) Davidson (author of *El Hajj Malik),* and it is hoped Dashiki will do more of Davidson's original work. Dashiki is well-grounded with good community participation, and should be effective for a long time (Info: Ted Gilliam, St. Frances de Sales Church, 2135 Second Street, New Orleans, La.).

(d) The BLKARTSOUTH Poets, discussed earlier, are now on their own. Influenced by the tradition of the FST, BLKARTS has since 1968 done performances of Black poetry in New Orleans, and in Mississippi, Alabama, Georgia, South Carolina, Arkansas and Texas. Much use of music, ensemble and dramatic effects. Most of their work is reflected in *Nkombo* Magazine. About 15 young writers. Many writing plays, particularly Val Ferdinand (Contact *Nkombo*, Box 51826, New Orleans, La.).

I do not mean to imply that these are the *only* new groups in the Deep South today, but these are the ones I know the most about. All of these groups have things in common:

(1) All, except Dashiki, are working mainly with poetry. Very important. Our people speak many languages, and it is the task of our writers to speak to our people in our own languages. When we began to do poetry shows with BLKARTS we discovered it was a much more fluid, flexible device for reaching our people than, well, plays. Like we worked up three or four shows, each with a different point of emphasis, and learned to study the audience, then decide which show to do just before going on stage. As well-organized and choreographed poetry shows continue to develop, they will point the way to new forms for Black theater.

(2) All are working to serve a particular locality. None of these groups are trying to duplicate or finance an FST-style tour. This is very much in the pattern of what has happened to the Movement since 1966. Economic/political projects are localized now, serving one city, or one region. John Buffington's CCCDP in West Point, Miss., Jesse Morris' PPC in Jackson, Miss., Ed Brown's MACE in Greenville, HOPE in Houston. These are typical current Black community organizations in the South.

(3) All, except Dashiki, employ an extensive use of Black music. Very important. The road to new and more effective forms.

One of the observations Larry Neal made in his TDR piece had to do with the need for communication between different wings of the Black liberation movement. Like, since the national civil rights organizations departed, the Black South has been out of it as far as national coverage is concerned. Or rather since Watts. I understand that the action now is supposed to be in the cities, in the ghettoes, with the Panthers, with the various forms of armed, or unarmed, rebellion.

But the South is moving, too, rather quietly and with a strong emphasis on economic development (demonstratin & gettin whupped over the head is out), but moving just the same. Who is involved? Black people, in localities, are organizing themselves to do the things the Movement inspired, but did not do. It's slow, it's; it's hard, it's; it's unspectacular. But, like West Point, Miss., alone has four economic co-ops, all done by people there, and when the white man wakes up and finds out what happened it's gonna be too late.

But for our new cultural projects, as well as the economic/political ones, to survive and grow, we must be considered *part of the national movement.* Not a duplication, or bad imitation, or poor little brother of the movement, but a vital and significant part. We need the analysis, criticism and inspiration from people working in New York City, Chicago, Newark, and/or Detroit so that we can keep ourselves going, so that we won't all trip up over the same mistakes while busy doing our individual things.

As for the South, as new theaters, artists, writers develop, we will add something too. We will add, hopefully, diversity to the Black Aesthetic. Don't expect our plays and poetry to follow right behind Amiri Baraka, Ed Bullins, Don L. Lee. It won't happen that way, because if these new groups, and groups that will soon spring up, are true to themselves, if they really search for effective forms, they will reflect the Black lifestyle of their region, and what that means. It's all Black, but there are a lot of beautiful flowers in that garden yet to bloom.

It'll be like our music, brothers and sisters.

THE BLACK ARTS MOVEMENT IN THE SOUTH:
The Task of Building Black Consciousness

Tom journaled everyday, where he would both reflect on himself and whatever was happening around him. In his journals we find a lot of the real world experiences that ended up in his creative work. Here are the seeds of Tom's most lasting play, Ritual Murder. (Unpublished)

One night a few months ago, I was driving through the largest black section of New Orleans and passed a large crowd gathering in front of a restaurant, the Dew Drop Inn. I could hear police sirens in the distance getting louder. Something had happened in the Dew Drop, and I swung around the block to get a better look. But the crowd had grown too large and the police were arriving like it was the holdup of the century, so I split the scene.

About an hour later, returning along the same route, the crowd was still there, about a dozen police cars and the morgue wagon. This time I parked, got out, and went over to find out what had happened. It seemed as if two kids had come into the restaurant, tried to hold up the place, and shot the cook through the head. They didn't get any money because they didn't know how to open the cash register.

A woman was crying. She worked in the restaurant next door and knew the dead cook, and was the first to reach him after the kids ran out. There was the typical police scene with white detectives walking around joking among themselves, the photographer shooting pictures of the body, and the one black detective trying to look like he was one of the boys.

A few people in the crowd were grumbling. "Another brother shot." "When are they gonna stop this stuff. "Slim (the cook) didn't mean no harm to no one." "When are our people gonna get together."

It was a scene all of us have seen in our cities, and with all its sadness we see increasingly, yet what struck me was the level of awareness coming from those grieving brothers and sisters in the crowd. It was as if something deep, some deep knowledge of what had taken place, some profound recognition of black impotence and self-destruction had for a brief moment of recognition surfaced.

I remember thinking that if the black theater could jump the gap between art and life it belonged here, right now, for this crowd, for Slim's body, and for the kids who shot him. For if our newfound cultural awareness is to mean anything, it has to bring a positive consciousness of ourselves or we are certainly a doomed people.

RITUAL MURDER

a one act play by Tom Dent

CHARACTERS

Narrator

Joe Brown Jr.

Bertha: Joe's wife

Mrs. Williams: Joe's teacher

Dr. Brayboy: a black psychiatrist

Mr. Andrews: Joe's boss

Mrs. Brown: Joe's mother

Mr. Brown: Joe's father

James Roberts: Joe's friend

Mr. Spaulding: anti-poverty program administrator

Chief of Police

SETTING

New Orleans, La.

TIME

Now

It is important that the actors make their speeches in rhythm to the background music.

NARRATOR

Last summer, Joe Brown Jr., black youth of New Orleans, La., committed murder. Play a special "Summertime" for him and play the same "Summertime" for his friend James Roberts who he knifed to death.

(We hear "Summertime" under the NARRATOR'S voice.) In every black community of America; in the ghettos and neighborhood clubs where we gather to *hear our music,* we play "Summertime;" and in each community the bands play it differently. In no community does it sound like the "Summertime" of George Gershwin. It is bluesier, darker, with its own beat and logic, its joys unknown to the white world. It is day now. The routine events of life have passed under the bridge. Joe Brown Jr. has been arrested, indicted, and formally charged with murder. It happened...it happened in a Ninth Ward bar—we need not name it for the purposes of this presentation. The stabbing was the culmination of an argument Joe Brown had with his friend. We have learned this, but the *Louisiana Weekly* only reported, "James Roberts is said to have made insulting remarks to Joe Brown, whereupon Brown pulled out a switchblade knife and stabbed Roberts three times in the chest before he could be subdued." The story received front page play in the *Louisiana Weekly*, and a lead in the crime-of-the-day section in the white *Times-Picayune*. After that, it received only minor news play, since there are other crimes to report in New Orleans. Play "Summertime" for Joe Brown Jr., and play the same "Summertime" for his friend James Roberts who he knifed to death.

(The music dies out.) Why did this murder happen? No one really knows. The people who know Joe Brown best have ideas.

(We see BERTHA looking at T.V. The sound is off, only the picture shows. BERTHA is young, about 20. She is

JOE'S wife. She is ironing while looking at the set—iron-ing baby things.)

BERTHA:

Joe just didn't have any sense. He is smart, oh yes, has a good brain, but didn't have good sense. The important thing was to settle down, get a good job, and take care of his three children. We been in the Florida Ave. project now for almost a year, and we never have enough money. Look at the people on T.V.; they make out okay. They fight, but they never let their fights destroy them. Joe didn't have control of his temper. He was a dreamer; he wanted things. But he wouldn't work to get them. Oh, he would take jobs in oyster houses, and he'd worked on boats ever since he was a kid. But he wouldn't come in at night, and sometimes he wouldn't get up in the morning to go to work. Sometimes he would come in and snap off the T.V. and say it was driving him crazy. It's not his T.V.—my father bought it, and besides, I like it, it's the only thing I have. This is just a 17-inch set, but I want a 21-inch set. Now I'll never get one because he had to go out and do something foolish. You ask me why he killed that boy? I don't know. But I think he killed him because he had a bad temper and wouldn't settle down. Joe was a mild person, but he carried knives and guns—that's the way his family is. I used to tell him about it all the time. Once I asked him, "When are you gonna get a better job and make more money?" He said, "When I get rid of you and those snotty kids." He could have done something if he had tried, if he had only tried; but instead, he wanted to take it out on us. I'll go see him, but now look; I have to do everything in this house myself: iron the clothes, cook the meals, buy the food, apply for relief and get some help from my parents—and my father ain't work-ing right now. Joe didn't want to have our last baby, Cynthia, but we couldn't murder her before she was even born, and now I got to take care of her too. Joe knifed that boy because he was foolish, wouldn't settle down and accept things as they are, and because he didn't have common sense.

NARRATOR:

Mrs. Williams, could you comment on your former student, Joe Brown Jr.?

MRS. WILLIAMS:

I don't remember Joe Brown Jr. very well. I have so many children to try to remember. I had him three or four years ago just before he dropped out of school. I was his homeroom teacher. Joe was like all the others from the Ninth Ward, not interested in doing anything for themselves. You can't teach them anything. They don't want to learn, they *never* study, they won't sit still and pay attention in class. It's no surprise to me that he's in trouble. I try to do my best here, but I have only so much patience. I tell you, you don't know the things a teacher goes through with these kids. They come to class improperly dressed, from homes where they don't get any home training, which is why they are so ill-mannered. We try to teach them about America—about the opportunities America has to offer. We try to prepare them to get the best jobs they can—and you know a Negro child has to work harder. I teach History, Arithmetic, English, and Civics every day, and it goes in one ear and comes out the other. It gives me a terrible gas pain to have to go through it every day, and the noise these kids make is too, too hard on my ears. I've worked for ten years in this school, and I don't get paid much at all. But next month my husband and I will have saved enough money to buy a new Oldsmobile, which I'm happy to say will be the smartest, slickest, smoothest thing McDonough No. 81 has ever seen. Two boys got into a fight in the yard the other day and it was horrible. It pains me to hear the names they call each other—irritates my gas. Some of them even bring knives and guns to school. It's just terrible. I'm only relieved when I get home, turn on my T.V., take my hair down and face off, drink a nice strong cup of coffee, look out at my lawn in Pontchartrain Park, and forget the day. You ask me why Joe Brown murdered his friend in a Negro bar on a Saturday night and I tell you it is because he was headed that way in the beginning. These kids just won't listen, and don't want to learn, and that's all there is to it.

> *(Lights on JOE BROWN JR. He is wearing blue jeans and a tee shirt. He is seated. He faces the audience. There is a table in front of him. On the table is a small transistor radio, but the music we hear is Gil Evans's "The Barbara Song.")*

NARRATOR

Here is Joe Brown Jr.

JOE BROWN JR.

Once I saw a feature about surfing on T.V. Surfing on beautiful waves on a beach in Hawaii, or somewhere...

> *(The lights shift to another man who is seated on the opposite side of the stage. He is a much older man, dressed in a business suit. He is a negro. He is DR. BRAYBOY, a psychiatrist. His chair does not face the audience; it faces JOE BROWN JR.)*

NARRATOR

A black psychiatrist, Dr. Thomas L. Brayboy.

DR. BRAYBOY

At the core of Joe Brown's personality is a history of frustrations. Psychological, sociological, economic . . .

JOE BROWN JR.

. . . and I wanted to do that . . . surf. It was a dream I kept to myself. Because it would have been foolish to say it aloud. Nobody wants to be laughed at. And then I thought, I never see black people surfing . . .

DR. BRAYBOY

We might call Joe Brown's homicidal act an act of ritual murder. When murder occurs for no apparent reason but happens all the time, as in our race on Saturday nights, it is ritual murder. When I worked in Harlem Hospital in the emergency ward, I saw us coming in bleeding, blood seeping from the doors of the taxicabs . . . icepicks and knives . . .

(These speeches must be slow, to the rhythm of music.)

NARRATOR

Play "Summertime" for Joe Brown Jr., and a very funky "Summertime" for his friend James Roberts, who he knifed to death.

JOE BROWN JR.

. . . And then I thought, I don't see any black folks on T.V., ever. Not any real black folks, anyway. There are those so called black shows like *Good Times* and *The Jeffersons,* but they are so far removed from the kind of folks I know that they may as well be white too. I see us playing football, basketball, and baseball, and half the time I miss that because they be on in the afternoon, and I'm usually shelling oysters. "Where am I?" I asked my wife, and she answered, "In the Florida Avenue project where you are doing a poor job of taking care of your wife and children." My boss answered, "On the job, if you would keep your mind on what you are doing...count the oysters."

DR. BRAYBOY

...Ice picks and knives and frustration. My tests indicate that Joe Brown Jr. is considerably above average in intelligence. Above average in intelligence. *Above* average. Vocabulary and reading comprehension extraordinary...

NARRATOR

(to audience)
Our purpose here is to discover why.

DR. BRAYBOY

...But school achievement extremely low. Dropped out at 18 in the eleventh grade.

JOE BROWN JR.

I began watching all the T.V. sets I could, looking for my image on every channel, looking for someone who looked like me. I knew I existed, but I didn't see myself in the world of television or movies. Even the black characters were not me. All the black characters were either weak and stupid, or some kind of superman who doesn't really exist in my world. I couldn't define myself, and didn't know where to begin. When I listened to soul music on the radio I understood that, and I knew that was part of me, but that didn't help me much. Something was not right, and it was like . . . like I was the only cat in the whole world who knew it. Something began to come loose in me, like my mind would float away from my body and lay suspended on a shelf for hours at a time watching me open oysters. No one ever suspected, but my mind was trying to define me, to tell me who I was the way other people see me, only it couldn't because it didn't know where to begin.

> (*The scene shifts to the desk of the CHIEF OF POLICE. He may be played by a white actor, or a black actor in white face.*)

NARRATOR

The Chief of Police.

CHIEF OF POLICE

The rate of crime in the streets in New Orleans has risen sharply. We know that most of our colored citizens are wholesome, law abiding, decent citizens. But the fact remains that the crime wave we are witnessing now across the nation is mostly nigger crime. Stop niggers and you will stop crime. The police must have more protection, more rights, and more weapons of all types to deal with the crime wave. We need guns, machine guns, multi-machine guns, gas bombs and reinforced nightsticks. Otherwise America is going to become a nightmare of black crime in the streets.

> (*Lights up on MR. ANDREWS, Joe's boss. He is sitting behind a terribly messy desk with papers stuck in desk holders. His feet are on the desk. He is eating a large muffelleta sandwich. His image must be one of a relaxed, informal interview at his office during lunch time. If there are no white actors, the part can be played by a black actor in whiteface, but instead of eating lunch, he should be smoking a huge cigar.*)

NARRATOR

Joe Brown's employer, Mr. Andrews.

MR. ANDREWS

I have trouble with several of my nigra boys, but I likes 'em.

(*He almost chokes on his sandwich.*)

Joe was a little different from the rest . . . what would you say. . . dreamier . . . more absent minded. Joe was always quitting, but he must have liked it here 'cause he always came back. You can't tell me anything about those people. One time, during lunch hour, they were singing and dancing outside to the radio, and I snuck up to watch. If they had seen me they would've stopped. It was amazing. The way them boys danced is fantastic. They shore got rhythm and a sense of style about them. Yes sir...and guess who got the most style...ole Joe.

(*bites and eats*)

That boy sure can dance. I loves to watch him.

(*bites*)

Recently, he been going to the bathroom a lot and staying a long time. I ask the other boys, "Where's that doggone Joe?" They tell me. So one day I go to the john and there he is, sitting on the stool...readin'. I say, "Boy, I pay you to read or shell oysters?" He comes out all sulky.

(*smiling*)

He could be kind of sensitive at times, you know. I been knowing him since he was a kid . . . born around here . . . kind of touchy.

(*ANDREWS has finished his sandwich. He takes his feet off the desk, throws the wrapper into the trash, and wipes his hands. A serious look comes over his face.*)

As for why he killed that boy, I can't give you any answers. I think it has to do with nigras and the way they get wild on the weekend. Sometimes the good times get a little rough. And them

(pause)
you don't know what a boy like Joe can get mixed up in, or any of
them out there.

(waves towards the door)
I don't understand it, and I know and likes 'em all, like they was
my own family. My job is to keep 'em straight here . . . any trouble
out of any of 'em and out the door they go.

> *(The scene shifts to another white man. He is well dressed
> with his tie loosened, sitting behind an extremely disor-
> dered desk. Black actor can play in white face. He must,
> throughout his speech, wear a public relations smile. He
> must speak with a winning air.)*

NARRATOR
Mr. Richard Spaulding, Director of the Poverty Program in New
Orleans.

MR. SPAULDING
Last year we spent 3.5 million in five culturally deprived areas
of New Orleans. This money has made a tremendous difference
in the lives of our fine colored citizens. We have provided jobs,
jobs, and more jobs. By creating, for the first time, indigenous
community organizations controlled and operated by the people
of the five target areas, we have, for the first time, provided a way
to close the cultural and economic gap. Social Service Centers are
going up in all these areas. We will develop a level of competency
on par with American society as a whole. In the Desire area alone,
750 mothers go to our medical center each day. We have, in short,
provided hope. Of course, there are still problems.

NARRATOR

Any insights into the murder of James Roberts last Summer by Joe Brown Jr.?

MR. SPAULDING

We are building community centers, baseball diamonds, basketball courts, little leagues, golden agers facilities, barbecue pits, swimming pools, badminton nets, and…if our dreams come true…well supervised and policed bowling alleys. It is our firm hope that sociology will stay out of neighborhood bars.

NARRATOR

Thank you, Mr. Spaulding.

(The scene shifts to a middle aged woman sitting on well worn couch. She is wearing a plain dress. There is a small table with a lamp and Bible on it next to the couch. She is MRS. BROWN, Joe's mother. Across the stage, sitting in a big easy chair is a middle aged man in work clothes. He is MR. BROWN, Joe's father. He is drinking a large can of beer, which, from time to time, he will place on the floor. He listens to what MRS. BROWN says intently, but there must be an air of distance in his attitude towards her and what she says, never affection. The audience must be made to believe they are in different places.)

NARRATOR

(solemnly)

This is Joe Brown's mother.

(A spot focuses on MRS. BROWN. There is enough light however to see MR. BROWN.)

MRS. BROWN

Joe was always a sweet kind boy, but Joe's problem is that he... stopped . . . going. . . to . . . church. I told him about that, but it didn't make any difference. When we climb out of Christ chariot we liable to run into trouble. I tell the truth about my own children, like I tell it on anyone else. Once, before Joe got married he came home in a temper about his boss and his job. Talking bad about the white folks. Said he wished something from another planet would destroy them all. Said he didn't like the way his boss talked to him, that he should be paid more, and like that. We all get mad at the white people, but there is no point in it. So many colored folks ain't even got a job. I told him, "If you think you can do better, go back and finish school." But no, he didn't finish school, he just complained. "Stay in church," I told him, but he started hanging around with bad friends. Bad friends lead to a bad end. Talking bad about white people is like busting your head against a brick wall.

NARRATOR

Mrs. Brown, do you feel your son would kill for no reason? There must have been a reason.

MRS. BROWN

When you hang around a bad crowd on Saturday nights, troubles are always gonna come. I told him to stay out of those bars. I don't know what happened or why. A friend told me the other boy was teasing Joe and Joe got mad. He was sensitive, you know, very serious and sensitive. He didn't like to be rubbed the wrong way.

NARRATOR

Mrs. Brown, the purpose of this program is to discover why your son knifed his friend. No one seems to have answers. We are using the scientific approach. Do *you* have any answers?

MRS. BROWN

(despairingly)

I don't know why. I don't understand. You try to protect your children as best you can. It's just one of those things that happens on Saturday nights in a colored bar; like a disease. You hope you and nobody you know catches it. The Lord is the only protection.

NARRATOR

And your husband? Would he have any information, any ideas?

MRS. BROWN

(sharply)

I haven't seen that man in four years.

(Both MRS. BROWN and NARRATOR look at MR. BROWN).

MR. BROWN

I plan to go see the boy...I just haven't had a chance yet. I have another family now and I can't find any work. I help him out when I can, but. . .

(pause)

...I can't understand why he would do a thing like that.

NARRATOR

If we could hear what James Roberts has to say.

(We return to the "Summertime" theme and the scene of the crime, the barroom where the play began with JOE

*BROWN JR. standing over JAMES ROBERTS' body and
all other actors frozen in their original positions as in the
opening scene. After the NARRATOR speaks, the body of
JAMES ROBERTS begins to slowly arise from the floor
aided by JOE BROWN. It is important that BROWN helps
ROBERTS get up.)*

JAMES ROBERTS

(begins to laugh . . .)

It was all a joke. Nothing happened that hasn't happened between
us before. Joe is still my best friend…if I were alive I would tell
anyone that. That Saturday was a terrible one. . . not just because the
lights went out for me. I heard a ringing in my ears when I woke up
that morning. When I went to work at the hotel the first thing I had
to do was take out the garbage. Have you ever smelled the stink of
shrimp and oyster shells first thing in the morning? I hate that. The
sounds of the street and the moan of the cook's voice; that's enough
to drive anyone crazy, and I heard it every day. That day I decided
to leave my job for real. . .one more week at the most.

JOE BROWN JR.

(getting up from the bunk into a sitting position)

Damn. The same thing happened to me that day. I decided I was
going to leave my job.

JAMES ROBERTS

(looking at JOE with disgust)

Man, you are disgusting. You all the time talking about leaving
your job.

NARRATOR

(to ROBERTS, then to JOE)

Get to what happened at the cafe please. We don't have all night.

JAMES ROBERTS

We were both very uptight. . . mad at our jobs—everybody . . . everything around us.

JOE BROWN JR.

(excitedly)

I know I was…I was ready to shoot somebody.

JAMES ROBERTS

Shut up. This is my scene.

JOE BROWN JR.

You won't even let anybody *agree* with you.

NARRATOR

Please.

JAMES ROBERTS

Joe went on and on all evening and all night. We were getting higher and higher, going from bar to bar. We went to Scotties, then to Shadowland, to the Havana…we had my sister's car…Joe getting mad and frustrated and talking 'bout what he was gonna do. By the time we got to the Ninth Ward Cafe, we was both stoned out of our minds. Joe getting dreamier and dreamier. He was talking about all his problems, his wife, his job, his children. I could understand that.

JOE BROWN JR.

You really couldn't because you don't have those problems.

(We hear Otis Redding's "Satisfaction" from the album Otis Redding Live.*)*

JAMES ROBERTS

Joe was screaming about the white man. He said he was $1500 in debt. . . working like hell for the white man, then turning right around and giving it back to him. He said he couldn't laugh no more.

(From this point on, there must be little connection between JOE'S thoughts and those of JAMES ROBERTS. The Otis Redding recording continues, but must not drown out the speeches.)

JOE BROWN JR.

I had a dream...I had a dream...I dreamed I had 66 million dollars left to me by an unknown relative...

JAMES ROBERTS

(Slow, to the music. As much pantomine as possible, as though he is re-enacting the scene.)

We were in the Ninth Ward Cafe sitting in a booth by ourselves. There was something on the jukebox, I believe it was Otis Redding. It was a hot night. Joe was talking about how there was nowhere he could go to relax anymore. Then suddenly, his mind would go off into outer space somewhere, and I had to jerk him back. I would ask him what he was thinking about, and he would say he wasn't happy with himself. He didn't know himself or where he was headed to anymore.

JOE BROWN JR.

...I always get screwed up when I try to figure out the *first* thing I'm going to buy...a new car...maybe...Mach IV...a new house...a brick one with wood paneling...a new suit...a tailor made three piece...new shoes...some high steppers...a new transistor radio...a big Sony that plays loud with big sound . . . Then I'd give everybody a bill. . . but I can't figure out what I'm going to buy *first*...

JAMES ROBERTS

I said, man what are you talking about. I don't understand all this blues over what happens every day. He said he wanted to believe there is hope. I told him there is no hope. You a black motherfucker and you may as well learn to make the best of it.

JOE BROWN JR.

...People always tell me I can't make up my mind what I want, or I want things that don't make sense, or I want too much instead of being satisfied with just a little. People always tell me I ask too many questions . . . especially questions that no one can answer...and I am just frustrating myself because I can never find the answers. The way I figure it you may as well dream 66 million as 66 thousand. The way I figure it, you may as well ask questions you *don't* have answers to; what's the point in asking questions everyone knows the answers to. Life is just a little thing anyway . . . doesn't really amount to much when you think about time and place.

JAMES ROBERTS
(intensely and quicker)

Then he just blew. Screamed nobody calls him a black motherfucker. I just laughed. Everybody calls him that cause that's just what he is. There nothing wrong with calling anyone a black motherfucker. We been doing it to each other all our lives, and we did it all evening while we were drinking. I just laughed. He jumps up, pulls out his blade and goes for my heart. I could outfight Joe any day but…

JOE BROWN JR.

High steppers…

JAMES ROBERTS

…He got the jump on me and I couldn't get to my blade. It was ridiculous. He was like a crazy man…a wild man . . . turning on me for no reason when I done nothing to him at all. . . and shouting, "There is no hope."

JOE BROWN JR.

High steppers…

JAMES ROBERTS

Before I knew it I was stunned and weak and there was blood all over the chest of my yellow polo shirt…I felt the lights darken, and my whole body turned to rubber…

JOE BROWN JR.

High steppers on a Saturday night. . .

JAMES ROBERTS

…But I couldn't move anything
     (pause)
Last thing I heard was Booker T. and the M.G.s playing *Groovin'*…
Joe…his eyes blazing…everything turned red.

NARRATOR

(to ROBERTS after pause)
You mean this caused such a brutal act? You called him a name?

JAMES ROBERTS

That's all it takes sometimes.

NARRATOR

And you think this makes sense? To lose your life at nineteen over such an insignificant thing?

JAMES ROBERTS

It happens all the time. I accept it. Joe is still my friend. Friends kill each other all the time…unless you have an enemy you can both kill.

NARRATOR

And you Joe?

JOE BROWN JR.

What is there to say? It happened. It happens all the time. One thing I learned: when you pull a knife or gun, don't fool around, use it, or you might not have a chance to. Better him dead than me. He would say the same thing if it was the other way around.

NARRATOR
(to JOE BROWN JR.)
What did you mean when you said there is no hope?

JOE BROWN JR.
(evenly)
I don't know. *There is no hope.* Here in this jail, with my fate, I might be better off dead.

NARRATOR

One more question.
(to JAMES ROBERTS)
Do you feel you died for anything? Is there any meaning in it?

JAMES ROBERTS

Yes, I died for something. But I don't know what it means.

NARRATOR

(to JOE BROWN JR.)

And did your act mean anything?

JOE BROWN JR.

(softly)

I suppose so. But I can't imagine what.

> *(The music of a bluesy "Summertime." The NARRATOR comes out to downstage center, as in the beginning of the play. He addresses the audience directly in even tones.)*

NARRATOR

Play "Summertime" for Joe Brown Jr. and play a very funky "Summertime" for his friend James Roberts who he knifed to death.

> *("Summertime" theme continues as NARRATOR slowly scrutinizes the people he has just interviewed.)*

Our purpose here is to discover why. No one seems to have answers. Do you have any?

> *(NARRATOR moves to actors who play BERTHA, MRS. WILLIAMS, MRS. BROWN, JOE BROWN SR., and DR. BRAYBOY, asking the question, "Do you have answers?" To which they respond:)*

BERTHA

Joe knifed that boy because he was foolish, wouldn't settle down and accept things as they are, and because he didn't have common sense.

MRS. WILLIAMS

You ask me why Joe Brown murdered his friend in a Negro bar on a Saturday night, and I tell you it is because he was headed that way in the beginning. These kids just won't listen, and don't want to learn, and that's all there is to it.

MR. BROWN

I plan to go see the boy…I just haven't had a chance yet. I help him out when I can, but
        (pause)
I can't understand why he would do a thing like that.

MRS. BROWN

It's just one of those things that happens on a Saturday night in a colored bar. . . like a disease. You hope you and nobody you know catches it. The Lord is the only protection.

DR. BRAYBOY

When murder occurs for no apparent reason but happens all the time as in our race on Saturday nights, it is ritual murder. That is, no apparent reason. There are reasons. The reasons are both personal and common. When a people who have no method of letting off steam against the source of their oppression explode against each other, homicide, under these conditions, is a form of group suicide. When personal chemistries don't mix just a little spark can bring about the explosion. Icepicks and knives, and whatever happens to be lying around.

NARRATOR

When murder occurs for no apparent reason, but happens all the time, as in our race on a Saturday night, it is ritual murder.

(The following lines should be distributed among the actors and delivered to the audience directly.)

That is, no apparent reason.

There are reasons.

The reasons are both personal and common.

When a people who have no method of letting off steam against the source of their oppression explode against each other, homicide, under these conditions, is a form of group suicide.

When personal chemistries don't mix just a little spark can bring about the explosion.

Icepicks

Knives

And whatever happens to be lying around.

NARRATOR
(moving downstage facing audience directly)
We have seen something unpleasant, but the play is over. Yes, we see this thing
(gesturing to stage behind him)
night after night, weekend after weekend. Only you have the power to stop it. It has to do with something in our minds.
(Pause. "Summertime" music gradually increases in volume.)
Play "Summertime" for Joe Brown Jr., and play a very funky "Summertime" for his friend James Roberts who he knifed to death.
(NARRATOR walks over to DR. BRAYBOY and shakes his hand as lights fade to black.)

THE END

SONG OF SURVIVAL

by Tom Dent and Kalamu ya Salaam

*Tom had an idea for a play, and was stuck. He shared the idea,
and I said, "We can do this with it." I never would have come
up with this play on my own, because it was based on the rural
reality of Black Power era Mississippi, which included many small
jurisdictions, that had been controlled by whites but now had black
officials. Most people don't know anything about Black Power in
small towns across the Deep South, but it was an amazing reality.*

(RILEY *is cutting* JAMES'S *hair.* EDDIE *is looking in the
mirror, trimming his mustache.* AL *is sitting in a chair.
The barber shop is a typical Negro affair; radio is on not
too loud.*)

RILEY

Soon as I finish James here, that's it for the night.

EDDIE

Uh huh.

RILEY

Yeah, I believe I get on down the way and do some TCBing tonight.

AL

Ah, you ain't got nothing to do.

RILEY

You don't know that!

AL

Yeah I do.

RILEY

How you know?

AL

I know cause you couldn't do nothing if you wanted to, Nigger, you ain't nothing but old dreams and hot air.

JAMES

Watch out, man, don't mess up my head.

RILEY

Boy, I know what I'm doing. I was cutting hair before you had a head.

JAMES

Yeah, just don't take too much off and mess it up.

RILEY

Can't make no damn money these days anyway. Lookit that!
(pointing to JAMES'S hair)
Naturallis. They don't want to cut their hair anymore. Even my own son tells me, "Pa, we don't need you no more; all we want is a shape up, not a cut."

JAMES

Lemme see the mirror, old man, before you have me walking out here bald.

RILEY

Sit there, just sit there. I'll let you see in the mirror when it's time.

AL

When I was a boy colored folks didn't love they hair. They went around bald, to get a job.

JAMES

Yeah, well the times done changed. You ain't got to be a boy no more. Now you can be a man and wear your hair any way you want to and still get a job.

RILEY

Maybe, but the hair don't make the man, the man make the hair.

EDDIE

Don't make me no goddamn difference one way or the other. They want it trimmed. I take a half hour to trim it and charge the same as they want it all off and walk out of here bald. Don't make me no difference.

AL

Yall colored barbers gon always be in business cause niggers ain't never, never gon be satisfied with they hair. Looket James there, wearin his hair long like some damn African or somethin. He be spending hours trying to get that stuff even and keepin it clean and such. I see my grandson. When it be that long they have to come back every other week to keep it even. So this way yall makes more.

JAMES

Mannn, don't you be messin up my head. Watcha doing now? You mess my head up, and I might have to kick some ass.....

RILEY

Boy, I wouldn't be talkin that way if I was you while I got this here razor in my hands.

JAMES

Yeah, just don't mess up...don't none of you old folks know how to cut hair noway. Yall lucky yall the only barbershop in this old town otherwise you wouldn't have no business at all.

RILEY

Be quiet a minute before you make me cut your throat with this razor.
        (A knocking is heard on the door.)
Tell em we closed. It's nearbouts ten o'clock.

AL

Closed! Closed for the night!
        (knocking continues, more insistent)

EDDIE

Goddamn it, we closed. Go home.

VOICE

I'd just like some information.

RILEY

Who the hell is that? Eddie, check it.
        (EDDIE goes to the door and opens it. A white man in his early thirties and a white youth in his early twenties stride in.)

SID

(to RILEY)

I'm sorry, sir. Could you tell us which way to Harrison Street?
We're lost.

RILEY

Yes, justa minute.

(taking barber's cloth from around JAMES'S neck)

There you go.

JAMES

Bout damn time. How much?

RILEY

You know....

RUDY

(pulling gun)

All of it. This a stick up, niggers.

(Everybody raises his hands except JAMES.)

SID

O-k, Niggers, let's have it, and don't try nothin funny.

(moving toward cash register)

If anyone knocks, just tell em you closed, understand!

(Cash register is emptied.)

This ain't much.

(to RILEY)

Nigger, you sure you don't have more stashed away somewhere.

RILEY

No, sir.

RUDY

O-k, we got it. Come on, let's go.

SID

Wait a minute. I want everybody's wallets on the floor in the middle of the room.

> *(RILEY, AL, EDDIE, and JAMES throw their wallets on the floor. SID goes over and picks up the four wallets, stuffing them into his jacket pocket without even looking inside them, and then turns to JAMES.)*

Boy, raise your hands.

> *(JAMES raises his hands. He is shaking, obviously scared.)*

RILEY

You got the money; now won't you let us be? We ain't got much. I don't see why you want to rob us. We ain't got nothin.

RUDY

Come on, let's go.

SID

Naw, hold yo horses.
> *(smiles at RILEY)*

You one of them smart niggers, huh? We know what we doin.
> *(to JAMES)*

Boy, sit back down in that chair. Now Nigger, finish cuttin that boy's hair, you ain't through.
> *(smiling at JAMES now)*

EDDIE

Ah, mannn.

(catching himself)

Sir, why don't you just take the money and split.

SID

(to RILEY)

I said cut his fuckin hair, Nigger!

(to JAMES)

You want your hair cut, don't cha, boy.

JAMES

Yessirrr! Yes Sir!

SID

See there, that's what that boy came here for, a haircut. Needs to get shit off his head.

RILEY

Mister, you done took our money; now why don't you leave us alone.

SID

Nigger, is you back-talking me?

(No one says anything. RILEY slowly folds his arms.)

RUDY

Come on, Sid; let's go.

SID

Naw.

(to AL)

Nigger, go turn that radio up loud. We gon have us a good time tonight.

(AL turns the radio up and stands still, his arms half way up.)

RUDY

Somebody comin, Sid.

SID

Just be still, boy. They closed, ain't nobody comin here. Besides, this here boy waiting on a haircut.

(They remain silent 30 seconds.)

RUDY

They done gone on by now.

SID

Good.

(to RILEY)

Now cut that nigger's hair. That nigger can't get a job with long hair! Make that nigger respectable.

RILEY

I already cut James' hair once today. I do a good enough job for at least a week.

SID

Nigger, you better cut some hair or you might not be seeing no more weeks.

JAMES

Go cut my hair, Riley. He gon kill you if you don't.

RILEY

No he ain't. He just trying to scare us.

SID

Nigger, I'll scare you to death if you don't cut that boy's hair.

JAMES

(almost crying)
Cut it. He gon kill you.
(AL makes a funny noise, and SID turns to him.)

SID

(to AL)
Boy, you dance while this here boy
(pointing to RILEY with the pistol)
cuts that ugly nigger's hair.

(AL starts buck dancing.)

RILEY

Man, why don't you go head on.

SID

(voice full of violence)
NIGGER.....

JAMES

(pleading)

Cut it.

EDDIE

(to RILEY)

Do it, man, before he kills you.

(AL is still buck dancing.)

RILEY

I ain't gonna cut the boy's hair.

(AL stops dancing, and the action freezes.)

RUDY

Come on, Sid. Leave them niggers alone.

SID

Naw, this boy gon get his hair cut, or they gon be some dead niggers around here.

JAMES

Riley, please. I don't want to see him kill you behind my hair.

(Nobody says anything.)

SID

(to RILEY)

Nigger, you gon cut that boy's hair, or do I have to blow yo brains out?

(RILEY does not answer. SID raises his gun.)

EDDIE

Wait a minute. I'll do it. I'll cut the boy's hair!

RUDY

Sid, the sheriff coming up the street.

(SID looks to the door.)

SID

All right! All right, hurry up and cut the boy's hair!

EDDIE

(moving very, very slowly)

I'm hurrying.

RUDY

Sid!

(He breaks out the door and starts running. SID goes to the door and looks down the street.)

SID

Damn fool. Now the sheriff done seen him.

(He runs out.)

(Silence, nobody looks at each other. After a while JAMES runs to the door.)

JAMES

Aw man yeah. Aw yeah. Go on Sheriff Johnson, go getum. Aw man. That's Black Power! He gone get um. Aw man, wow.

(He runs out.)

RILEY

Damn, I hope Jack catch um. That's a whole weekend's work gone there.

AL

He better be careful; that was one mean cracker.

EDDIE

Jack got a gun, and he know how to shoot.

AL

Yeah, but both of them white mens had guns.

EDDIE

So what?

RILEY

I hope there don't be no shootin; ain't no callin for that. All I want is my money back.

JAMES
    (running in excited)
Sheriff Johnson done caught um, and he bringing em down here.

EDDIE

He need to lock um up for life.

AL

Them sho was some mean white folks.

SHERIFF
(leading the two white men ahead of him at gun point)
This here the boys what held you up?

RILEY
Yeah, that's them.

SHERIFF
Well, yall can get your money tomorrow morning. Yall, OK, huh?
They ain't assaulted nobody, did they?

EDDIE
Yeah, we OK.

SHERIFF
(to two white men)
OK, let's go.

(They exit.)

JAMES
Wait a minute. Ima come help you identify them.
*(runs out the shop behind the sheriff with the barber's cloth
still around his neck)*

RILEY
Damn, this been some night. Let's close up.

JAMES
*(comes back into the shop slowly, the cloth folded in his
hands. He hands it to Riley. He stutters a little)*
Than…Thanks…Mr. Riley…thanks a whole lot.
(he runs out)

EDDIE

You didn't even get paid for that one.

RILEY

Yeah I did. That boy called me Mr. Riley.

THE END

New Orleans

Power to the Parade

Contrary to Thomas Wolfe's famous assertion, Tom *did* go home again, both physically and, more importantly, psychologically—but not before putting time and space between himself and New Orleans. Indeed, the deeper truth is that many of us leave our birthplaces on a pilgrimage to find ourselves, or at least to find a place where we can be ourselves, when our literal homes can't afford us that freedom.

That was certainly Tom's reality as the son of the president of Dillard University. As a young man, Tom conformed to his family's expectations and values, matriculating at one of the black elite's more famous "finishing schools," Morehouse College, which counts Spike Lee, Samuel L. Jackson, Julian Bond, and Dr. Martin Luther King, Jr. on its long list of illustrious alumni. In graduate school at Syracuse University, where he completed all but a dissertation in political science and international affairs, Tom was likewise groomed to take his place as a member of the talented tenth.

But instead, Tom heeded the counsel of African liberation theorist and revolutionary leader Amilcar Cabral, committing class suicide by returning to the source. Tom's personal orientation and heritage may have been petite bourgeois, but his chosen lot was cast with the working class masses of his people, those trapped at the economic and political bottom of society. "Never trust anyone over thirty" was the catchphrase of the day when Tom boldly defied his pre-ordained path and dropped out of his master's program. By the sixties, America was a nation in tumult, its citizens and politicians ferociously at odds with each other. Ignited by the bold idealism of the times, Tom bucked the standards of the generation that raised him and blazed his own path.

In New York, Tom chose to work as a journalist and social activist on both national and international levels, serving as a publicist for the NAACP and supporting burgeoning independence movements in Africa. He also became a founding member of Umbra, the first post-fifties, and ultimately highly influential, black literary collective. These opportunities and activities would not have been available to him in the New Orleans of the late fifties and early sixties. After several hectic years in Manhattan, Tom intended to spend a few months getting himself together in his provincial hometown before jetting back to urbane, sophisticated New York City. But then, unexpectedly Tom fell in love.

Tom found himself seduced and enraptured by the city of his birth, the same locale he had left and not expected to ever be permanently domiciled. His friends and comrades were in New York, not to mention the cornucopia of earthly wonders available there on a daily basis in the pinnacle metropolis of the USA. But he was seeing his childhood home for the first time as an adult. When Tom had departed for schooling in Atlanta, he had been too young to fully appreciate the intoxication of working class black New Orleans, where there were neither expectations nor disappointments about how Tom chose to live.

The cultural depth of the music and the black, neighborhood social organizations—neither of which generally caring from whence one came or, for that matter, to where one was headed; whether you were a fourth-generation resident or an immigrant newly arrived from overseas—New Orleans fed your spirit and embraced you as though you were a long lost friend. Indeed, Tom's deep appreciation of New York notwithstanding, for him New Orleans was not only the city of his birth, but unexpectedly also became the site of his maturing as a writer and cultural activist. On his second time around, New Orleans became the cradle of Tom's rebirth.

As a cultural worker approaching New Orleans with both eyes open, Tom could peer beneath its surface, realistically appraising the place he frequently referred to simply as "New O"—the "O" being an exclamation of wonder, astonishment, surprise, or conversely sometimes an acknowledgement of disappointment or disapproval. Tom knew that New Orleans could simultaneously be both serious and silly, naive and decadent, carefree and cruel. Hence the handful of essays in this section don't just gape at New Orleans in awestruck wonder; they also critically examine the social reality of Tom's complex and very often contradictory hometown.

Tom was not a fool in love. He knew that his relationship with the city of his birth was a difficult love. Tom understood why people left; if they were young, college-educated, and optimistic about a professional future, well, New York, L.A., D.C., even Boston or Chicago offered much better mainstream opportunities. But Tom didn't care if life was better someplace else—Tom cared about making life better in Big Easy. Hence his rephrasing of the trademark sixties slogan: Power To The Parade.

KALAMU YA SALAAM

NOSTALGIA:
St. Joseph's Day Celebrations, or the Origins of Super Sunday

Tom had a profound interest in the people who made New Orleans work, and not just in the culture in the abstract. The conversations he is having are with two of the most important culture makers, Tootie Montana and Danny Barker. Both of these men ushered in the modern expression of their respective cultures: Tootie for the Mardi Gras Indians, and Danny for rekindling young people's interest in New Orleans street music.

   Published in the New Orleans Tribune *in 1986.*

You are driving through town in rush-hour traffic as dusk falls. Suddenly you run up against a cluster of Mardi Gras Indians parading across the street silently, as if they are an apparition that refused to dissolve on Carnival night.

   "Surely, this is a dream," you tell yourself, well knowing the Big Easy's ample capacity for the unreal. It is then that you realize this must be St. Joseph's Day, March 19th—the traditional day for a minor repeat masking by the Indians.

   No matter how rushed you are, you may as well stop for a few minutes and enjoy one of the miracles of New Orleans culture—the luscious colors and startling designs of the Indian costumes.

Later, you may wonder about the origins of this improbable tradition. Why on St. Joseph's Day, an essentially Italian festive occasion that falls smack in the middle of Lent—a time of supposed abstinence and restraint— why do the Indians suddenly reappear?

This question led me into a brief search of the history of St. Joseph's Day, its relation to Carnival, and its even more unlikely connection to the Black New Orleans community.

In the section on St. Joseph's Day in *Gumbo Ya-Ya,* the fascinating repository of New Orleans history, myth, legends and lies compiled by the Federal Writers Project during the early 1940s, I discovered that St. Joseph's Day is indeed an Italian religious holiday of Sicilian origin, set on March 19th by the Medieval Papacy.

Observances to "St. Joseph, the carpenter" actually began hundreds of years before St. Joseph was assigned a commemorative day in the Franciscan calendar. It was in 1870, however, that · Pope Pius IX declared St. Joseph the patron saint of the Roman Catholic Church.

In the Sicilian tradition, altars to St. Joseph were offered to protect the giver against evil, disease, pestilence and, particularly, to protect travelers. Altars were constructed with the image of the saint in the center, flanked by an incredible variety of breads and pastries. At heart, the holiday was considered a respite from the heavy restrictions of Lent, a day of even bacchanalian relapse into the pleasures and celebrations of Carnival.

Carnival, which has always been connected with the coming of spring and the rebirth of vegetation, predates Christianity. It began in Egypt as a commemoration of the renewal of life brought about by the yearly flooding of the Nile and spread into Greek and pagan Roman societies. Once Christianity became accepted in Rome, the Papacy merely incorporated the pagan rites they could not stamp out into their scheme of rituals, celebrations and holidays. St. Joseph's Day was one of these.

In New Orleans, St. Joseph's Day took root in the late 19th and early 20th centuries, brought over by generations of Sicilian and Italian immigrants. Many of these immigrants settled among the numerous, widely dispersed Black communities of the city, establishing small groceries and bars—establishments that became integral components of the daily lives and memories of the Blacks who inhabited those neighborhoods. "Generations of Italians came, settling in Black neighborhoods with their corner groceries," said Danny Barker, one of the city's most esteemed jazz banjoists and historians. "The newer immigrants were supported in their businesses by family members who had preceded them."

It is Barker's impression that the Italian immigrants didn't understand or completely accept the racial prejudices common to the American South, so they got along fairly well with their Black neighbors and customers, though it was not the custom of Blacks to visit Italian homes—which were usually in the rear of, or above, the groceries. According to Barker, St. Joseph's Day was probably the only day of the year Blacks were welcome. On March 19th, many Italian families constructed altars and held open houses. That's how St. Joseph's Day probably got introduced to the Black community.

Though all of New Orleans commonly acknowledged special devotions and celebrations on March 19th, among non-Blacks, the holiday was rather exclusively limited to those of Italian ancestry (New Orleanians of Irish descent celebrate St. Patrick's Day, March 17th). However, by 1900 Blacks were celebrating St. Joseph's Day with unusual enthusiasm. It was the occasion for parties, balls, and masking (though rarely for altars). In short, it was an outburst of Mardi Gras frivolity for one brief reprise.

According to Barker and Allison "Tootie" Montana, Chief of the Yellow Pocahontas Black Indians for the past 37 years, 40 to 50 years ago parading groups from the traditional Carnival clubs like the Baby Dolls, the Saints & Sinners and the Dirty Dozen were familiar sights on the night of March 19th.

Since it was still recognized as a working day, "St. Joseph's Day celebrations in the Black community were almost always at night," said Montana, "though some uptown Indians came out in the afternoon to get a few more hours in their costumes."

Both Barker and Montana pointedly recall the railroad lanterns the Indians carried so that they could be identified at night. A lantern in the distance meant the Indians were coming. Barker said the police required the Indians to carry lanterns, but Montana doesn't remember being harassed by police on St. Joseph's night.

Carnival Day, with its warlike atmosphere among the Indian tribes, was a different story. "On Carnival night years ago, the emergency ward at Charity Hospital used to be full of wounded Indians," says Danny Barker.

"On Carnival," Chief Montana agrees, "you weren't supposed to give way to anyone because you represented the pride of your tribe and neighborhood. On St. Joseph's night, it was mostly our habit to parade in quiet walks within neighborhood. All you could see were lanterns, the shininess of the costumes and hear the jingles of the metal pieces on suits." The Indians visited traditional neighborhood stops, ending their ritual journey at a neighborhood ball or bar. If there was a humbug, the second liners started it with their chants and boasts proclaiming the greatness and fearlessness of their respective chiefs and tribes.

"That was St. Joseph's Day in the old days," sighs Chief Montana. "It was really something to see and enjoy."

Today, very few of those who mask on Carnival mask again on

St. Joseph's night. Only a few of the Indians still come out, and those are mostly the uptown groups. Festivities on March 19th among Blacks have receded into the past (save for a few altars and dances), as have the once ubiquitous Italian corner groceries and the "credit slip" held by "Mr. Johnny."

As times and cultural patterns change, however, they sometimes mutate into a more glorious manifestation. For many years, Chiefs like Tootie Montana and younger Blacks who grew up engrossed in Indian culture deplored the violence that was all too characteristic of Indian encounters on Carnival Day.

Jerome Smith is one of these younger Blacks. He grew up in Montana's St. Bernard-St. Claude-Claiborne neighborhood. In his early twenties, Smith was a key figure in the Louisiana direct action civil rights movement, representing the Congress of Racial Equality (CORE).

During his civil rights period, Jerome became convinced that the African culture-rooted Indians of New Orleans represented a serious, prideful and unique aspect of Afro-American culture. Nowhere else in America do similar groups appear, though similar costuming and rituals do exist in the Caribbean.

When his Movement days were over in the mid-sixties, Smith, along with fellow CORE leader Rudy Lombard, founded the Tambourine and Fan organization to highlight Indian culture and tradition, and to tie that hundred-year-old tradition to athletic and positive Black cultural training for youth in their Seventh Ward neighborhood.

Using Hunter's Point (the field at St. Bernard and Claiborne Avenues) as his base, Smith has, in two decades, built a strong program that serves New Orleans youth as no other before or since.

It was Jerome's dream to use Tambourine and Fan as a vehicle for building better relationships among Indian tribes throughout the city—to eliminate "tribalism" and long-standing hostilities.

In 1961 he began trying to set up meetings that would bring all the chiefs together, but it was impossible to ever get more than two or three to attend. Smith's aim was to have all the tribes march together on St. Joseph's night.

Gradually, with the constant support of Montana and Tom Sparks of the Yellow Jackets, and with ten years of persistence, objections against a unified parade wore down.

"We had to contend with the extreme neighborhood mentality of New Orleans," Smith recalls. "But because they knew I had worked in the civil rights movement, and because I knew guys from all over town from my days on the riverfront in the banana workers' local, we were finally able to get enough chiefs to see that what we were advocating was in the interests of Black pride and the education of our youth."

A unified parade on St. Joseph's, Smith argued, would spectacularly demonstrate the genius of Indian costuming as a unique New Orleans phenomenon and signify a new time of brotherhood and cooperation. The basic idea was creative exchange, not competition, though there would certainly be an appreciation for costume beauty and creativity.

In 1971, seven or eight of the chiefs agreed to convene with their tribes at Hunter's Point on St. Joseph's night and parade together, complete with chanting and second lines to the Municipal Auditorium for an affair commemorating the event.

"That first march was a huge success," remembers Jerome. "People along Claiborne Avenue couldn't believe what they were seeing—all those Indians in one parade together," recalls Montana. "The next year we were amazed. We didn't have to beg the chiefs to come to a meeting—they called us about wanting to be part of the parade."

Thus the origin of the most beautiful parade held in New Orleans today. Now all the Indian tribes active in the city have joined the St. Joseph's parade, along with traditional second line dubs, Mardi

Gras clubs, various drummers, kazoo bands, individual maskers, and at least three marching bands, including Dejan's Olympia.

By the mid-seventies, however, Smith recognized that such a massive parade could not be fruitfully held on St. Joseph's night. So a decision was made to hold it on the Sunday following March 19th, which is now known as "Super Sunday."

The 1984 and 1985 Super Sundays were long, multi-faceted, spectacular events involving the Creole Wild West, Seminoles, Cherokee Braves, Wild Magnolias, Flaming Arrows, White Eagles, Golden Stars, Mohawk Hunters, Yellow Jackets and Yellow Pocahontas. Second line clubs who marched included the Moneywasters, Sixth Ward Swingers, Bucketmen, Mellow Fellows, Kazoo Band and the Jammers.

In a massive, four-hour procession from Bayou St. John and Orleans Avenue, from Orleans to Claiborne Avenue and on to Hunter's Point, each group had a chance to strut their stuff in a gloriously colorful display before thousands of admirers.

This year, weather permitting, Super Sunday will be March 23rd. It is the parade to end all parades—St. Joseph's Day raised to a level of magnificence never envisioned in Sicily or old New Orleans. Through Super Sunday, the genius of Black New Orleans culture has spun off from the old Catholic holiday to produce its own altar of ever-nourishing spiritual and celebratory bread.

A CRITICAL LOOK AT MARDI GRAS

In New Orleans, there is an interesting dichotomy. Black people traditionally talked about Carnival, much more than they talked about Mardi Gras, as if they were two different things. In many ways they were, and this is what Tom explores in his critical look at Mardi Gras. Tom had an academic background and a street sensibility—he was comfortable with the musicians not just as artists, but as individuals. Jackson Advocate, *Feb 18-24, 1982.*

Growing up in New Orleans, I believed that Mardi Gras happened everywhere; it was a part of life one learned to look forward to and lived with. But it didn't take me long, even as a child, to become bored with it all—Mardi Gras meant a day off from school and endless traffic jams.

When I left New Orleans to go away to school, and later when I lived in New York, memories of Carnival were, frankly, dim. In the northeast where acquisition of the precious dollar must go on relentlessly, the idea that an entire city would devote an annual season to a massive party and a delirious leap into fantasy seemed incomprehensible and, finally, unintelligible. And yet, you would meet those who, upon learning of your New Orleans childhood, would say, "Oh, I always wanted to go to the Mardi Gras. How wonderful it must be to have grown up in New Orleans." Well, I don't know.

*   *   *

Returning to New Orleans years later gave me a chance to perceive Mardi Gras anew, from both the perspective of memory and the distance of separation. First, I noticed what should have been obvious: black Mardi Gras is different. Oh, blacks go to the parades—after all, it's a free show one must see at least once during the season, but for most once is enough. No one I knew was really into parades. I found the floats both gross and absurd, and the trinkets diminished in quality, if that is possible. The only blacks who really follow the parades are teenagers who run behind the hip black school bands, indulging themselves in a free second-line, at the peril of police nightsticks and, as we have come to discover, bullets.

But as I experienced it again, I began to find the *idea* of Mardi Gras interesting. Giving the devil his due is a concept blacks accept very easily. In fact, the concept may be African in origin. Of course, Carnival is a holiday of Catholic derivation, but the genius of Catholicism has been its capacity to absorb unto itself those elements of what it calls "pagan" cultures that the church cannot eradicate. The application here seems to involve a recognition that the wares of Satan are formidable, therefore, it is on the side of wisdom to arrive at some sort of detente with the devil, at least on the Tuesday before Lent begins. The more I thought about it, the more it seemed to make sense. It made more sense than a lot of things I saw in New York.

*   *   *

Carnival for blacks, I continued to discover, was pretty much a time of parties, seasonal balls, and, on Carnival Day, costuming—the most interesting manifestations being the Indians and, with reservations, the Zulus.

Parties were held either at home or on one of the spacious neutral grounds converted into a semi-picnic ground for the day—the tragedy here being that downtown Claiborne Avenue between Orleans and St. Bernard was the most desirable stretch—still used, but virtually ruined now by its paving over due to the expressway overhead. It is a time of good cooking: seafood, gumbo, red beans and rice, potato salad, plenty of wine—pots many friends can share. Finding a good spot on Claiborne is still ideal, for Claiborne twists S-like through the black community as its spine, from the Jefferson Parish line to Jackson Barracks.

From the vantage point of Claiborne Avenue, either in a family resting spot or on foot (only fools attempt to drive Claiborne on Mardi Gras), one can see all the Carnival sights worth seeing: The various costume fantasies, the Zulu Parade, the Indians.

I found it interesting that blacks *do* costume, love to costume, really don't have to wait for Mardi Gras to costume—imaginative and outrageous dress seems to be endemic to black people in New Orleans. People make their own costumes. And blacks love Mardi Gras fantasies. My favorite all-time Carnival scene was one I saw on North Rampart: A small contingent of marching black youth returning from Canal Street tooting on those toy trombones with all the conviction of the Olympia Band, marching in perfect time and rhythm, oblivious to the insanity around them. And who can find fault with that? In a city where unemployment is rampant, where housing is decrepit and where there is no improvement within range of a telescope, the more capacity for fantasy, possibly the better.

*   *   *

And then there is the Zulu Parade. As a child I didn't have a consciousness of ever having *looked* for it, nor possibly did anyone—it just came reeling around the corner at you. Yet the Zulus, in my memory, provided the only Mardi Gras trinket worth a damn— coconuts. The danger one risked of getting hit in the head leaping for one was worth the prize: good eating and something worth showing.

When I returned to New Orleans I made a point of seeking out the Zulus on Mardi Gras morning. For one thing, I was interested to know how, in that time of new black American-African con- sciousness, they came to use the southern African name "Zulu", a people who, incidentally, had contributed few members, if any, to the slave trade. I was surprised to discover that the Zulu Social and Pleasure Club was formed about 1910, and the Zulu name was chosen somewhat accidentally—if anything it had more to do with self-derision based on Tarzan myths than on African pride or knowledge. The grass skirts, the totally unnecessary black face, the "wildness", etc. What had been nice about Zulu, however, was its intended derision through caricature of European royal pre- tensions, so evident in the white parades, a satire blacks might not so easily have gotten away with on any other day. "It's all in fun, boss." I liked the fact that the inspiration for Zulu had come from something incorrigible in black culture, despite the lack of positive Afro-American or African assertion. In fact, historically, part of King Zulu's appeal had been his incorrigibility, his unpre- dictability, particularly in his meandering route through town, and his veiled threat to the American ruling structure order of things, so brilliantly explored by Robert DeCoy in his fascinating but weirdly titled *The Nigger Bible*.

But by the 1960s the NAACP, or someone, had begun to say the Zulu Parade was much too unsavory, the Zulus ought to clean up their act. Then the satire was toned down, the floats, rather than creative, handmade, and distinct, became weak imitations of the white parade floats; in fact, they *were* second-hand floats from earlier parades. The route became planned, even announced in the paper like the white parades. By 1980, the Zulu Ball had become the most prestigious of black Mardi Gras balls, themselves mirror images of the white balls, replete with King, Queen, Maids, Court, Debutantes and formal dress—which were mirror memories of a lost European age, the same age that perpetuated regal grandeur from the profits of the slave-trade and New World plantation culture. We seemed to be trapped in a circle we knew not the origins of. And, finally, blasphemy of blasphemies, the coconuts were painted gold and handed out to favorites along the route rather than tossed to the hungry populace. They were still coconuts alright, but you felt like a fool if you cracked one open on the spot and ate it.

*   *   *

If the Zulu Parade had become more imitative than satire, then the black Indians are more African than Indian. At least, that is my educated guess. Certainly they are the most interesting phenomenon of Mardi Gras, an annual ritual rooted in black cultural function.

How the Indian tradition got started is, of course, worthy of an entire essay and considerably more serious research than anyone has yet done. My guess is that the hundred-year tradition of the Mardi Gras Indians descends from the gatherings at Congo Square, the great New Orleans meeting place before and directly after Emancipation for those of African descent furthest removed from Creole heritage. Because of the preponderance of West African dance, music, drumming, to some extent dress, and whatever survived of African languages at Congo Square, it is the most important New Orleans site of African remnants, and probably the most significant ancestral site of jazz and other indigenous forms of New Orleans black music.

From my reading, it is interesting to discover that there were ritual observances and costuming extremely similar to the New Orleans Indians in West Africa and the Caribbean. The name "Indians" is particular to New Orleans, but the similarities are noticeable. In the Caribbean, it is also noteworthy that traditional black cultural celebratory days are associated with Catholic rituals, or are modifications of original European Catholic festive occasions. Over a period of years these became occasions when slave cultural reversion was approved by the church and colonial authorities, out of a policy of control through tolerance. It is interesting that when such reversions presented no threat, the Latin-colonial owners were titillated by what they observed, from a safe distance, of course.

I certainly would look closely at New Orleans, Caribbean, West African festive occasion cultural similarities with respect to: (1) organization into tribes or nations, (2) the existence of chiefs, sub-chiefs and a hierarchal structure, (3) dress, particularly the imaginative use of feathers, (4) chants (which are probably of African origin), and (5) the secrecy of the clubs, requirements or membership and methods of organization.

If strong similarities exist, as I believe they do, the question, then, is why the New Orleans Indians call themselves "Indians." The great Caribbean poet and historian, Edward Kamau Brathwaite, has developed a theory around the process of African survival in the New World that I find instructive. He says the mother culture, to survive under extreme duress in the New World, must go through a submarine or tunneling stage, during which it is masked in more acceptable and innocuous forms when confronted by the dominant European culture and power structure. During the period of submersion the mother cultural practice undergoes transmutation, so that years later the original phenomenon reappears in a completely new form, though it contains the soul of its original form. Thus African culture has survived in the New World to the extent it has masked (submerged) itself in new forms that will not be destroyed by the dominant white culture.

There are endless examples of this in the Afro-American experience: traditional African religions reappear here in the form of the black Baptist Church, the penchant for African social organization becomes a black American love of societies and complicated club life, traditional African spirituality turns up as black American "soulfulness." The African genius for orality is obvious in our playfulness of language and love of slang as a form of racial solidarity and sophistication; African pantheism transforms here into an extremely elastic and endlessly imaginative concept of "what the Lord can do," and so forth.

This cultural submarine process sheds considerable light on why the Africanity of the black Indians is masked as "Indian." It was more innocuous to say "We are Indians" than "We are Africans." We certainly may also speculate on whatever contact blacks had with Native Americans during the first century of New Orleans, however slight. Native American settlements, before they were obliterated, would have been the only ones to offer asylum to escaping slaves, and, in fact, in the very earliest days, an attack on the city by an alliance of escaped slaves and Indians did occur. There would have also been instances of intermarriage when runaway slaves settled permanently with Indians, though integration of blood was not as extensive as it was in northern Florida with the mating of escaped slaves and native Seminoles. Whatever the case, an interaction between blacks and Indians would have been one of natural allies against a common enemy. Even when contact was only the slightest, as in the case referred to along Red River country by Solomon Northup in *Twelve Years A Slave*, such contacts were never hostile.

For blacks in New Orleans with a heritage of strong African traditions, a heritage under siege due to the high value placed on European culture by not only the dominant whites but the more favored Creoles of Color, to call themselves "Indians" is not only explainable, but in the light of history, fascinating and poetic. Calling themselves "Indians" was a way of acknowledging a symbolic alliance of resistance between the greatest racial victims of the brutalities of the colonial and American regimes. That this deeper purpose is achieved through the real and symbolic act of *masking* is altogether fitting, and provides a far more viable function to the Mardi Gras ritual than appears at first glance. It also provides a clue to the resilience of the black Indian tradition, and to why it renews itself year after year, whatever the cost of costuming.

*   *   *

One of the things I always liked about Jerome Smith and Tambourine and Fan, which was created in the sixties, is the attempt to utilize the potential for black pride inherent in the Indian tradition and to build programs around it. To a large extent, Tambourine is credited with ending the incipient tribal feuds and self-destructive violence that Indian Carnival activity was notorious for, shifting competition between tribes to a rivalry based on originality, elaborateness and beauty of costuming. Tambourine has also evidenced a heightened consciousness of the need to preserve the traditions against the incursions of commercialization, as several of the Indian groups recently seem to have become fascinated with discovering ways of making money off themselves.

*   *   *

And finally, it is indicative of the pervasiveness of black culture that in music city, the soul of Mardi Gras is now signaled by the music by Professor Longhair, a genius of post-traditional New Orleans music. Longhair's music has supplanted as unofficial carnival anthem the old "If Ever We Ceased to Love", or whatever it is, and good riddance. The playing of "Mardi Gras in New Orleans" on radio and jukeboxes marks the real beginning of the season—it isn't even necessary to hear the entire tune, just the first trill of notes. When we hear the notes of that marvelous piano we know it won't be long, and, well, who can avoid it? And if the insanity gets to be too much, I found I could always go see the Indians again and marvel at the sanity and purpose that lies deep, deep underneath the costumes of Satan's own day.

REPORT FROM NEW ORLEANS: Resisting the Poised Wrecking Ball of Progress

Janus looks forward and backward. He could be the patron saint of a New Orleans sensibility that Tom articulates here. (Unpublished)

New Orleans is a weird town, now wavering in the breeze of history. An old place, one of the few towns in this country where one can look at the layers of two or three centuries in one glance. Then there is also the poised wrecking ball of "progress."

One hundred and fifty years ago New Orleans was primarily a black city, as it is becoming again now. The city was largely built by black people skilled and unskilled, slave and free. It was, and has always been, a river city, a seaport that made it on the sugar and cotton trade, and later on oil. But all that is changing now. Now the city wants to make it on reputation, that is tourism, and if possible on the grand scale. This is the reason for the domed stadium, the largest in the world with all the problems that white folks have when they decide to build something too large. It is also the reason for the new hotels and office buildings and even for the current obsession with Preservation.

And as New Orleans wavers, like a rickety old building, in the winds of time and change, a young black dude thinks about it all and then thinks about his plans to leave. He is any young man, just turned twenty, married or getting married, and he can't get a decent job, if he can get one at all. He's heard things might be better in LA or Chicago or Detroit or wherever in California his family has relatives.

As for New Orleans, he wonders what "progress" means for him. He even wonders about the new black politicians, and what they're doing for him. He sees them on TV now and then talking about this and that but they don't touch his life as anything real. He also wonders about the rash of new movies on Canal Street with his people running around pushing dope, or breaking up dope rings, or being beautiful secret agents, or cowboys; he wonders what that has to do with his life and livelihood. He wonders about the two soul radio stations: "your black giant booming you the latest in news and sounds" with steady advertisements from Mr. Tee's jewelry store offering beautiful diamond rings with nothing down if you're getting married. He has a buddy who got one of those rings and they sat down one night and figured out that he will be paying for it for at least four years. But the music is good… when they play music.

And as he strolls past the downtown Howard Johnsons he notices that it is open again, with the same stupid sign outside, this time SUPPORT YOUR SYMPHONY ORCHESTRA, BEAUTIFUL MUSIC, and he wonders about Mark Essex, but not too much because he figures that Essex just stopped wondering and decided to *do* something, and what he did to this day gives him a tinge of pleasure, and he could very well imagine himself coming to the point where he would do the same. As New Orleans wavers in the wind he wonders what will happen to the *niggers* of New Orleans, will it be their city too, will it be a good city for niggers. Or whether there will come a time when there are his people and his music but no more niggers.

Suddenly he hears Baptiste's trumpet sound the call. He feels the excitement run through his body same as always; the Olympia is ready. The beat, the jump, the swift movement of rhythm, the entire crowd of his people carried away into unity of motion, singleness of purpose, individuality of motion. The second line is everybody's thing together and everybody's thing for themselves.

Umbrellas raised, the huge throng moves before, behind and with the band as if convulsed *into* it, become a part of it, reunifying movement and sound. The drumbeats echo like shots underneath the Claiborne Avenue overpass. Traffic stops before the blk throng. Our dude feels like he is a part of an irresistible and undeniable force. He has heard people condemn the parades, the music, the funerals, the dance, but he realizes there is something deeper, and he is a part of it, something old and certain about what it means and what it celebrates. Something he cannot put in words.

And for the first time in a long time he really didn't want to leave New Orleans because as the trumpet of Wallace Davenport darts out, echoing off the sunrays, he knows there won't be anything like this in LA or Chicago or Detroit, there is something about this moment that can't be defined by money or jobs or progress or new buildings.

Quickly our dude moves closer astride the band, his umbrella up high bobbing with him. And he imagines that this parade never ends—it marches right on to City Hall and through it on Monday morning, through the courts, through Parish Prison and Central Lockup, then winds its way through the library, up and down Canal Street, through Maison Blanche and Holmes, through Mr. Tee's taking a few diamonds along with it, and right over to Tulane and Broad to the police station bursting the eardrums of the polices so that their brains fly right out the side of their heads in both directions and the music oozes in to impart finally some sense.

And then there were no more niggers because the niggers *were* the city: what his people had learned long before him was the order and the music was the law.

But he noticed that the Olympia had stopped playing, the excitement had cooled down, and the good dream got lost. Soon, when the parade was over, he would have to get back to his plans to leave.

So much for the weird town, this nineteen hundred seventy-third year of the anglo calendar, wavering in the wind of history.

Tom Dent
Fall 1973

NEW ORLEANS VERSUS ATLANTA:
Power to the Parade

Deflating the myth of 20th Century American Progress. Which would you rather do: participate in a political election or dance your ass off in a second line? Although they are not mutually exclusive, most politicians can't dance. (Unpublished)

Politics in New Orleans has always been fascinating because the game is played with such cynicism. New Orleans politics is *trickster* politics; ideology means nothing; rhetoric is a tool of the poseur. It is only natural that the person on the bottom—the black who is barely surviving in this society—is the most cynical of all toward the electoral system.

Certainly blacks know that electoral politics, even in the last decade with the elections of Moon Landrieu, Edwin Edwards and Dutch Morial, has not been their road to power and independence as a people. In the American political system, independence stems from economic power—politicians don't represent the "people"; they represent the economic interests that elect them; these interests in return expect protection and the services of the system. Economic power is exactly what the black community of New Orleans does not have, so in the end black politicians either represent white interests or opt for rhetoric, which, however sincere, is usually impotent.

Black Atlanta, on the other hand, has for several decades been a strong economic community, reaping the consequent political benefits. In fact, in Atlanta the power interests of black and white money often coincide. Atlanta *is* middle-class America, and the blacks there seem very satisfied to emulate the whites. Not only an emulation in style of acquisition, but in values, lifestyles, even speech. This is the real reason why Atlanta is "the city too busy to hate." They are busy making money.

What they do with the money is something else, but suffice it to say that middle-class black Atlanta would never pause during the good day's work to join a parade. Nor is the thought considered anything but New Orleans foolishness and if not immoral, certainly recidivist. Black Atlanta ties into a system of middle-class respectability fully supported by the big churches and the six colleges. Their suppression of black culture or any lifestyle that white America cannot identify with is typified by an attitude toward the power structure of "we're just like you," and in its more highly developed stages, "we're more like you than you if you knew the best in you." In this system, black Atlantans look upon African heritage like some long-suppressed family illegitimacy. Even the down-and-outs who wander up and down old Hunter Street (now the new Martin Luther King Boulevard) wear suits and ties, the better to pick up a free drink.

Compared to Atlanta, New Orleans is a breath of fresh air—but if air cost money, a lot of homefolks would suffocate. The food is great, but it is becoming more expensive; the music is great, but one cannot eat music. If New Orleans had a large black middle class, possibly their interests and the interests of the white power structure would coincide as in Atlanta, but I doubt it. As it is, the policies of the New Orleans white power structure seem to be designed to keep the black community underfoot while giving up nothing, making no concessions, not even to the twentieth century.

Dr. James R. Bobo, a University of New Orleans economist who has watched the direction of the New Orleans economy with alarm, noted in his exhaustive and well-publicized 1975 study, "The New Orleans Economy: Pro Bono Publico,"

> we really have two economies and two societies, one conventional and one unconventional (the under-world of economics). The most distinguishing charac-teristics of the underworld economy are: 1) incredibly high unemployment, 2) abject poverty and poorness, 3) relatively low educational attainments, 4) the deg-radation of welfare for many, 5) human, social and physical blight, and 6) substandard housing.

Bobo gives documentary support to what struggling blacks here see all the time: the expensive renovated uptown houses in contrast to the prison-like Desire Housing Project downtown, the buses primarily ridden by blacks, the tourist trade at the expensive New Orleans restaurants seen only when the kitchen door swings open; Parish Prison, Central Lockup and the criminal courtrooms filled daily with blacks. Black youths wash the dishes, sweep the floors, cook the fast foods, polish the image of New Orleans glam-our. And a lot of these jobs are work-this-week-off-next-week.

In 1969, 38.2 percent of New Orleans' black families lived below the poverty level, as compared to only 25.2 percent in Atlanta, 26.8 percent in Houston and 26.5 percent in Dallas. Since then, the relative position of New Orleans has probably worsened. Bobo concludes that,

> ...low labor force participation rates, economic dis-crimination, the relatively low educational prepara-tion of the labor force because of the disadvantages of

poverty and being poor, with its attendant high rates
of unemployment, underemployment and unem-
ployability, have contributed to our relative impoverishment, a condition of impoverishment greater in
degree than for all major metropolitan areas, Atlanta,
Dallas, or Houston, or for that matter, the entire
nation.

The overwhelming thrust of Bobo's criticisms has to do with
fundamental New Orleans economic weaknesses and the long-
standing failure of the power structure to recognize them—and
to recognize, with the exception of the police force increases, that
the entire city suffers from the consequences of the condition of
its black poor.

Economic inequities are not the only distinctions between
blacks and whites in New Orleans. We must begin to view the
descendants of freedmen as a people who inherit not only the
horrible legacy of slavery, but the strong positive legacy of African
cultural retentions, especially in music, dress, the various racial
societies, dance, cooking, parades, funerals, and the joy of something we might call the theater of the street. (To some extent these
qualities exist in all large black communities of the South, but
they are ever more so in New Orleans.) The gaiety, the love of life
that whites (and many blacks) perceive on the faces of blacks here,
particularly during cultural celebrations, is often misinterpreted
as a sort of mindless contentedness, as if the people had not the
sense (or the cause) to be angry.

It is my feeling, however, that this attitude toward life is a
cultural strength that makes it possible for people to survive the
hard times despite their frustrations—though white New Orleans,
especially some of the younger enthusiasts of black music and
culture, usually sees black culture as devoid of political and

community consciousness in the same way their elders thought
the beatific look on the faces of black musicians was due to their
own "tolerance," the kindness and indulgence of the ruling class.
Culture, music, parades, funerals—all of it—as it operates among
black people in New Orleans never eschews political or economic
considerations, however much these aspects may be suppressed.
On the contrary, culture can be the very instrument that best con-
veys the political and economic interest of the people, though it
has not been generally viewed this way.

The appeal of culture is why so many blacks remain in New
Orleans, or return, seemingly against all economic reason. "It's a
good town," many a black New Orleanian will tell you even away
from the city. "Can't make no money but no other place like it."
Then they will talk about the good times: the music, red beans
and rice, the parties, gumbo and what happened at carnival, or
the mystery and intractable perversity of the place, the rains, the
family histories of entangled bloodlines, then the music again.

*   *   *

All this means that full black political strength in New Orleans
must begin to include people with lifestyles and interests at odds
with middle-class America: the second-liners, the people who
walk the unemployment lines, the people who were born in and
have never left the projects, the welfare mothers and the welfare
children, the people who wash dishes in the famous Quarter
restaurants, the people who live in rundown New Orleans housing—the people to whom the vote now means nothing. They have
been the *cynical ones*, and for good reasons. Most of the nonpar-
ticipants, the non-voters, feel that politics is "white folks' business."

Will politics ever become "black folks' business?" If so, what will
make it so? Black New Orleans culture *is* at odds with mainstream

American culture, a historical reality not only not likely to change, but in my opinion, not desirable of change. The extreme poverty, the raging unemployment in hard-core black New Orleans, makes it almost impossible for the community to elect representatives who will further its interest in traditional political ways. Once the black community elects someone, it is difficult to hold that representative faithful after she or he is exposed to the lure of greater amounts of money from competing mainstream econom- ic interests, whether in plain ole dollar payoffs or jobs which offer huge increases in salary. "Opportunity" for newly elected black politicians, themselves poor, appears in shiny traps wrapped in red ribbon.

In addition there are the problems created by the skillful direc- tion of the potential black vote through outrageously gerryman- dered districts—or brilliantly gerrymandered depending on how you look at it. Although the Supreme Court recently ruled that the present at-large, five district representative structure of the City Council is constitutional, it does not shake the conviction of most blacks that both the councilmanic and state legislative districts are now and have always been drawn with aim of diluting black voting strength. Black voting blocs have also been discour- aged by the racial housing pattern of New Orleans: in the old city, since the abolition of slavery, blacks have lived in just about every neighborhood. It is said this pattern developed because so many blacks worked as servants and the whites wanted them to live nearby; in the same way, in the French Quarter, slaves lived in the rear of the houses of their white owners.

The potential black vote is even further defused by the tradi- tional practice of buying off neighborhood organizations—well, if not pennies, for rent money. During the last decade, SOUL (The Southern Organization for United Leadership) attempted to put a stop to this, but what has happened to SOUL is a case of history repeating itself. SOUL grew out of the concentration of black voters in the lower Ninth Ward. As the first really strong black New Orleans political organization in the twentieth century, SOUL was, for a time, a solid step forward, built largely on the small black homeowners and middle and low-middle-income blacks who populate the area below the Industrial Canal, a commercial waterway that runs between the Mississippi River and Lake Pontchartrain. The Lower Ninth Ward represents mostly post-World War II growth, offering an opportunity for black home ownership not possible in the inner neighborhoods of New Orleans, and the lifestyle of a small town as satellite of a great city. SOUL also reached across the Canal to organize the area around the Desire project. (The area Tennessee Williams wrote about in *A Streetcar Named Desire*—part of the area was then Polish—is also the area where whites were most active in resisting the beginnings of school desegregation in the early 1960s.) Desire, however, is much more poverty-stricken and politically impotent than the Lower Ninth.

In a sense, SOUL was a child of CORE (Congress of Racial Equality), the civil rights organization that attempted to organize New Orleans in the early sixties. It was also a product of the extremely active sixties legal firm of Nils Douglas, Lolis Elie and Robert Collins (now the first black federal judge in the South), CORE'S local legal defense firm and the meeting place for New Orleans veterans of the civil rights movement. Nils Douglas was the first to test the political waters in the Lower Ninth in 1966 with workers buttressed by Movement veterans. Douglas lost this election, but within a few years he put together a formidable organization which controlled the ward's state representative office and became a power to be reckoned with in all city political affairs. Meanwhile, Douglas' law partner, Robert Collins, created COUP (the Committee for Organizational Politics) in his native Seventh

Ward (primarily creole blacks). COUP often endorsed candidates in tandem with SOUL.

By 1970, when Moon Landrieu ran for mayor and Edwin Edwards for governor, SOUL-COUP had such a strong position it could guarantee the delivery of at least 80 percent of the city's black vote. Landrieu won the mayorship almost entirely because of the black vote, receiving less than 30 percent of the white vote. Edwards, after a messy primary, won a close gubernatorial race because of the solid bloc of black supporters delivered by SOUL-COUP and other black groups in New Orleans.

As a result of Landrieu's mayoral victory in 1970, SOUL struck some deals that most people feel were beneficial to the New Orleans black community. It is generally believed that in return for their support, Landrieu agreed to black control of federal community action and model cities programs; in addition many blacks gained prominent city jobs including, near the end of Landrieu's term, Chief Administrative Officer Terrence Duvernay.

Certainly the Landrieu-SOUL marriage was an extremely bene-ficial one for both parties and through it the very face of City Hall, previously so hostile white, seemingly stocked by straw-hatted, cigar-smoking Irish or Italian bosses, blackened before our very eyes, blackened in ways whites who liked the way things were be-fore Landrieu could not accept. On the other hand, it should never be forgotten that it *was* a bargain; during his crucial eight years Landrieu was able to win almost every key election he had a stake in because of his dependable bloc of black support—of which a large part, but certainly not all, was orchestrated by SOUL-COUP.

After such notable successes, the quick demise of SOUL (COUP still exists as a fairly potent force) is difficult to explain. In a sense it can be explained by saying the leaders followed the classic pat-tern: lacking a strong economic base, they took whatever jobs— from judgeships to independent business opportunities—became

available during the Landrieu years and used the political organization to protect their new-found economic opportunities. Early
in the game, severe splits emerged within SOUL over direction
between the rank-and-file and the leaders, between those from
Desire on one side and those from the Lower Ninth and Gentilly
on the other; the inclination of the leaders to further their own
interests at the expense of the rank-and-file did not inspire unity.

In addition, leader Nils Douglas, though a fine strategist and
conceptual thinker, never seemed able to articulate SOUL policy
in a way that could transcend the labyrinthine organizational
endorsements. Finally Douglas, always a rather phlegmatic politician, left the leadership role, and with his departure went what
remained of organizational cohesion. By the time Landrieu's term
was ending in 1978, SOUL had split into factions and was fighting
itself in the courts, a sad spectacle indeed.

Ironically and possibly tragically, it was during a period of
setbacks for black political organizations in New Orleans that
Ernest M. Morial was elected the first black mayor in 1977. Morial
possesses a distinguished record as a civil rights attorney and is a
protégé of the late A. P. Tureaud, the preeminent black civil rights
attorney in Louisiana during the legal battles against segregation.
Morial is also a product of black New Orleans' strong creole
legacy, a people who have historically suffered from confusions
and indecision about racial identity, often preferring, even when
self-professedly black, to see themselves as a third group between
the whites and the dark-skinned African-retention blacks of
Congo Square heritage. Culturally, the creoles of color of earlier
generations looked to France, not Africa (or America) as the paradigm of civilization.

Morial has always identified black, but his career has eschewed
alliances with black political organizations; he has always seemed
to move in splendid isolation. Nevertheless, he became the first

black state representative in the late sixties and soon after narrowly missed a bid for City Councilman-at-Large.

When Morial announced for Mayor to succeed Moon Landrieu he was considered by most blacks to have no chance. What happened was almost unbelievable. Morial ran an excellent campaign in the first primary, coming out strong as a "black" candidate, identifying his aspirations with such as Tom Bradley of Los Angeles and Maynard Jackson of Atlanta. It soon became obvious that Morial would be one of five candidates to be taken seriously, and it accrued to his advantage that he was the only black in the race.

In the first primary, Morial carried almost 90 percent of the black electorate, to the dismay of three of the white candidates who had reputations as racial moderates and hoped for at least a part of the black vote. Morial has always had his enemies among blacks in politics here, but he in fact received an almost unanimous endorsement from the black electorate without begging for it or having it delivered to him by an ongoing organization; it was, as some said, "a secret black bloc." Therefore, totally unexpectedly, Morial ran first in a closely fought five-man primary, and very importantly, the three white moderates split their vote, throwing the one rather conservative white, Councilman Joseph DiRosa, into the runoff against Morial.

After a few debates and an aggressive and sometimes bitter campaign in which Morial gave no quarter, it became obvious to the power structure he was the only choice; one who would be able to hold, if not actually improve on, some of the "progress" gained during the Landrieu administration.

Yet Morial's election means almost nothing to the blacks on the bottom rung, those who have never been involved in the political process. As if to underscore the meaninglessness of any substantial gains for the black community, upon winning Morial has steadfastly maintained he is not and will not be a "black" mayor, owing nothing particularly to the black community. Such rhetoric is hardly necessary, since the black community has no method of calling in debts. In a sense, Morial, in contrast to Maynard Jackson of Atlanta, presents the spectacle of a "black" mayor whose prime distinction is that he does not act like a black man.

*   *   *

If there is to be any meaningful change in New Orleans, we may have to arrive at a politics not of profit or extraordinary power, but of *survival*. The person who puts together this new black political structure might be the person who, after winning, does *not* take a better job, does *not* move "up" as the fruit of political labors. We are not talking about a new, more radical ideology (however desirable this may be), but a new breed of community political activist, one who does not identify as a political "professional," one who has the luxury of not needing to convert political efforts into immediate cash reward, jobs or contracts, who has no desire to be the object of political glamour or to acquire a judgeship or appointive post. Hopefully, this person will work for years on the building of black organizational coalitions and their skillful use. Until one day the sight of a plum becomes too sweet...

All this may sound dreamy, but if it ever happens it will probably happen this way. The only real political salvation for the black community in New Orleans is self-help, the building of strong coalitions, and the retaining of dedicated people at the level where they have to answer primarily to the interests of the community— not the power structure.

*   *   *

Meanwhile, when it comes to politics these days it's all Atlanta. Black New Orleans has a big corner to turn. But when it turns

it won't be the same corner as Atlanta, which is the same corner
the rest of America always turns, it will be its own. Then, as one
prominent black Southern politician—a native of New Orleans
who left to go elsewhere—said, his eyes opening wide as he com-
prehended the idea of political leverage *plus* culture, "*then you
would have a monster!*"

Griot Work

"trying to fight through the prison / of indifference"

We never made much money, Tom, myself, or our contemporaries. The twin predators of despair and depression were ever-present at the back door of our lives, just waiting for a misstep on our part so they could jump onto our backs—they loved the taste of our brains, leaving us mentally maimed as they licked their lips. Surviving as a black writer serious about one's life and the lives of our people is damn near an economic suicide mission.

Yet putting money first would have landed us in the same league as our historic slave masters, whose morality, such as it was, was based on the infamous nine-tenths of the law: all that they could earn, steal, or con; the booty, the loot, the wealth, the luxury—none of that, myths notwithstanding, was based on honest, hard work, but rather was mammon incarnate.

Tom was from the big house. Me, from the stables. But we recognized kindred spirits when we looked into each other's eyes. We knew neither of us was going to sell out, was going to cross over or lose our resolve. We were runaways committed to frugal living on the margins, a lifestyle precious few of our people would voluntarily choose. We had choices, opportunities, and yet here we both were on the lam, running away from fame and fortune. That was our conscious decision. We both knew what rejecting the mainstream meant.

The subtext of all of our literature was not the Bill of Rights—not in the face of our history in the United States, where we were literally property for nearly one hundred fifty years, during which time we had no rights that whites were required to respect, as the Dred Scott decision explicitly stated. The brutal bottom line as enunciated by the United States Supreme Court was unequivocal: we were never intended to be included as citizens. As Tom testifies in one of the poems included in his masters thesis, "those of us who seek a / tribe of free black people / know no nation."

With this precedence in place, no one should be surprised that as former chattel, we self-identified our literature as warfare as much as aesthetics—as much more than art for art's sake. Moreover, we knew the system was not going to pay us to intellectually retrieve our property, i.e., ourselves, from those who not only stole us and sold us into slavery, but also benefitted economically, accumulatively and over generations, from our exploitation.

Our freedom could not be founded in wealth, not in the way that most Americans amassed it. Even if we wanted to, even if some of us tried, we could not exploit our people the way America had exploited us. Indeed, the best and most talented of us, the Frederick Douglasses and Sojourner Truths of us, the DuBoises and Garveys of us, the Ida B. Wellses and Fannie Lou Hammers of us, the Malcolm Xs and Angela Davises of us, and yes, the Martin Kings and Dorothy Heights of us—all of them understood that we could not succeed by simply following the American arc of capitalist assimilation, an arc based on the super-exploitation of those of us at the bottom.

Is it really any wonder that our art was based on social relationships, rather than capital acquisition? On content and context, rather than craft and classics? Our art, which mainstream critics characterized as being obsessed with race, was actually an art obsessed with ending racially-based exploitation. Our situation was an original, all-American catch-22: we were subjugated as a race, then condemned as hacks and propagandists when we used our art to address our oppression. We were supposedly sullying our art with an overemphasis on race, when really art was our shield and spear to fight back against white exploiters, those who actually overemphasized race and systematically profited from that design.

This necessarily adversarial work of documenting and advocating for our community, if one was serious about the task at hand, was tantamount to taking a religious vow. To be a serious black writer, you not only had to ask and answer the near universal question in our community (*why am I treated so bad?*); you also had to figure out why you would continue giving your all to your work when you got only meager returns.

I remember Tom telling me that those of us who were good at writing were invariably also good at other tasks: people were willing to pay writers to do other things, but seldom would they pay us to write. For writers who refused to confuse entertainment aimed at the mainstream with the creation of conscious art reflective of our own lives, this was especially the case.

There was neither bitterness nor resignation in Tom saying this; rather, Tom observed a matter-of-fact truth of which most non-writers were ignorant. Not only did we toil in poverty, but worse yet, most people in general, and mainstream cultural critics in particular, paid our literature no mind.

Even so, Tom would just lower his head a little and whisper conspiratorially: *You just got to keep doing it.*

In 1983, through an improbable series of circumstances, I was selected to become the executive director of the New Orleans Jazz & Heritage Foundation. I had served on the board of directors during the seventies, with Tom serving before me. By 1987, I was leaving the directorship and encouraged the appointment of Tom as my successor. It was a prestigious position and I was elated when Tom won the job.

That I would walk away from the job after only four years was no surprise to anyone who knew me. But then Tom also resigned in order to work on *Southern Journey: A Return to the Civil Rights Movement.*

Since moving back to New Orleans in the mid-sixties, Tom had struggled financially. Leaving the Jazzfest was not a decision lightly made—it was a crapshoot. Tom chose the uncertainty of a book project, whose treatment is included in this section, over the comfort of a prize position in the city's leading music-producing organization. Following through on such a noble decision takes a level of ideological commitment that most of us don't have. Tom was willing to make deep sacrifices.

Begun in 1991, comprising literally thousands of miles traveled by car and hundreds of hours of taped interviews, the document that chronicled the post-Civil Rights conditions of the cities and towns that had been critical hot spots of that struggle finally came out in 1997, and then slowly sank into oblivion. *Southern Journey* was not a commercial success, even though it was one of the most honest and painstakingly researched assessments of what we as a people gained and lost in the eighties and nineties.

I never knew specifically how much work Tom did until I took up the task of putting together this reader. I had shared so much with Tom, seen so much of his work in draft form, discussed so many literary ideas, traveled across the South visiting people from east Texas to North and South Carolina, journeyed with him to the severe northern climes of Ohio and back down to the sun and sand of Miami. Tom shouldered the griot's task without any guarantee that the work would be valued in the future. Much like our enslaved ancestors, Tom toiled against staggering odds to create a legacy for a hoped for but uncertain future.

Most people under fifty have never heard of Tom Dent or his book *Southern Journey*; Tom died before the book was even two years old. Sometimes writing our literature seemed as futile as throwing snowballs at the sun—and that's really futile in a town where it snows only every ten years or so. And yet, over fifteen years after Tom's death, his work is being revived. He could not have known this book, *New Orleans Griot: The Tom Dent Reader*, would be produced. Tom simply did what he thought needed to be done.

Tom taught me the griot way, taught me to value our history and to relate to our contemporaries who were history makers themselves. This griot orientation motivated Tom not just to explore the obvious subjects such as Mardi Gras and New Orleans music, but also to consider personal memories like tossing the football with Paul Robeson, or such speculative meditations as getting into the head of a musician who had committed suicide.

The last major example of Tom's writing (accessible in the Amistad archive) is an essay that is pieced together from extensive notes. In 1987, Tom took a journey to West Africa, with his friend Dr. Gabou Mendy as his guide. Tom's travel to Gambia, Senegal and Mali was no quest of a starry-eyed idealist; Tom was a mature man with a realistic grasp of the ways of the world. His African notes reflected reality rather than romance.

Over a quarter-century later, the writing remains fresh in its critical insights and implications—"critical" because the focus is on hard truths rather than platitudes, misplaced optimism, or even understandable (albeit inaccurate) nostalgia. After all, Africa is not just an ancestral motherland: Africa is also a contemporary wound whose healing will take significant time, resources and therapy.

On a visit to the famous Gorée Island and the infamous "door of no return," Tom noted a cruel dialectic:

> Later I am still reflecting on the experience of visiting
> [a] slave house. It was discomforting; I had wanted to

leave very soon after entering, and I did not remain long. As a shrine, can slave house properly be a tourist attraction? I think not. My overwhelming emotion was one of shame at Europeans visiting the horribly painful site of our humiliation. Historical humility; immeasurable shame. The paradox of that bitter history existing on this beautiful island forever. Like the tragedy of all African history, all of modern Africa— beauty trapped within exploitation. Exploitation thriving within beauty.

Tom neither sought nor garnered fortune and fame. From time immemorial, most griots have done their important work in historical anonymity, with a humility much different from the one Tom mentions above. We don't know their names nor much about their lives; indeed, in the oral traditions of ancient Africa, we don't even have their words passed down in books or recorded songs.

Yet the griot was nevertheless a relevant model for what it meant to be a writer in the twentieth century. In this new millennium, as we revisit the work of Tom Dent, we realize how fortunate we are to inherit this rich, written legacy.

KALAMU YA SALAAM

POETRY AND CONTEMPORARY BLACK LITERATURE

What these poems really represent is Tom making a transition from a formal text-based poet to a blues and jazz poet, in which he plays with not only the meaning, but the sound and placement of the words, i.e. the rhythm.

Submitted in partial fulfillment of the requirements for the degree of Master of Arts, Goddard College

Thomas C. Dent
August, 1974

GODDARD COLLEGE Plainfield, Vermont 05667
GRADUATE PROGRAM
STUDENT SELF-EVALUATION FORM

Student's Name: Thomas C. Dent
Date: August, 1974

Using this page, and its reverse side if necessary, please present a thoughtful and concise critique of your own graduate work. You may organize this in any way you wish, just so long as you evaluate your growth over the time you were in the Program, the strengths and weaknesses of your present level of development, and the thoughts you may have about where you should go from here.

NARRATIVE SUMMARY OF WORK—MASTER OF ARTS DEGREE

I. Main Objective: a Thrust

The basic substance of my project was the completion of twenty or more new poems comprising a distinct body of work, submitted herewith.

My Goddard workyear poetry was written with emphasis on:

1) The oral tradition in Afro-American poetry, beginning with the African oral narrative, continuing through oral imperatives in black music, black linguistic inventiveness and dialect in America, and culminating in the 1960s when orality has become an important force in contemporary black American poetry. I have been working from the theory that my poetry is as much to be heard as to be read. My concern is not with "literary" language but a language the people can understand, in forms familiar rather than obscure. Poetry for me is always an act of communication. My models then are black music, letters, street talk, dialect, and private speech more than public speech.

2) The world I have known since birth: the deep South, New Orleans, the concerns and conflicts surrounding the black community of New Orleans with its strong musicality and African retentions, symbols such as the river, the music, the dance. I would describe my work as consciously ethnic rather than transethnic, speaking to certain people, certain things that interest me, and

hopefully the people that share community with me or are interested in that community. Most of the poems are rather short, but
my work includes one long poem about Louisiana history with the
Mississippi River as a central symbol. I would note the poem for
Louis Armstrong, "For Lil Louis," poems for friends, poems eulo-
gizing musicians and poems about black movement experiences.

3) I have molded the direction of my creative work from specific reading and study.

I have read at least one book during the workyear by every
major black American poet, with particular study of the work
of my mentor Keorapetse Kgositsile, who bridged the African
and Afro-American experiences of the 1960s. Also, well-known
contemporary poets whose style is not akin to mine but whose
work I respect like Sonia Sanchez, Marie Evans, Alice Walker and
Sarah Webster Fabio. The style of the Puerto Rican poet, Victor
Hernandez Cruz, has strongly influenced mine. I have also spent
considerable time studying the work of Ewe (Ghana) poet Kofi
Awoonor, whose symbols I found very interesting and helpful in
dealing with New Orleans material.

Books by the above authors are *My Name is Africa* by Kgositsile,
Snaps and Mainland by Victor Hernandez Cruz, *Night of My
Blood* by Kofi Awoonor, *i am a black Woman* by Mari Evans, *Jujus/
Alchemy of the Blues* by Sarah Webster Fabio, *We Are a BaddDDD
People* by Sonia Sanchez, and *Revolutionary Petunias* by Alice
Walker.

4) My reading of contemporary creative work was augmented
by the reading of the essays of Ezerkiel Mphahlele, especially
the long critical essay, "Voices in the Whirlwind: Poetry and
Conflict" from *Voices in the Whirlwind and Other Essays* by
Ezekiel Mphahlele. Mphahlele, like his younger colleague,
Kgositsile, is an exiled South African writer. His lengthy and
brilliant essays look at the history of Afro-American poetry

and particularly the poetry of the sixties from the perspective of the pan-African experience and the African and European literary traditions. In my opinion, Mphahlele's essay is the best critical work ever done on contemporary Afro-American poetry. I found his African perspective particularly helpful to me in providing information about writers I was not familiar with and in providing reactions to black American literature from the literary African perspective. This has deepened my sense of how Afro-American and African culture can be bridged, a major concern of my own creative work.

5) I have received close assistance and critical help from my field faculty mentor, poet Keoragetse Kgositsile, and from my core faculty supervisor, Craig Eisendrath. Kgositsile has been especially encouraging and helpful in suggesting directions for my work and the work of other writers who would help me in the process of self-definition; Eisendrath especially encouraging and helpful with detailed criticisms of the work herewith submitted.

II. Additional Writing

In addition to the poems that comprise the basic body of my work, I am including two articles written during the work year:

a) "Black Theater in the South: Report and Reflections," to be published in September 1974 in a special issue on the media of *Freedomways, A Quarterly Review of the Freedom Movement.* This piece is the latest of several essays I have written during the last eight years in the South and the Free Southern Theater.

b) "Report from New Orleans" is a narrative essay that contrasts the black cultural strengths of New Orleans with its lack of economic opportunity, especially for black youth. It is a conflict central to my concern with the city.

III. Other Activities

a) Edited a special issue of *Nkombo*, a journal of the black arts in the South, which I co-edit and co-own with Kalamu Salaam of New Orleans. The special 1974 issue contains poetry by many young black writers, fiction by Keorapetse Kgositsile and myself, and an interview with senior poet Octave Lilly of New Orleans about his days with the Federal Writers Project during the New Deal, his collegiate years at New Orleans University, and the struggle of a black poet to publish when writing carried little possibility of remuneration and encouragement. This issue of *Nkombo* was published in June 1974.

b) Organized a writing workshop among young black writers in New Orleans. We began meeting in the spring of 1974 and now meet weekly. The group is called the Congo Square Writers Association. It is hoped that we can expand to include a new literary journal, regular readings, the sponsorship of appearances by non-New Orleans poets, and hopefully a theater primarily committed to performance of creative work from the workshop.

c) Attended the Phyllis Wheatley Poetry Festival at Jackson State College in Jackson, Mississippi in October 1973. The Wheatley Festival was designed to commemorate the first black woman American poet and to bring together for the first time twenty of the outstanding black woman poets for three days of performances and discussions.

d) Received a Whitney Young Fellowship for 1974-75, which will allow me to begin work on a novel.

e) Participated as workshop leader in writing workshops at the Goddard College 1974 Summer Colloquium, at the November 1973 Washington Regional Colloquium panel on Literature and Politics (with Penny Hogan), and at the Memorial Day Washington Colloquium.

RETURN TO ENGLISH TURN

this
barren place on
river road english
turn
where deep river turn

this
cemetery small old wooden
crosses
weeds this spot
where Bienville convince english
this land french
sign say
1699

nothing but the woosh
of occasional strong
breeze
levee green
it
is
here
it all began

the french push
the people
who live here
out
go west young indian man
and come up this river turning

here
in droves pushing themselves up
over and over those years
at the bottom
groaning leaning straining to
the river current
us
the music of our ruptured memory
beat out by the music
of
chains

plantation thrived
here
off the work of Leroy and
Beulah orange trees
great house
cotton and sugar
and chains

songs and shouts
the forgotten pains
the rebellion
and the hangings
at every parish church
above and below this
barren place

then the boats
up and down this
muddy snake with
the sugar and the cotton

and the corn
up and down
past this barren place
to France and England and
Cincinnati
Memphis
Chattanooga
Philadelphia
trying to bring this river under
machine control
commerce thrive
we work the boats
live in shacks by the new tracks
and look to the river
where will it bring us
what will it bring us

then
something went wrong
something went strange
something went weird
the plantation begin to slip away
the foundation

begin to rock
to the pulse
a the rivuh
current oh muddy
rocking slipping straining
slipping rocking swinging
oh current oh
crazy muddy rivuh

what you doin
what you doin!
whas happenin
you done moved in
on us oh crazy rivuh
its de *moon*
de ju ju
crazy le bas
leavans be look down on dis
what is it in this night
everything fallin fallin
slipping away
floating down de
old crazy rivuh

bells/steeples/cotton mattresses
hoes/sickles/draywagons
China from Europe
rugs from Turkey
picture of painted faces
mirrors/columns/moss-covered oaks
stuck in the moon mud
chains/whips/flintlocks
cypress doorways/stained glass windows
thin iron fences/spiral staircases
stuck in the mud
stuck in the mud
and the river wouldn't stop

\#   \#   \#

so see us now in the city
to the direct north
the crazy city the city
of de pleasure unpostponed
city of raindreams
of raindreams
moon-night mare city

city we built
tradesmen and mechanics and craftsmen
with Dahomey-honed crafts
city we carve from de swamp
and in tall plaster glass steel
building fortunes made and lost
but not ours
our music stolen made
circus show for drunk
whiskey dreams not ours
while straw-hatted newly
americaine rulers sweat
through dey sear-sucker suit
wipe brows over oyster
contemplate next move
we seethe in project heat
the glass broken the steel
jutting at us the plaster chipped
our streets mud
our whiskey dream endless
our music drowns the rain
soothes the cuts from shards

we seethe in project heat
we seethe in memories
ship hull ship boiler
cane field weeded shack
city dock city factory
orange tree
brick over cemetery
forced river journeys
past this place
this barren spot
making the sharp turn
over and over and over

and now we look to the old craggy
river
we look for deliverance
as the spirit of our ancestors
hovers above this place harvesting memory
may our gods watch over the long journey
may our god of music
bestow grace on us
as we journey until the river
goes wrong again in the night

then may
centuries of building
on forced journeys
return to the silence
of this spot now
nothing but the woosh
of occasional strong   breeze
levee green

ship mast in the distance
where river
turn

INTROSPECTION NO. 3 (for sarah webster fabio)

message to you that
I am fightin myself agin
yes kicking my ass all over the place
you said just let it be
but I won't

this comes from rushing
being rushed pushed shoved
and like Willie Mays at bat
I do not know my strength
here I am
winning games again
marching through cities the conquering
hero
my eyes fighting my soul again

and I lifeless
see this writing that we do
a lost art, a non-functional useless thing...
what are we doing
to jot down these insistent painful
memories that become dots of
ink of woodpulp

what are we doing?

but my message to you
lost up there somewhere in
the mid-American desert
is that we do it anyway...

death will come soon enough
and then memory, then memory
all this celebrating act
will have drifted like dust
in the rushing wind

we don't know why we do
there is no heroic commitment
to announce
so here are some little
bits of me
and hello
how you be?

FOR KOFI AWOONOR

"Sew the old days for me, my fathers,
      Sew them that I may wear them
      for the feast that is coming
      the feast of the new season that is coming."
        from "The Years Behind" in *Night of My Blood*

Brother
your words speak to
who we are
who we were
who we will
be if this world be

we too
thousands miles away
share your heart's
invocation of tried & true
gods our journey too
has been arduous mystifying
we too wait
by the shores of the river
for deliverance

our god of songs
is alive and well
and now we ask him
to walk with the god of rivers
that we may never forget
the forced journeys of the forefathers
forefathers
fore
fathers
even as we look out at our green sunrise
at our green sunrise
of the coming
new
new...

we, too, brother.

VERMONT (for the members of the Goddard writers workshop)

the spewing ghetto of Hartford
spills out into the rolling hills
of Vermont
place of winding highways
hidden streams & lakes

that we came there
beside that hill
to argue about the
major contradictions of America
is Hartford Ghetto's hold
on us
but then
some of us were lonely people
& we stared out at each other
sharing something of ourselves
just relaxing down & sharing
& somehow we made it through
without too many promises
without too many lies
without too many manifestoes

it was a good time

AS THESE WARM MUNDANE DAYS PASS (for de workshop)

as these warm mundane days pass
my wish
that whatever I learned from
                de elders
be passed on to you
yr gain what little I know

like our musicians
master of the ancient art
we teach each other
we teach each other

as the sun-rising
marks the passing of day to day
we revere memory
we revere knowledge and memory
the hard times, bitter times
good times
we learn the things we must do
and must not do

may we make this
strong as stone
secure as cement
this spirit
so that you
too
pass it on
pass it on
as these warm mundane days
pass.

FOR LOUIS

slipping away from myself
from the surface city
at night

Louis like all black people
your essence is night
secret places and secret meanings
reserved for us
the mocker behind the
grinning mask
reserved

        for us

          &

            those

once were places
that still live within us

YOU ASKED: if I can't live with it when will it end?

the answer is
probably never

but if you wish
we could lie about
it that is
you could lie that
it ended
& we could lie that
you are right
but the river still turns
only when it wants to
the sky still explodes
only when it wants to
the forest screams
only when it wants to
& we can't really
do anything bout that to be
brutal
the hurts come
at all the wrong times
& when they go
away
it is too late
too late
too late fool
because then
you
are past
never

but if you wish
we could lie about
it

RUNNING & DIPPING POEM NO. 1

for
J. Don David and his gin
bottles
hid in the drawers and closets
of the *Houston Informer*
press room

may his soul rest
in peace
for the legends and truths he
told me
shoe
     string
black news
papers
small town Louisiana

may his soul rest
from the pain

and for Bob Brisbane
who did his best to make it
to class but didn't always
but when he did
told the truth

like the time he said
when they arrest and
handcuff DuBois
this country
in a bad way
may his soul rest in peace

and for Paul Robeson
not for being the big black
hero
the heroic celluoid image
or the social pro
phet just for throwing the
football around with me
when I was a kid
and later when I was a little old
er
for telling an Atlanta
reporter to
                kiss

                        his

                                ass
when he asked
him are you a communist
may his soul rest in peace
and for all the organ
                zashun
ale
ideolo   gists
who told me I had to do some

thing
other than

       w

      r

     i

      t

       e

if I wanted to liberate
black people and forced
me to believe
in the worth
in honest
written
word
for my people
for me
for mah people
for them that
forced me to work that through
may their soul rest in peace

and for the rumble
of New Awleens
cho-cho trains
that still
rumble
through my uneasy nights
may they rest in peace
and for Galveston
that resting watery place
place of barbeque and

memory
island no island
those waves, those tight dark streets

I come to you when I am full
up
and slow down/letting you ease into my
mind
as the ferry slides across the
bay
those waves
those beating waves
may they rest my soul in....

things like that.

MISSISSIPPI MORNINGS (for John Buffington)

early early early
before the eternal basketball game begins
John meeting & greeting the peoples
getting together the latest
  proposal
listening to Staple Singers
dark woods in the house where Feather lived
mingling & the picture of lean
Mississippi girl with hoe staring
somewhere the groan of tractor
the chickens, the country green earth smell
the memory of last night's gin folly
burned out by the new sun
soon everything moving & the
hustle is on
toward busy what?

& John's laughter at it all.

WHEN WE MEET

when we meet
it is funerals
natural disasters
the coming together
of wounded animals
like when we met for the people
murdered at Bynum's
drug store.

somehow we always
play the perimeter
same hymns, same intros
same chants
same speeches
somehow it is necessary
we make that circle again.

we walk around the edges
of the small crowd
moving in whispers
each of us known each
other for so long

to the side
on the glass-littered street
people
watch us
wonder what
                    it's a
bout.

seems like
we could just meet in silence
let our silence speak
our silence the heart
of our shock

the people
would know.

CITY LAUGHTER NO.1

but what do you do
what do you do
how *do* you

        on those rainy New Awlins afternoons
        those cloudy, muggy, thunderstruck
            summer aft/noons glued
            to dreams & the fluids
            that clog our dreams

what do you do

        when the moon all
        ready to run out & burst full
        on us in those balmy southern
        sweaty muggy

aft/noons
the dreamy woman to
the teenager
with the sex fantasy on
        his hand...

Tennessee Williams is a gas/
specially on TV

CITY SKETCH #1

young body
old eyes
space sounds of the stars
shot bloods
years of long nights
young fragile body
old old eyes

CITY SKETCH #2

the mother the seat of
                the family

sits satisfied
at the lakefront
while
daughter braids
                her hair

young brother
brother?
boyfriend?
sits beside
looks away
impatient.

such it is with families
& such it will be.

[UNTITLED]

Victor Cruz poems
explode off the page
into your skull
blowing the dam
of form
flooding
all over the page
of your mind

Victor's poem
raw   uneven
core life
scooped from
middle

FOR KGOSITSILE

From "To Mother"

"We claim the soil of our home
runs in our blood yet we run
around the world, the shit of others
drooling over our eye."

Ah
but we too are aliens
there is no home
no home
even Africa the Afrika
                        of our elaborate
dreams

those of us who seek a
tribe of free black people
know no nation
we float through the cities of the west
like a man trying to place memories
while the world slips away
we watch the curvature of the moon
what that portends...

we will die here like other animals
dross scattered to the wind
that we dreamed
that we dreamed
the soul of our domicile

but who will inherit dreams
    who will inherit dreams?

STATUS REPORT THE LATE NIGHT SELF

these days
trying to fight through the prison
of indifference
trying to keep my balance
as I row against the river
current

these days
wanting to go unclothed
yet I wear suits of the
quick change artist

these days of
little caring but
golden sun clean note attempts
to make these days
ours

COLTRANE'S ALABAMA

yes, Coltrane
it is a woeful song
you sing

times of rain
& memories of fields
rolling by from the Southerner
& the loneliness
the shacks
the curious
staring black
faces
the rain
the rain-filled
land

red mud sticks
to my brain
shards of broken
glass
puncture my heart
it is raintime
woetime
& the flood cannot
wash
the blood
away

INTROSPECTION NO. 2 (for Bobbi)

Sunday aft/noons the lakefront
is peaceful like someone blessed it
possibly some secret god
blessed not just the sheet of sunwarmth
or the breezing trees or the
blue of that tranquil treacherous lake
                              with all its undertricks

it is a place graced by
Pharaoh's insistent and groaning sounds
of organized sunlight
recording like waves the
beauties of all movement
        all movement
        all move
ment
tations

all this comes after knowing the destruction of
cities of bits of glass flying through space
of legs and eyes flying alone through
steel, implanted in steel, buried in steel
of dress suits taking over
giving command orders
of funerals piled on top of funerals beyond
all memory including ours
of hundred year hopes taking power dives into
the sand

and now peaceful

so sudden
so sudden
so un expected
this peace
is it real
like someone blessed this place in time
and space
it is real for the magic
clothes our people
like a great god had rode in from the lake
and said peace, peace unto you my people
be beautiful
and flashed all the beauty colors of nature
jest for the hell of it
and it for once worked

could we float
melt into this?
I mean
we need no other thing
than to melt to be a
part of this
to be one with these people
here in this time and place
Sun in Aquarius
in Aquarius
in Aquarius
us
us

MAGNOLIA STREET

Dear Miss Lucas
I remember you
when I pass Felicity and
Magnolia
yes Old Magnolia

                      that rickety winding street
                      that smells New Orleans
that is open fish-markets
people lounging
memories of numbers tickets strewn
like confetti over the sidewalks

                      that rickety winding street
                      that sounds New Orleans

which is music
loud
music for siesta and dreaming
and funerals
and sun-happiness Saturday nights
and your clumsy heavy winding
                      stairsteps
and the circular room that looked
like a lighthouse
and gumbo
                      that broken winding street
                      that breathes naw/lins

which is everybody knowing your bizness

Miss Lucas
is it not?
and you cousins and your aunts and your nieces
they all came to your
                        wedding, your hospital bed, your fund-
                        raising Saturday night fish fry
which was old wood meeting old wood meeting
old unpainted wood
which is the truth
is it not
Miss Lucas
and the smell of the acrid tar in the summer
in the street told you it was not hot
and I remember your sweating face
and your heavy hand wiping the sweat

                        that old winding street
                        which was your home

is gone now
Miss Lucas.

FOR COOL PAPA BELL

Hey Cool Papa
I see picture of you in your later
years
tall black skin withered
straight
proud
you must have been a streak of black gold
flashing around the bases like some
great African warrior misplaced
it is said you scored from first on a bunt
against the all-white major league all-stars
you were forty summers then
and they wanted to know how you did it
was it magic
was it voodoo
was it a freak of segregation
was it special compensation for
                national mental inferiority
                in the labs of Stanford?
was it something that only happens in colored ball
                a Saturday night mutation gone insane
                in the white man's game?

you must have been the genius black musician
of Daho/Sippi carving his own instrument
so now at seventy
they parade you out from
your job as janitor St. Louis
City Hall
and place you in the retroactive
Hall of Fame...

and forgive us if we don't cry
Cool Papa
forgive us if we don't get excited
for with you we share the night
of that memory those memories
all the bitter years and buried triumphs
because you did it man
and no one can take away
bitter years
buried triumphs.

FOR LIL LOUIS

Louis I'm trying to understand what you were
here
and how you left this place
how you gave the people bravura music
how you could survive it all
even bucket-a-blood
where the frustration of our people
        boiled into daily laughter
but then New O is an old town for that:

> don't you think it's a moon-town
> where the imagination of violence
> sparks easily to life?
> what festers in the minds
> of the grandchildren of the
> people who knew who languish
> now in the projects?
> bucket-a-blood was demolished
> the people banished to the project
> your old town:
> the city's new progress
> your old house:
> the city's new jailhouse
> such the way it is the city
> tells you what they think of you
> and everyone like you and still the
> people dance and progress looks on afraid...

Louis I'm trying to understand what you were
really like

in the dark moments away from the stage.
rumors have it you were not pleasant
to be around,
the shit-eating grin nowhere to be found:

>   did the moon-blood intrude
>   the sleep of your nights
>   even sleep of your days
>   did you carry moon-blood
>   memories to the grave?

Louis I'm trying to understand but never
mind
it's enough that you said don't bury me in
New Orleans
and it's enough to hear your trumpet
laughing at it all
it's enough that you played de-truth-de-truth-beeeeeee
and the sweaty handkerchief
always honest   honest
it's enough
it's enough
but Lou/est

>   someday the dancers will explode
>   and all this little history
>   will shatter as all the
>   shit-eating masks fall...
>   and only the moon will know

A MEMOIR OF MARDI GRAS, 1968

There is a man walking between the gutters and the streets. He is not dancing, but his body vibrates with each beat. His eyes are cameras, his ears are recorders. Tom Dent is written on the side of the box that contains what he saw and what he heard. Let's leave it at that. (Black River Journal, *1988*)

It was time to depart the French Quarter for another place. I decided to walk over to the intersection of Orleans and Claiborne Avenues, where most of the downtown Black community congregates on Carnival Day. As I cross Rampart at Dumaine, there is a group of young black people, men and women, marching in tight formation, single file, toward Esplanade. They had purchased tiny imitation instruments Orleanians call kazoos, sliding trombones which when played produce buzzing notes. They are blowing kazoos, oblivious to the world around them, strutting majestically behind the young man who is acting drum major. I want to enter their fantasy, suspend for a while my terrible, unrelenting reflection. The God of Foolishness is not necessarily the God of Fools. I stride past the old Basin Street turn, past Congo Square, past the site of the old Parish Prison, past the present Municipal Auditorium. More private theaters: a couple riding a bicycle-for-two, someone in a skeleton suit with skull mask, a string of elderly women in pink and scarlet hot pants, deep into their cups, staggering all over the street waving greetings to everyone.

At Orleans and Claiborne the crowd is all-black, generally non-costumed, merely casually dressed, though youths, vibrantly indulging their youth, wear a little something special: combs sticking from their hair, large red handkerchiefs, and among each group a fifth of wine—wine being the traditional intoxicant of the day, cheap wine, though the smell of marijuana is everywhere in the air.

Claiborne Avenue is the sight of much of the Carnival I remembered during childhood. From the balcony of a family friend we viewed the fantastic and ridiculous eating ourselves half to death: red beans and rice, fried chicken and potato salad, gumbo and chili. Everyone had a pot on. It was a day for walking. Attempting to drive was insane, though there were people who tried it, to their chagrin. Here on Claiborne it is not so much a day of total excess, but a fun day, a day of relaxation dropped in the middle of the week, relaxation from the rigors of the work week—a day, if nothing else, of relief from routine. No one works on Carnival except those who are selling, besides the police, and they don't work very hard.

In the forties and fifties, Claiborne was the perfect site for Black community Carnival, the expansive oak-lined neutral ground dividing the street into two parallel thoroughfares. The Claiborne neutral ground became everyone's front yard; front yards rarely existed in inner New Orleans; the houses invariably reached out to the sidewalk. That was then. In the sixties the city chose to construct its new expressway above the neutral ground, obliterating the greenery of what was once the "front yard." Oaks and neatly trimmed grass lawn became concrete pavement paced by ugly posts supporting the elevated expressway.

The pavement below reduced to a wasteland of parked and abandoned automobiles, an ever-present rumbling that sounds as if one is trapped beneath an airport.

*   *   *

Despite this awesome urban transformation, ritual does not die out. Claiborne neighborhood residents have set up card tables with portable chairs beneath the expressway, as their parents did on the former neutral ground, parking their autos in choice spots. With homemade food and coolers for drinks, portable record players for the necessary blare of music, they have secured the perfect site to witness the day's events.

The music, the music was predominantly the work of a genius named "Longhair." That is, "Professor Longhair," a thin, dark-skinned, unsmiling rhythm and blues pianist now in his fifties. Longhair, whose real name is Roy Byrd, wrote a song called "Go To The Mardi Gras" about twenty years ago, which has become the theme song of Carnival through sheer popular explosion in the black communities of New Orleans.

His lyrics, *You ought to go see the Mardi Gras / When you see the Mardi Gras / Somebody will tell you what Carnival for / Get your ticket in your hand / You will see the Zulu King / On St. Claude and Dumaine,* make you feel you are the vortex of some crucial event, a folk miracle. Longhair's song is a self-realization of black uniqueness, a rare event in American culture. Non-existent, for instance, in New York, except in the West Indian communities of Brooklyn. Carnival and Longhair's theme song are deeply en-twined, even since the beginning of Carnival in Egypt more than two thousand years ago, who know when? Longhair's music is everywhere, but where is Longhair, and why is he known by such a strange name?

Is Longhair alive? He isn't performing anywhere, as far as I know. He seems to be one of those black musicians in the South who surfaces for a brief period with a flash of genius, leaves an indelible imprint, but never achieves a "career" or the income

associated with a "career." Then they fade back into faceless masses, living out their lives unrecognized, unacclaimed, unnoticed.
Such stories are commonly heard in New Orleans.

There are men standing on the corner of Claiborne and Dumaine,
conversing. Maybe Longhair is one of them, listening to endless
repetitions of his own recordings blare forth. Possibly, if he is here,
he understands the meaning of his gift to the people. The people's
culture has imbued him with a spirit that he in turn has transformed
into music, the soul of the music echoing in expanding circles to
repossess the spirit of the people, a beacon of our times, of our
lives. Like one tuning fork activating another in turn activating another and another around an awesome aural circle. Musicians like
Longhair do not originate solely from their own creativity; they are
mediums whose genius is transformation, conversion, sublimation.
On today I long to actually see the man, not necessarily to speak to
him, for any conversation we might have would be meaningless. I
only wish to gaze upon him as one might an old building now in
the process of becoming a magnificent ruin, a historical miracle
that has crucially determined the course of who we *are* in this place.
A junction. We must always act out who we are. In America, it's not
always easy to know. Not for us.

Now I hear the music of the Black Indians, the chants of "Handa
Wanda" and "Indian Red." Longhair saluted them in his tune, "Big
Chief"; they are part of the beauty, the integrity of black Carnival.
The cry of Bo Dollis' chants, the singing chief of the Wild Magnolias,
an uptown tribe, and Longhair and Earl King's bluesy singing amidst
drums and tambourines are voices possessed by Congo Square
spirits and the searing historical knowledge of having labored for
nothing on plantations under a relentless sun, a cry we recognize
as from there, that cry unknown in the world of commercial music.

At Orleans and Claiborne, I realized, with an impact that only
comes from experiencing it, how different this world is from the

world of the French Quarter, though the two areas are virtually
adjacent. I might have crossed half the earth. I had always believed
this aspect of New Orleans, of neighborhoods totally disparate in
ethnic, even linguistic entities, to be an unpleasant reality, a pity, a
tragedy that forever plagues the city. It was part of the aspirational
ethos of my generation that we as Afro-Americans would become
an integral part of a unified America. New Orleans: one city. We
must ever endeavor to blast away ethnic territorial boundaries that
are endemic to the way the nation, the city, grew. Afro-Americans
were on the outside of the economic and political nerve center of
the nation—forcibly so—and we wanted in, to be a participant in
the rush of American life with a lowest possible recognition of
color, of cultural distinctiveness.

Now I was beginning to believe the existence of nations within
the American nation not necessarily undesirable. Or politically
"wrong." Or tragic. There is no intrinsic virtue in national ethnic
homogeneity. The Afro-American nation of America, of New
Orleans, is itself beautiful and logical, if it only had political and
economic strength. All over the South now we are trying to effect
"integration," but we don't really know what that is, or why it would
be preferable. Mostly we see integration as a practical social reality wherein all peoples live at peace in society, each able to count-
er-balance the other in economic and political power—but more
specifically, what do we anticipate for our new dream South? Will
there be no more Negro schools, Negro churches, Negro social
organizations, no more history, or Negro music in the dream state
of integration? If all things strictly Negro, strictly Afro-American
are by definition inferior, as so many Afro-Americans are sincerely
convinced, shouldn't we give up our cultural distinctiveness willingly? What would then happen to the recalcitrant New Orleans,
the blacks who refuse to integrate?

MARDI GRAS EVE/1968

Much too warm a night for this time of year, whites roaming the Quarter in packs. Approaching Bourbon on Toulouse, youths racing toward Bourbon, many policemen in their wake—blue lights flashing fire on Bourbon, the sound of police sirens teasing blue lights, a navy police van racing up, backing into St. Peter, a military policeman jumping out, a white kid wandering through the street half-drunk "looking for his cousin's car," Tony trying to sell everything in his Dumaine at Burgundy corner grocery "because I can't be open tomorrow," the dour-faced newspaper man hawking the *States-Item* on Rampart: "I'll be glad when it's all over." Small children out roaming the streets in expectation, the screech of fire engines from the fire station on Dumaine across Rampart. Big Daddy says, "I'm gonna stay home tomorrow, too many people make me nervous." The French Quarter streets stink of stale and spilled beer. The eve of Mardi Gras draws to a close, in preparation for the grand madness of Shrove Tuesday. The God of Foolishness has not shown his true hand as of yet; he has not driven the people completely into madness, but they are in a state of preparedness, a state of imminent possession. I have decided I will observe tomorrow fully for the first time since I returned to New Orleans, trying to resist becoming possessed myself, passing the day like a detached scientist.

MARDI GRAS/1968

First I want to see the Zulu Parade. Haven't seen it since I was a child. I remember it then as a lot of fun, a straggling conglomeration of homemade floats with dancing Zulu club members in grass skirts heaving coconuts to the crowd. Their parade route in the old days was known to be a joke, an improvised wandering through the streets of the black communities, which were every-where in the old city, stopping at bars and clubs and a few funeral homes that offered a toast to the King and Queen. These ritual stops were the occasion for imbibing, greetings, compliments, then off to another such stop, winding their meandering way until finally Zulu wore down somewhere downtown, usually in the vi-cinity of Dumaine and Rampart, where I was living.

The Zulu Parade has nothing to do with Africa, or the Zulu peo-ple of southern Africa. Maybe rumors of Africa. Stereotypes of Africa—the Africa of white American stereotypes: jungles, Tarzan movies, Wild Men. The Africa we "escaped from" via the histori-cally novel method of delivering ourselves into bondage and the civilizing influence of Europeans. That Africa.

The original idea, from the nineteen teens, was to hold a parade that parodied Rex, the most prestigious of the elite white society parades. The newspapers dubbed Rex the "King of Carnival." So from its earliest days Zulu rode the back streets, bestowing his "royalty" on his fellow Afro-American subjects, a joke; Rex rode the glorious Avenues, stopping for no one or no thing except City Hall, where the King and Queen were toasted by the Mayor, and at the Pickwick Club on Canal Street, where highfaluting toasts were offered by old, moneyed New Orleans families, a serious matter, you must understand. Rex is a more elaborate parade with almost three dozen floats, loaded with junk to throw to the populace. But I wasn't interested in all that.

I finally catch up with Zulu on Tulane Avenue, right across from the Trailway Bus Station as it was warming into a beautiful day, in the seventies. The King's float is preceded by a dancing advance guard of secondliners. This means there is a band in front of the float, and there they are: The Olympia Marching Band, accom-panied by the lining boys and men all wearing the black youth Carnival day costume of jeans and jean jackets, some wearing black and red handkerchiefs tied around their heads. The King's float is also preceded by a police car inching ahead slowly in preparedness to stop whatever imminent black madness might break out, two huge police dogs nervously pacing the back seat. Someone taunts the policemen: "Let 'em out." As the King's float passes before me I can see he is adorned in immaculate black facial paint, gold and silver finery, slowly waving his scepter to the sparse crowd. He is quite dignified, whoever he is, dignity having replaced "actin' a fool" in today's Zulu. Louis Armstrong, who was chosen King during the old underground Zulu days and came home from New York to assume his throne, wouldn't know what to make of this.

Now Martin Luther Kingism had overcome the Zulu parade and swept into the new age of black pride. Not that the people in the parade were middle class or racial leaders; they were the same longshoremen and waiters and cooks of the old days. But this is an NAACP-approved parade, with a designated route, the ultimate deviation from tradition. Today they hand coconuts to the crowd instead of tossing them. The coconuts are painted gold with eyes and nose and printed message: "Courtesy of the Zulu's, 1968."

The floats are disappointingly second-hand. Obviously used by previous parades because they carry totally incongruous Anglo-Saxon or Greek mythic images. The contrast between the Afro-Americanism of the Zulu signs hung on the floats, and designs of the floats themselves, which cannot be obscured, renders the entire parade deflatingly absurd for anyone interested in more than merely catching beads.

Now the Queen's float passes, preceded and followed by police escort. Each float is dragged along by a tractor, the Queen's with an amused country-looking driver in the saddle. "What the hell am I doing in this parade, even if I am getting paid?" The Queen of Zulu is, thank our gods, unpainted, a middle-aged woman dressed in elaborate finery, her maids tossing a few beads to the populace, reaching down to pass out an occasional coconut. The Queen is very smug, and maybe a little exhausted.

Float No. 3 carries the huge proclamation: "Big Shot of Africa," no doubt a display of stubborn Zulu Club recidivism in reaction to the new Martin Luther Kingism. "Big Shot" with Derby Hat, gargantuan cigar and black facial paint run amok, is a classic Zulu Parade, a much sought-after annual prize among club members. I never knew whether "Big Shot" parodied Africa or Rex or the idea that anyone from the mythical nation of Zulu could be a Big Shot. Pretensions and self-grandeur have no racial boundaries of course, so maybe the club in a rare display of wisdom voted it was necessary to keep this essential character in the Parade even while they moved on toward middle-class respectability.

Then the other three floats jerk slowly by, the crowd on Tulane Avenue mostly white at this, the backwater of pieces of parades that wander up and down Canal Street. King Rex, the feature performer, has yet to make his awaited appearance. Someone on a float throws a bead a long way down the street, like an outfielder to the plate, to the lone scream of a joyful recipient. Then Zulu is gone.

On Canal Street, two blocks away, several homemade floats are parading for an audience of about a hundred thousand, jammed together like impatient sardines. Most of these handmade floats are really decorated trucks, with costumed families and friends playing royalty by throwing beads and trinkets to the grateful citizenry. People leap and fight for beads as if they are competing for nuggets of gold. Yes, the athletic youths usually win, as do those who have positioned themselves on ladders along the grand route of the avenue, which was once a canal. All New Orleans was once water, you know. Before it became the swamp it now is.

I decided to forego Canal Street, since it was virtually impossible to walk it, for the French Quarter adjacent to the Village of Burgundy, where the really serious madness was taking place. Early this morning, as I looked out of my apartment window in the Village, I saw a drag queen ambling down the street in elaborate costume, complete with train, impervious to the slowly passing city bus moving in another world. I was reminded of Sedonia's loud comment, hands on hips, Sunday, "effen you wants to see the real freaks, you'll see 'em at Carnival, but Sedonia don't care, she stayin right inside her house all day long." In fact, the entire Village seemed unexcited by this Carnival, acting more like a town suffering inundation from a flood of madness it could not prevent than a participant in the madness itself. The madness would soon go away, then everything would return to normal, the Village hopefully still intact, a coastal town weathering an annual difficult storm.

This is the day for drag queens, all sorts of sexual fantasy. As I walked down Bourbon Street toward Dumaine I observed men in cowboy suits with their pink behinds showing, men in huge, elaborate, feathery peacock-like constructions, men in heavy makeup with elaborate hairdos, women in the scantiest of dress, the Indian Summer seventies-degree weather a sure promise of Spring.

Is all this the people's revenge against Catholicism and Christian piety, a reversion to a "pagan" spring ritual with origins in Egypt, old Rome? Maybe so, but it is the immigrants, the visitors, the tourists, who seem to throw themselves into Carnival most intently, believing no doubt they must 'prove' their worth through deeds to their share of the madness. The Quarter, the home of transients, even wealthy transients, is the center of Carnival insanity. I wondered how many of these Quarterites, particularly gays, have moved to New Orleans and the Quarter in full anticipation of the license of Mardi Gras, relishing their freedom from the small, strict, tight little towns and circles of professional relationships in Mississippi or Alabama or Minnesota or Tennessee they have left behind.

Now, on the Great Day, the gays have concocted a massive drag-queen contest on a stage placed smack in the middle of the blocked off intersection of Bourbon and Dumaine. I could see that the drag queen contest was a vicious take-off of that dauntless American tradition, the beauty pageant, pursued here with vigor, imagination, outrageousness, and narration by a master of ceremonies. Maybe this is the final destination of the sequin-bedecked-with-train person I observed from my window early this morning.

Royal and Bourbon are littered with drunks. Desperate humans staggering through the narrow streets screaming for other humans on balconies to throw them something, throw them anything, throw them themselves. Loudspeakers from Bourbon apartment balconies blare out New Orleans tunes and popular soul music, though no blacks live here.

Many hippies have descended on the Quarter from all over the nation, if not the universe. Among serious hippies everywhere, Mardi Gras is a well-known destination. "Ahh, man, you didn't make it to New Orleans for Carnival? I got so high I didn't know where I was for three days." For a week now the Quarter has been filling up with youth who hitchhiked here, on-the-roaders complete with backpacks and bikes, even a black hippie sporting a shoulder-strapped guitar. These "tourists" the Chamber of Commerce is hardly enthusiastic about. They arrive broke, unable to afford the expensive hotels, the snazzy restaurants that depend on Carnival to put them in the black for the year. The city administration seems to have decided to jail 'em to death, throw 'em in for not having identification, not having money, not having a place to stay—whatever. Tulane University students have opened up housing for these young transients, but hardly enough. Jackson Square, the founding site of the city situated squarely in front of the aged, austere St. Louis Cathedral, has become a sort of convening place for the hippie world. Quarter residents and businessmen respond by calling press conferences to complain that the invaders are desecrating Jackson Square by indulging in public sex there and are generally making of themselves a public nuisance right under the nose of a stone-faced Andy Jackson, who would surely ride against them if he could—the Square must be locked.

Not that the "established" high rent-paying Quarterites are op-posed to Carnival. For a week now, almost every nightly parade has completed its route by weaving its way through the Quarter down Bourbon Street to Orleans Street in the Quarter, where it turned toward Basin Street and its Municipal Auditorium (at old Congo Square) destination. Those who live in the Quarter, partic-ularly those with prestigious upper story balcony apartments, pos-sess front row parade seats. Schechner and his friends who live in apartments along the route eagerly awaited these parades, leaning out of their windows, standing on their balconies to catch beads. Below, preceding each float, black flambeau torch carriers strut and dance, toting from their hips the dangerous-looking oil-fu-eled torches to "light the floats with," one of those throwbacks to the pre-Edison days New Orleans loves. As the torch carriers put on a show with their dancing, the balconied Quarterites amuse themselves by pitching coins down to them. The flambeau carriers well-uphold the tradition of mindless mirthful niggers, somehow stooping without spilling burning oil on themselves to collect the change. Like the stuffed black mammies and Aunt Jemimas of the French Quarter praline shops and the black jockey statuettes in the front yards of many New Orleans homes, these are living ar-tifacts of the Old South. As are the tap-dancing boys of Bourbon Street, dancing for coins thrown into a cardboard box, tapping their behinds off to the music of Bourbon Street Dixieland bands (true Dixie). This is their "hustle" of course, along with shining the shoes of tourists; all of this resurrecting glorified images of the Old South where things are under control, specifically the nig-gers—as long as enough of them are dancing for coins, how can they ever become a threat? Despite the demonstrations, the urban explosions on the television screen elsewhere, we are assured New Orleans will never really change, aren't we?

How did our dance, drumming, music—traditions so deeply embedded in the mother culture—become distorted into a dance for spare coins from New World neo-Europeans, I pondered, even in the midst of this revelry. Poverty? Destruction of psyche, spirit, memory? Possibly, but all that still seemed too much, the sum being greater than its parts. And it worried me, for it meant whatever we thought the "New" South had the potential to become, it could never achieve until some of this perversion ceased. But then, if the members of our theater walked over to Bourbon Street from the Village to demand that the boy-dancers stop dancing, what would we have to offer in return? They were tapping for coins, sure-enough coins, not promises, and we hardly had coins to offer. My mind flipped to the great clarinetist Sidney Bechet's autobiography, *Treat It Gentle*, and the story of his grandfather, Omar, at Congo Square. Omar was remembered in the Bechet family as a masterful danc-er and drummer. Bechet, a dark-skinned Creole, made a point of noting that grandfather Omar never ceased to consider Africa his ancestral home; knowledge of the motherland was torn from him with a burning pain. With those early slaves, African knowledge, either through memory or firsthand storytelling, was still strong:

> Sometimes, if they dreamed, things would come to them out of Africa, things they'd heard about or had seen. And in all that recollecting, somehow there wasn't any of it that didn't have part of a music-form

in it…when he got to the south, when he was a slave,
just before he was waking, before the sun rode out in
the sky, when there was just that morning silence over
the fields with maybe a few birds in it—then, at that
time, he was back there again, in Africa. Part of him
was always there, standing still with his head turned to
hear it, listening to someone from a distance, hearing
something that was kind of a promise, even then…[1]

Omar became the lover of a girl named Marie, a slave whose
owner desperately tried to smother his own infatuation for her.
When this man learned of Omar's amorous nightly visits to his
plantation, consumed with jealousy, he spread the rumor that
Omar had raped the girl, inducing a militia alert for Omar's
arrest and detention. Fearing for his life, Omar escaped New
Orleans to the swampy environs around Bayou St. John near Lake
Pontchartrain. There he lived the life of a maroon, along with
other escaped slaves and occasional outcast whites in makeshift
camps. From this point on, Omar's story may be mythological. It
closely parallels the fate of the legendary Bras Coupe. Venturing
in from the swamps, under cover of night, Omar continues to visit
Marie. On one of these trips, he is betrayed by a slave, a supposed
friend, for the price upon his head. This slave shoots Omar in his
sleep but never receives a reward from the owner, who treats him
with disdain. Marie is pregnant; Sidney Bechet's father is born
from the dangerous union of the lovely Marie and the slain Omar.

It is Bechet's celebration of Omar's inner freedom, even while
in legal bondage, that fascinates me. Omar's sense of inner freedom derives from his sure sense of the meaning of Africa, music,
rhythm, from his determination not to become other than himself.

Memory was the key. Memory was invoked through dance,
drumming, music.

The only thing they had that couldn't be taken from them was their music. Their song, it was coming right up from the fields, settling itself in their feet and working right up, right up into their stomachs, their spirit, into their fears, into their longing. It was bewildered, this part in them. It was like it had no end, nowhere even to wait for an end, nowhere to hope for a change in things. But it had a beginning, and that much they understood . . . it was a feeling in them, a memory that came from a long way back.

This quality of memory I find suppressed in the Village of Burgundy. It is there but buried deep, deep into the subconscious, even though the inhabitants of the Village are the spiritual if not physical descendants of the people of Congo Square. I did not know how I could free up a quality of memory equal to Omar's, or Sidney Bechet's, from people like Sedonia or Big John. Maybe that was what made Bechet and his ancestor great artists, that ability to give expression to innermost memory, profoundest emotion.

*   *   *

When I was a youth, the underworld, the inner recesses of this black nation, was always colored by my family and teachers in dark and dangerous lives. Violence always lurked in that underworld. Possibilities for personal and social advancement were nil. Mrs. B, the principal of our upwardly mobile, Methodist, colored high school, warned us in a voice drenched in acid: "Stay away from South Rampart Street, or you'll end up there. A hint to the wise is sufficient."

Fiftyish, medium dark-skinned, never overweight, certain of her voice and step, her spectacles hanging from her neck by golden chain, Mrs. B presented a fearsome image filled with a staunch pride that both attracted and repelled me.

We all wanted to be "wise," and we did not misunderstand the urgency in Mrs. B's admonition, but the lures of South Rampart Street were difficult to resist because Rampart was the commercial center of the struggling black nation within the city we had all emerged from and were now, attitudinally, being trained to escape from. Rampart Street would not so easily go away.

On those long, lazy afternoons, the St. Charles Avenue streetcar rode the neutral ground, transporting my heavy baggage of dreams. The streetcar route home from school was most favorable to fantasy—it traversed the center of a high-prestige boulevard of sprawling nineteenth-century mansions and spacious lawns, rocking from side to side as it crawled along the track, clanging its bell at intersections, stopping every two blocks for passengers. I would reflect on the encounters, disappointments, incomprehensibles and undecipherables of the school day, a day I never relished in the mornings upon awakening or on the long, multiple-transfer bus rides to school on a different, quicker route. In the afternoons I deliberately chose the St. Charles Avenue route home because it was longer, because it allowed dreaming, reflection. We seated ourselves on the wooden double-seats in the rear of the capsule after depositing our $.07 fare and obtaining the necessary paper transfer, after assessing the placement of the wooden stenciled sign: FOR COLORED ONLY. We might move the sign forward or further toward the rear, depending on the balance of racial streetcar riders. Fortunately, in the afternoons, there were few riders at all except me and my schoolmates and a handful of whites who sat so far to the front, we never saw their faces.

In the fall and spring I liked to throw the shutter-like, shellacked brown windows up to enjoy the beauty of the warm air and relaxed promenade of the avenue, where it seemed no persons of color resided or could ever hope to reside. St. Charles was the street where many of the mothers and grandmothers of my class-mates worked: five dollars a day plus round-trip carfare—14 cents. A magical ride through a forbidden city representing the grand "out-thereness" that we might aspire to—the dream world of possi-bilities Mrs. B and visiting speakers always alluded to, a world be-yond the barriers of FOR COLORED ONLY, beyond Negroidness or Negroid reality. A world fueled by movies of the great American dream life at the Canal Street Orpheum and Loews State, which we viewed from the balconies as outsiders looking across a vast territory from afar, ever eager to one day traverse the boundaries ourselves, though we didn't have the faintest idea how this would be accomplished.

As I rode past Louisiana Avenue toward the intersection of Washington Avenue I thought I saw Mrs. Chatman, a tall, elderly, dark-skinned woman in white uniform, walking along St. Charles. Of course it could not be her. Or maybe it was her. Mrs. Chatman *was* to me an elderly long-distance runner, a survivor. To all of us, in our mid-teens, she seemed old enough to have been born during slavery. Maybe she had endured slavery, I surmised, but due to her sterling virtues, which must have originated from the church, and the new possibilities created by the school and Mrs. B, Mrs. Chatman had liberated herself from the kitchens of the man-sions to instead work for the uplift of the race by making lunch sandwiches for us; she had gone into business for herself.

On the spacious backyard of the school, once the site of a Reconstruction black college, she set up her table lined with French bread, oysters, shrimp, and fish she had fried at home that morning. At noon we lined up eagerly to buy out everything she made, sharing with students who didn't have "lunch money."

Mrs. Chatman was no fast-food cook. The culinary genius lost forever to the kitchens of wealthy white Garden District families was our triumphant gain. We saw Mrs. Chatman as more than a cook; she was a kind of folk heroine-surrogate mother, who would offer soothing, reassuring words, no matter how baffling our trials or how badly Mrs. B had scolded us for ever-occurring transgressions. After all, she had seen enough of the world to know "talking in class" was hardly the most mortal sin we could commit in our lives.

Her asking, "chile, do you want a ham & cheese on French dressed *wit* mionaissaze, or wit*out* mionaissaze, make up your mind" seemed to reduce all our silly troubles to the basics of life— who could resist her?

As the streetcar rocked past Washington Avenue, Jackson Avenue, past the numbered streets, along its relentless, ever-repeating journey, I tried to focus on what the world of Mrs. Chatman had been like, what she had risen from. A hopelessness of rural poverty, a vague, gray, depressing eternity of involuntary servitude? Hard as I tried, I could not relate to such a past.

Do you too fathom the immense psychological expanse separating generations within our harried race? Sometimes it seems the impact of this generational gap is as enormous as the physical and psychological severing and suffering of the forced journey from the Old to the New World: a tearing, ripping apart of everything a people, a generation, has known.

The very ground we stand upon, the sky, the air we breathe, the water we drink, the language we speak, torn by each new generation proclaiming a new world, new terms of existence. Endlessly and accusingly reminded by Mrs. B that we, the younger generation, enjoyed privileges and luxuries of time to study and grow previously unavailable to our race, we were told we hardly seemed to understand the concomitant responsibilities. *Were* we ready for such historically new responsibilities? I didn't think so; I wasn't. Furthermore, I enjoyed the illicit racial luxury of idle dreaming.

Dreaming while others were forced to work. I wasn't sure what "work" my dreaming would lead to, if it led to "work" at all. The act of identifying with the elders, the Mrs. Chatmans, our grandfathers and grandmothers, and what their lives might have been like was akin to traveling backwards in time along a river shore trying to discover where the shores had shifted, where was once land, where was once a muddy river. I knew instinctively I must attempt to perform that feat of disentangling, of historical delineation, for what reason I was not sure at fifteen. Mrs. Chatman, the survivor. We, in our youth, in our blue school uniforms, in our jocular streetcar afterschool rides, possessed "possibilities," the hope of some vaguely perceived notion beyond the racial horizon.

My very tendency to dream, to fantasize, limited my "possibilities," as Mrs. B would have surely warned me. I did not know what "possibilities" existed for me. "Because of the deplorable condition of our race," she would have said if she had known the deplorable extent of my fantasizing, "there is no place for dreamers. Unless they are *purposeful* dreamers. You must work, work, work. Too much dreaming, too much thinking, too many questions, especially too many questions, do not, do not I remind you, build personal or racial uplift."

So at an early age, probably beginning on the St. Charles Avenue streetcar, I learned to mask the extent of my dreaming and to luxuriate in my secret life all the more because it was forbidden. Mrs. B wouldn't know; elders wouldn't understand; only a few student-friends might suspect. But none of them would ever know the extent of my slothfulness, which seemed to expand in direct proportion to Mrs. B's exhortations of purposefulness in her almost daily Special School Assemblies.

A native of Cincinnati, Mrs. B was not a Mardi Gras person, nor did she believe in it. The independent wife of a prominent Methodist minister, she did not underplay her ecclesiastical connections in her endless campaigns to win public support for the school, whose survival the governing ministerial Board persuaded her to assume. Our parents loved her. She kept us in line with her scorn, the threat of her rarely used but much talked about leather strap, and her admonitions.

Mrs. B did not limit her behavioral lessons to lectures. We were instructed to wear "proper" clothing to school, which meant the girls must wear blouses with skirts long enough to cover their musty knees. Boys must wear shirts and "proper," not overly fashionable, trousers. "Not overly fashionable trousers" meant no drapes or trousers wide at the knees and tight at the ankles, the stylistic rage among black men of the street. To enforce these rules, Mrs. B, assisted by the huge football coach Mr. E, often awaited us in the mornings at the Academy doorway on St. Charles Avenue, measuring tape in hand, turning away those who did not meet her standards with a "go back home and tell your mama you can't come inside this school unless you're properly dressed. You know what that is." She continually begged us to behave ourselves on the streetcars and buses to and from school, to please not spoil the "reputation of the school," for we were "watched everywhere we went." If we misbehaved anywhere in the city, she would hear about it.

She abhorred the popular music of the day, whether jazz or the rhythm and blues that pervaded the street like an ever-echoing musical accompaniment to the life of the people. For her, this music evoked Rampart Street and all its disreputable connotations of immorality, pimps, prostitution, and ship-wrecked love affairs. Nor did Mrs. B. take to her students engaging in close or overly sensual dancing at the occasional school dances, for that might lead to the worst of evils. All school "hops" were chaperoned; liquor was strictly forbidden, as were cigarettes. We were expected to become the walking, breathing opposites of any and

every presumed failing our unfortunate race had ever been accused of by the dominant race—if we were accused of congenital
immoral sensuality, then we must leave no doubt as to our morals;
if we were accused of being loud and unruly, then we must conduct ourselves quietly; if we were accused of being unwashed and
wearing soiled or torn clothing, then we must present ourselves
as thoroughly washed and wear neat and clean, if not expensive,
clothing. Conversely, if our leisure clothing was accused of being
ostentatious and sporty to a fault, then we must wear conservative
European dress so as to dispel possible aspersions. We must not
use foul language or in any way conduct ourselves as representative of the common derogatory image of the race—we must, in
short, be *different*. That was rule number one in achieving any
success we might attain in life, in improving our lot, and that rule
preceded learning or knowledge itself, notwithstanding the accul-
turating efforts of teachers like the lady who insisted we purchase
and study the plays of Shakespeare for her English class. The idea
was to become as like "them" as we could or, more precisely, become ourselves in a way that did not threaten or offend them.

We were to communicate our compliance through clear signals:
dress, vocal inflection, church membership, the spring in our step,
and, most importantly, avoidance of police encounters or those
places in the black community conducive to police encounters.
Not only must we as students know this; our parents must know
it too—otherwise our parents would be themselves unworthy of
the school despite the three dollars and fifty cents per month they
scraped up for the education of their children.

Often, when riding on the streetcar, I reflected on these primal
lessons. To me, at fifteen, they seemed unnecessarily harsh. It was
as if we were already locked into a societal prison of race; we were
only beginning to perceive where we could go and not go, what
we could do and not do. Inside the prison we were expected to

adhere to a code of prescribed behavior, to adopt well-worked out strategies for adjusting to the conditions of our largest prison, from which we could not escape.

*   *   *

All Mrs. B's preachings and warnings could not blot out the ubiquitous presence of the black laborers, especially those who lived uptown, those who we rode with to and from school on buses and streetcars, those worked the expensive homes, the kitchens, the docks of the Mississippi River—longshoremen, maids, cooks, small factory workers, garbage workers, street cleaners, brickmasons, those cutting the grass of the neatly tailored lawns of the mansions the streetcar steadily rocked past. Among them, decades ago, I might have found the young Longhair had I known him, for he lived on Rampart Street, not very far from St. Charles Avenue, his music the music of South Rampart Street. In my dream life, I already identified with him, though I did not know him. In my dream life I became a boy whose parentage was undeterminable, who moved among the "people" as one of them, enjoying the music, the dance—a music, a dance of relief from rigors, boredom, controls exercised over their/my daily life. Those not entrusted with the burdens of personal racial uplift sang, danced, dressed their fantasies, their imagined beings, indulging in whatever masks they chose, their "useless," "purposeless" fantasies much like my own.

In this world lived young Longhair, and though I might not have understood everything in his music, I understood he was not just trapped on the much maligned Rampart: he *was* it, he and those like him who created a music to sing and dance the psychological destruction of victimization away. Just as Omar did a hundred years ago at Congo Square—such apparent frivolity was the means by which they became captains of their own inner ship.

As the days of my high-schooling passed, the St. Charles Avenue streetcar ride grew into a dance of masks. I masked as one of Mrs. B's "hopeful" students, then as Mrs. Chatman's aged survivor, then as a boy among the people, faced with the awful burdens of poverty and harsh physical labor. In just one journey I might wear all three masks, interchanging them as my imagination flipped from station to station.

Each mask carried with it a corresponding music. Mrs. Chatman's music was the hymns of the Baptist and Methodist church: "Go Down Muses, Way Down in Egypt's Land," "Nobody Knows the Trouble I Seen." Rampart Street's music was Louis Jordan's "Saturday Night Fry Fish," "Caldonia, What Makes Your Big Head So Hard." The martial strains of "Onward Christian Soldiers" were surely an ample anthem for Mrs. B as she strode forward confidently, the weight of the school squarely upon her soldiers, with us following along behind her.

Cacophonous streetcar wheels seemed to represent the confusion, the clash of those three different but deeply entwined musics of our race. Within that cacophony lay all possibilities, all realities. Only the future would help me sort out my essential theme—if I were *ever* able to sort it out.

*   *   *

I heard shouts from the crowd as I peered down Orleans Street. Leaping, drumming, shouting gangs of youth were excitedly convulsing around slowly moving men dressed in finery with crowns of gorgeous feathers in the most subtly defined colors— the "Indians" arriving. Longhair's "Big Chief" come to life. Each approaching Indian, moving slowly because of the weight of their costumes, surrounded by tambourine drumming chanters, shouting the Hallelujah of their neighborhood tribal allegiance: Ninth Ward, Sixth Ward, Seventh Ward.

Down Claiborne another tribe appeared in the distance; I could see their feathers; "The Yellow Pocahontas," someone said. Once again I was a child as I rushed toward them to get a closer view of the Pocahontas, who were in a shade of pink. This tribe, which resided in the Seventh Ward near St. Bernard Avenue, was marching from their territorial home like some ancient African people on a ritual migration only they knew the meaning of. If the Zulus were decidedly not African, the Indians were more African than Indian, their masks working in reverse to expose, reveal a deeper, truer reality than these men, whether artisans or shoeshine "boys," ever revealed in "real" life.

The most elaborate costumes, like the beautifully designed pink on pink of the Pocahontas chief, Allison "Tootie" Montana, represented almost a year's work, and no telling what in cost. A predominantly male society, each tribal participant was responsible for paying for and sewing his own costume; it was considered sacrilegious by these veteran Indians to purchase a "made" costume. The value was not only the beauty of the costume but the work itself. Each participant's costume was different, I noticed, though each year, a tribe employed a color, a theme each member played a variation around—yet each costume was entirely distinct, the Chief's being the most elaborate.

These two tribes were apparently headed toward a street palaver at the junction of Orleans/Claiborne. "They always comes here to challenge," a woman cried. "Then they gets it *on*."

Then I heard a roar, a rush of excitement from Dumaine Street. A third troupe, costumed in black, was approaching to join the meeting at the intersection. No telling where they had begun, but here in the late afternoon they had arrived. The Fly Boys were leading the way as always with their cries of warning that their

Big Chief was not far off, clear the way! And clear the way they
did, often wildly swinging an elaborately decorated totem stick. If
the Fly Boy of the black-clad group wanted space he got space and
respect. In the old days, a meeting of tribal "Fly Boys" carried the
tension and drama of potential neighborhood war, an acting out
of ancient African Wars.

As the Fly Boys of the three tribes neared each other, their respective chanting, tambourining followers closed around them,
shouting and singing the words of age-old chants which may
have once been challenges: "here we come, the mightiest of the
neighborhood," or "if you offer peace, we bring peace," or "Indian
Red," an anthem of loyalty. The days when such Carnival day encounters led to small wars—knifings, clubbings, shootings—those
days had not entirely receded from memory. Now the "competition," the challenging, was in beauty of costuming, glory of tribal
chief dress, the strength, numbers and spirit of the backup "liners."
Now the chiefs were supposed to respect each other, the basis of
all peaceful relations.

I pondered again the meaning of this black New Orleans Indian
ritual. Once again, these are the people of the old Ramp, of Congo
Square, of the Village of Burgundy here in transformed state, the
flamboyant Afro-theater of Rampart Street performing an ever-re-
newing ancient purpose the "people" recognize as more crucial than
mere entertainment. The entire neighborhood exults in the stalking
marches of the Indians, shares the glory. This day they are once
again the warriors, the hunters, the secret societies of the African
motherland. After all, this is their parade, made for and conceived
by themselves, just as the Omars of Congo Square danced for themselves, in celebration of a past only dimly remembered, a loss that
made their dance all the more desperate, defiant, necessary.

The people exclaiming "beautiful," the Chief's second-liners
chanting, the crowd excitedly gathering around. Then, within

minutes, the Indians had departed for some other palaver. I wanted to follow them, try to suffuse myself in their ritual, but I could not; besides, I was exhausted. Dusk was fast approaching. Even Our God of Foolishness was standing back to quietly admire, a little overfull of it all.

In a few hours Comus, the final parade of Carnival, would be passing, but for me Comus was overdoing it.

Automobile traffic, determined to live out its nightmare of stalling cars, began to slowly forge through the sludge of paper, bottles, cans, discarded masks, trinkets, pieces of clothing, struggling people—the long-dream bacchanal was spending itself, stumbling to a close from sheer exhaustion.

When I arrived at my Burgundy Street building, I found that Sedonia had her door flung open, loud music blaring from her apartment. Big John had shifted from his usual spot on the corner, and had taken a chair in front of T-Boy's.

"How are you doin, Big John?" I asked. "You had a good day?"

"I didn't do nuthin," he answered pointedly. "But that damn woman Sedonia been drunk all afternoon, makin more commotion and racket than a decent woman ever should, that woman ain't nuthin but a shame!" A couple of his elderly friends quickly came over to add their assent.

When I entered the building Sedonia staggered to the door of her apartment. "Come on in, Slim," she shouted. "Les party."

"But Sedonia, I thought you weren't celebrating this Carnival?"

"Fuck that shit. Everybody else drunk. Why not Sedonia? I got wine for days."

"No, Sedonia," I begged off. "I've had enough. Been walking all over town."

"You see the fuckin Zulus and Indians?"

"Yep. Zulus and Indians. See ya later." I climbed to the third floor to my flat.

Later, when I walked over to Rampart Street just after midnight, I was surprised to see the sanitation "volunteers" with brooms and trucks busily clearing the street, pushing the accumulated debris aside, collecting it into containers. The old city undergoing a magical withdrawal from fantasy back into the "normalcy" of everyday life. It was depressing. Tomorrow, Wednesday, will be Ash Wednesday, day of Repentance for Sins, and forty days of Lent for true believers. I am not a true believer. But I too await the onslaught of the resumption of life's daily trials and trivia, the everyday crazy, but not with a little trepidation.

Endnotes

1. Bechet, Sidney. *Treat Me Gently*. Twayne, 1960.

INNER PEACE:
For Slow Drag
Pavageau*

One of the great New Orleans bass players, Alcide Pavageau, was better known as "Slow Drag."

Pavageau was a trad (traditional New Orleans jazz) player. A lot of New Orleans musicians play trad, but won't play Dixieland. For many players, Dixieland is associated with the most violent and terrible aspects of Jim Crow.

This meditation, written as a ramble after Pavageau's funeral, addresses some of the existential questions of life: especially, how do we make sense of ourselves and is there any salvation? Sometimes the sadness of life overwhelms the best of us. However, the best New Orleans musicians—indeed the best artists of all times, all genres, all forms—all are adept at finding the beauty in life's sadness.

(Nkombo No. 9, 1974)

Over the Mississippi River bridge from New Orleans. The old compulsion. New housing project to the right, looming like new factories. The plastic world of the West Bank Expressway: shopping centers, hamburger stands, service stations. The sun

---

* Slow Drag Pavageau is the name of a great New Orleans bass player; the funeral described is his actual funeral. He was about seventy when he died. —TD

obscured, heavy, fast moving clouds. Somewhere rain awaits. He is moving forty miles an hour in the heavy traffic, stopping occasionally for red lights.

Aaaaah, Slow Drag, you should have seen the crowd on Burgundy Street around your church. At first it was only a festive atmosphere, people milling around, tourists in the French Quarter who lucked up on something interesting. The Eureka and the Olympia began congregating around eleven. Many people were streaming in and out of the church. They wanted to look at your body. You would have cracked up over that, all those strangers running in to look at your body when no one even knew who you were when you walked the streets of Burgundy and St. Ann.

*   *   *

Dip into Harvey Tunnel. Burger King on the left. Nearing Lafitte Road, the old slave trader's route back to his palace in the swamps. Robinson Street on the right, which belongs to us. Traffic thinning now. Ames Street on the left, also ours. He picks up to fifty. He does not see the river now, but New Orleans is far behind. Passes Westwego.

*   *   *

At noon they brought your body out of the church and placed it in the hearse. The Olympia and the Eureka formed in front of the vehicles. Down toward St. Phillip the second-liners, black youth, waited. The tourists lined the sidewalks on each side of Burgundy, some spilling over into St. Phillip. Soon, one of the bands struck up "Nearer, My God, to Thee," drawing more people from other streets. A hush falls over the crowd as the instruments, straining, moan the hymn. Your procession inches forward down Burgundy

toward St. Phillip. That was a warm day in February, and the reflection from your hearse shined in the sun.

*   *   *

He hits sixty nearing the Huey P. Long Bridge: there'll be a sharp
left under the bridge approach. After the turn, Avondale shipyard,
and he is on 90-W. One street in Avondale belongs to us, that bar
over there. Now zoom on past the red light, ten miles of swamp
before he comes to Boutte.

*   *   *

Both the Eureka and the Olympia play different hymns at the
same time in lovely cacophony. It was as if they were speaking to
and answering each other, each surrounded by its own dancers.
The dancers move forward slowly, with a dance of upper body
as much as feet, some holding hat to breast. Umbrellas embroi-
dered with festival cloth flowers, open and high. Honor speaks in
graceful bows, the rhythm rocking like the constant wash of rivers. Overhead a jet banks, creating a sudden roar. One band stops
playing now, continuing only the bass drumbeat as the procession
moves like a giant amoeba to the turn at St. Phillip and Rampart.
Like a magnet, the band draws the people, and the procession
becomes with each block a larger throng. Far behind, your hearse
and the family cars follow. Now we are on Rampart, headed toward Canal Street. Traffic halts. Cameramen scurry around for
better angles. Secondliners pose, abstracting their dance. Canal
Street hangs heavy in the distance. The procession passed Congo
Square. A woman asked which cemetery you would be buried in.
The Marshalls, she was told, know the way.

*   *   *

Boutte is a nothing: a red light. It comes suddenly, a few bars to the right, a few service stations to the left. He turns right at the red light heading for Luling and the river road. He drives, transfixed, watching the small stilted shacks.

*   *   *

By the time the procession reached St. Louis No. 2 it had swelled tremendously. It seemed like people came from everywhere, the houses, the schools, the bars, the stores, as if the music were some magic signal. St. Louis No. 2 will be your home, your crypt is open. Several youths leap on the white-bricked wall to get a better view of your interment. One band marches through the cemetery gate playing a hymn. The other breaks formation, and the players wander off outside the gate to talk with friends. A very old woman who may have been your wife is led through the gate, supported by the arms of family. She is straining to walk, her face contorted: a hush surrounds her entrance. From the ceremony inside a few screams, a few moans. The mystery. Faded white structures with weeds growing in between. Another jet overhead. Oh, but Slow Drag, I'm sure you're not interested in all that. You would dig that on the way to the cemetery, far behind the Olympia and the Eureka, some young black cat pulled out a flute. He began to play like Coltrane, yes Coltrane, which maybe you don't understand, but he began to rip it off and the dudes around him began to dance, gettin' into something very deep and joyous…It was eerie, this light-skinned dude with the huge afro playin' this flute with his personal secondline. A woman said, "Isn't that horrible, they won't even wait until they cut loose the body," but I can see your sly smile, that twinkle in

your eyes as we talk outside Tony's. What happened to your cane?
Is it in the casket?

*   *   *

There's the levee, straight ahead. Just beyond the red light. The river
has rushed up on him. This is Luling. Left here. Go north. Luling is
a nothing too, a ferry and a red light. Now he is out into the open,
moving about forty, many, many curves, the road following the tem-
perament of the river. He feels a sudden mysterious freedom, as if
the glass and steel and brick of the city had been an unwelcome en-
cumbrance on the clarity of his life, and understanding could come
only with the turns, twists and space of this road. Time peeled off
like dead skin. Near Hahnville a sign speaks of Fashion Plantation,
now evaporated. A car here, a car there. An old courthouse. Then
winding slowly northwestward, past two massive chemical factories. He had learned to hate these, the odor harsh and suffocating.
He speeds up. Then Killona. Killona? Who came up this damn river,
he wondered. Terrible sharp turns. Killona a ghost town. A house
here, a house there, no person in sight . . . ever. A mile or two of
fields, then a sign, speaking of Acadian settlers. A sign tells of a
French priest killed by the Natchez Indians. Another sharp turn
and we are upon a black nightclub, several men standing outside
conversing. A young girl walks along the road carrying a carton of
milk. Several black teenagers sitting on the levee. To the left, several
rows of shacks. This is Lucy, as the water tank towering above tells
him. Who was Lucy? Why did the river bring her here?

*   *   *

The sound of Joe Avery's Stomp ricocheted through the brick
tombs without warning. Most of the people were still waiting at

the entrance of the cemetery, but one of the bands had slipped around to a side entrance, opened up, and was already heading for St. Louis Street. "They does that sometime," a woman complained, but you would have dug it. Peoples was running over each other to catch up. Edgard is a stone black town/the ferry doesn't work. When I caught up about a hundred cats was around the band, jumpin'. There we are, he thought, scattered along the river like dots no one can erase. The secondliners formed a mass in front of the bands, one great, individualized rhythmic army, beating from the pulse of both hands. Sounds and rhythm merged as one. The upper body becomes its own voice. Our speaking with the knowledge of ritual motion. There we are, scattered like dots along the river, like dots no one can erase.

The one-armed boy spinning, his arm flailing, in another world. A circle of dancers formed around a hat, knees bent, each dancer completing the circle. The whites faded into the distance, snapping pictures, scampering here and there. A hefty chick dances with her arms and tits bouncing. The marshal struts proudly. Evergreen plantation sits like a quaint mosaic, behind a white fence to the left of the road. It is a museum against the pulsing river. When the band crossed Rampart, one dude jumped up on a porch and did three handsprings to the beat. Death receded, and he felt your spirit overhead, as if embedded in the sun.

Another sign, nearing Vacherie. "Plantation claimed by the river." The river has its own ways. Then he felt drawn up the levee, his car inching up the dirt road slowly to the peak of the hill, and then down to where the road ended.

He got out of the car sweating, compelled by a mystery and need he surely did not understand, and walked toward the muddy and slowly gushing river whose bank lay before him like a patient, long forgotten, but ever waiting home.

Fully guided by what he knew he must do, he took off his shoes and then shed all his clothing to feel more at ease. To the sound of the surging water he walked gingerly, sinking and slipping in the mud to where he could kneel and touch water. There, racing backwards and forwards in time, he found an inner peace, and he felt as if something broken and separated in him all his life had finally come together.

(From *Pacific Moana Quarterly: An International Review of Arts and Ideas*, April 1979; and from *Nkombo* (N-9), June 1974.)

BLACK MUSIC IN NEW ORLEANS: Some Thoughts

Whatever you have heard, you haven't heard the half of it. (Unpublished)

It may not be apparent to New Orleanians, but this is a great town for blk music. There's plenty clubs, almost any night in the week, almost any hour, where you can hear a good solid band of good, imaginative, young musicians. Take my man Walter Washington, lead guitarist/singer with the Funky Four at the Off Limits. Nobody ever heard of him outside of New Orleans, but he's a young B.B. King right now. By this I don't mean he's imitating B.B. but that he can get where B.B. is in due time…and that's not easy. The blues is the most subtle, the most complex, the most ritualistic of blk musical forms; you can't get it in no one or two years, and no white musicians can master it. There's no way to describe a great blues musician other than to say he "knows" something, then listen. Walter knows something.

Take James Rivers. During the spring, actor Robert Hooks was here for the FST opening and we took him to hear James Rivers. When Rivers went into his thing, blowing it first as a wail, then upbeating it, then coming back and doing it as a mournful blues, Hooks said, "This guy is out of sight. I've never seen anything like this in New York." I don't believe Hooks was exaggerating. It was more than just

Rivers. It was the entire New Orleans blk musical mystique, for New O is a town where music, particularly live bands, are more than entertainment. Blk New O is a town, despite the demise of the great Jazz Age, intensely and functionally musical, where music plays an integral, almost necessary part in our lives, and where music is still closely related to dance. The powerful musician in New Orleans can always turn people on when he can bleed enough soul.

There's others. Porgy Jones, Willie T. & the Souls, James Black, Irma Thomas, Eddie Bo, Ernie K-Doe, Aaron Neville, the Neville family (the Meters), Eluard Burt, to mention a few of the most prominent. The gospel field is live and well too.

The problem is that these people are hardly known outside of New Orleans. People outside of New Orleans think blk music here is at best dormant. There's talk about Detroit, Houston, Memphis— those are recording centers—but when blk people think about music in New Orleans the mystique of jazz history comes to mind, or maybe, if they're old enough, Fats Domino. There's a lot more happening than that.

Washington, if he stays in blues, has a serious problem. In his book, *The Urban Blues*, Charles Keil quotes a blues A & R man in Chicago: "Even if a young B.B. King walked in here today I'd have to show him the door because there's no future in it." What he means is there isn't a big market for the blues, even among blk people. And the record companies that deal in blues decide what few musicians will be sold to that market. Even blues masters, like King & Bobby Bland, don't make anything like what Aretha Franklin and James Brown pull down. Ray Charles retains his original blues style, but he long ago invaded other territories to achieve his tremendous financial success.

But there are some interesting new developments. One is Jimi Hendrix, who though in his twenties, took enough of the blues to be black and hammed it up with gimmicks to appeal to the white hippie (Beatles, Dylan) crowd, using all the souped up electronic equipment that goes in white rock for musicianship, mastery and rhythm. Hendrix is getting rich in a hurry. A more important development is the tremendous success of B.B.'s recent record, "Why Do I Sing the Blues," the first notable expansion of blues material into what I believe are the fertile areas of racial protest and consciousness, even though King's treatment is very subtle. King, unlike most blk non-jazz musicians, is his own boss. Protest material is something the white A & R men have been telling blk singers for years they should stay away from ("the radio stations," white owned, "won't play it"), but the success of James Brown's "Black and Proud" blew this myth to shreds, and blues singers who have always treated blk pride and consciousness material so subtly that you have to be in-in to get it, should now come out swinging and really develop this still undeveloped area. I'd love to see Washington with this kind of material. (The Impressions have been there for a long time—they blew the lid off with "Moving On Up" in their New O show at the auditorium).

It's just that New Orleans lags in terms of aggressive, imaginative young businessmen. Maybe it's more a jungle than I think it is, but why doesn't some bright cat who knows how to do it (I could name some) put together a recording company and exploit New Orleans (not exploit the musicians) and build us a real blk commercial musical power from here. It could be done. If all these musicians were in Atlanta or Houston it would have been done. You know what I mean.

The talent is right here, waiting for the cat who knows what to do with it.

T. Dent
10/69

THE ADVENTURES OF KING ZULU: Mardi Gras, 1970

Explaining why you can't predict the unpredictable. (Unpublished)

It was slightly before 8:00 Mardi Gras morning, at Shakespeare Park. The air was brisk with anticipation. King Zulu was about to reign again. The King was on his float, looking proud & happy. He was ready. The floats were rolling into place on the river side of LaSalle. In the park, the Carver High School band of Pascagoula, Mississippi, was striking up pieces of tunes, then ripping off tremendous drum bursts that echoed over the field like a ceremonial preparation for tribal battle.

Black burnt cork stared from blk faces like a minstrel satire on a minstrel stolen from a minstrel. There were real people back there, behind that cork. A few officials in parade vehicles, neatly decaled "Krewe of Zulu," fingered doubloons, which drew rushes of people to their cars in expectation of getting one. A group of white nuns stood on the neutral ground with smiles of smug satisfaction: they had missed the landing at Canal St., one explained, but were now here to be present for the beginning of this historic occasion.

The King turned and looked toward the rear to see if everything was in order. He night have been looking for the King's baggage float, but it got lost some years ago. The King's Baggage was replaced by the George W. Carver float. A blk street vendor sang out: "pee-nuts, *pee*-nuts, nickel a bag."

Way up front, at the head of the parade, the Tuxedo Brass Band staggered into formation. The blk members of that old, traditional band were over sixty & looked ready; the three white recruits were under thirty & looked like they were about to be marched forcibly into deepest Africa.

An old drunk, reeling like a recluse from an old movie, fell into place carrying a sign: "Chairman, Parade Committee." One of the well-dressed parade officials leaped athletically out of his convertible, snatched it out of his hand and stuck it under his car seat.

Suddenly a great cheer went up. The Queen had climbed into place on her float and was wiggling around getting the feel of her throne. She looked majestic and was not enameled with blk cork. Behind her on the Queen's Maids float, one of the maids reached way over into the street, almost falling off her float, to hand a friend a gold coconut.

On the side of the floats, the Green Junior High School band went through about a dozen tricky funky steps, to the cheers of their friends. They were dipping & bopping so enthusiastically the floats reeled. Their director, a young blk cat with an afro and a brown trench coat, watched his charges with a bored expression.

Then the Tuxedoes struck up the Saints, and the secondliners marching with the band started jumping soul. Zulu was off!

The parade moved at tremendous speed, picking up secondliners & fans until it reached the Geddes Funeral Home at Jackson & Simon Bolivar. Here, in front of the funeral home, the King offered his ceremonial toast: *Long live the Queen*, and the parade was off again, stopping three buses on Jackson until it reached Dryades, where it turned toward Canal.

When Zulu reached Felicity, Rex was going by toward St. Charles with about fifty floats, so naturally the cops stopped Zulu to let Rex by. Somehow the drunk who had the "parade chairman" sign had regained his place and sign, and was last seen staggering toward Rex.

Finally Rex was gone, and Zulu lurched forward, with officials racing between floats shouting instructions, toward Lee Circle, St. Charles, and its meeting with white America.

At Lee Circle a tremendous crowd of white spectators waited in wooden bleachers, screaming for coconuts & doubloons from the entourage of the burnt cork king. Zulu waved his magic wand at them, and in the spirit of friendly relations between estranged nations, the crowd cheered, while his entourage sold coconuts for $2 a piece.

On St. Charles the parade came to a stall. During the stall the Mississippi band played tunes while the secondliners danced in the street. All their marches sounded bluesy, like they sprang forth from the Mississippi mud. Their director was a young cat just out of college, who graciously accepted congratulations on the excellence of his band. "By the way," he asked someone, "just how long does this parade last? We haven't had anything to eat." Everyone laughed. Someone offered him a sip of wine. "You gonna be marching a looooooooonnnnnng time. You need something to sustain you."

Then Zulu was off again to wave his magic wand at Schirro, who was playing master of ceremonies at Gallier Hall. Schirro sounded like he always wanted to be a traffic cop. When Zulu arrived Schirro and all the officials applauded enthusiastically. Some cat on the Mayor of Africa float danced a jig in a grass skirt, weighing coconuts in either hand. A white official called out for one, but the cat in the grass skirt just taunted him. The white official looked like he was trying to suppress the urge to leap off the platform onto the float to grab him a coconut. Finally, Schirro said into his mic, "Throw me a coconut."

The cat in the skirt said, "They told us we couldn't threw 'em anymore."

"Oh, that's okay, you can throw *me* one," Schirro said.

So he threw one, and Schirro caught it. That's all they got.

On Canal St. the parade turned toward Claiborne, but it ran into another long stall. Everyone looked distressed. Every now and then, the Queen would wave her wand, looking like an ad from *Ebony* inscribed: "The Negro Family Goes to Church." The crowd applauded. The King smiled. The women on the Queen's Maids float lay down so no one could see them. Occasionally a trinket or doubloon would come flying over the edge of the float, as if catapulted from a machine.

There were plenty blk cats & chicks on Canal St. walking around, staring at Zulu and saying: "What's he doing on Canal Street?" They didn't know what to make of it. One young girl was overheard to say, "Now that it's all right to be black, why do they need to paint their faces?" Far to the rear, the Mississippi band laid down the blues. One cat said: "If they just put all the black bands in Zulu, they could forget the floats and still have the hippest parade."

Then the parade raced off toward Claiborne at a tremendous speed. The last float was entitled: "Martin Luther King." By then that sign had been half torn off to reveal underneath: "Big Shot of Africa."

When last seen, Zulu was headed downtown. A few years ago he might show up anywhere, depending on how the spirit hit him. Now that he has a prescribed route, approved by the city, no one know which way he might go.

THE LEGACY OF
PAUL ROBESON:
To the Blk South

Paul Robeson (1898-1976) was a major figure in American theater and music. His role in the American psyche cannot be overstated. Lawyer, athlete, thespian, and singer, he was a cultural and political activist on a national and international level. Robeson refused the narrow boundaries prescribed for talented blacks of his era, and insisted on his due as a man in full. His list of victories and causes are too many to name, but he led efforts in American involvement in the Spanish Civil War and African Affairs.

One of the first times Tom Dent said "Throw me something mister," Paul Robeson was tossing him a football. (Freedomways, *1971*)

I remember meeting Paul Robeson when I was very young. He had come to New Orleans to do a concert and was staying at Dillard. I remember him then as a massive, physically impressive man (from my vantage point), huge, dark and imposing, yet kindly and strangely reflective. At that time he was a world-famous singer, a great hero of our race, and we were deeply honored to have him visit our home. But at that age I was more impressed by the fact that Robeson had been a football star, the first great blk all-American. Someone steered him out to the athletic field where the Dillard football team was practicing, and it wasn't long before Robeson was throwing and catching passes and drawing a large crowd of admiring students. Ah, that was an exciting day.

That was a time of undisputed racial heroes (everyone seems more controversial now), the time of the "talented tenth," those few blk folk whose accomplishments were accepted and acclaimed by white America, in fact the entire Western world. Joe Louis, Marian Anderson, Roland Hayes, Charlie Drew, Jesse Owens, Percy Julian, Bill Hastie, Robeson. Later Jackie Robinson, Ralph Bunche and Leontyne Price would join this group.

Think....what an *interesting* collection of heroes. (Calvin Hernton once asked, "Why is it we have only one Marian Anderson when I find singers just as talented in the Baptist church choirs all over the South?"). Great people, but most or all were acclaimed for accomplishments that did not challenge America in any real sense, accomplishments in areas white Americans thought laudable, like performing European music, athletics, law, medicine. The theory of "overcoming" was current then, blk people overcoming barriers and handicaps, as if we were afflicted with some sad and unfortunate disease that only the truly talented could transcend. And then too, wasn't it *wonderful* that America was such a great country that even the ("yes, the *Negro* in our melting pot too") blk man could find success and happiness if he worked hard enough, if he was talented enough, and if he said the right things (or at any rate, didn't say the wrong things).

Others, like DuBois, Richard Wright...well, we weren't so sure about them, we were told America was the "land of opportunity," and they weren't sure about that at all. Still others...Leadbelly, Count Basie, Langston Hughes, well, really they weren't that important; they were "race" artists, and one had to be "universal" to be a Negro hero in white America.

And then Robeson opted out. To us in the South, to those of us becoming of age, attending the southern blk college, being encouraged, exhorted to "make it," to make "successes" of our-selves, to "prepare for integration by being well-prepared," to us in those days Robeson became a figure who made us think (some of us) about what we were doing like no one else of that time. The charge "communist" was bandied around; we didn't know what it meant; we knew it sounded terrible. Our teach-ers were dumbfounded. Why would a man turn his back on all that hero-worship to say America was *not* a land of opportunity, but one rampant with racism and economic exploitation? Why would a man say that America would never achieve its promise unless it treated the blk man fairly? Why would a man say that the blk man, so busily striving to belong, should not lay his life down any longer in foreign wars for a country that considered his life worthless at home? He was upsetting the apple cart. And just when our teachers thought we were in.

We, in our youth, did not know if Robeson was a communist, but we knew that he didn't have to be a communist to know, certainly as a blk man, that there was something sick about America that any honest man, blk or white, ought to speak out against. Not necessarily brave, brilliant, militant, Marxist: just honest. Like, babe, ride the bus. And if you can't do that, look out the window.

And we knew that *any* blk man, particularly in the South, who spoke out against racism and oppression was branded a "commu-nist" by southern politicians. That's how they stayed in office. To be an outspoken opponent of racism in the South was to accept that you would be labeled a communist. Which was the final in-sult on top of the lynching: the blk man didn't have sense enough to protest being beat in the head & murdered on his own, he had to be *seduced* into protest by "foreign commies" from Russia.

Robeson returned once more to New Orleans in the years after Peekskill for a concert that I believe was his last in this city. I was away at that time but my mother attended. When I asked her about the concert she said, "Well, he didn't sing much. He spoke most of the time. He talked about America, about the way our people are treated, about the need for peace with Russia, about American imperialism." She thought it was an "unusual" concert, but beautiful. "He talked very informally," she said.

The change in American public opinion toward Paul Robeson once he began to speak out for freedom and equality gave us an unforgettable insight into how blk heroes of that time were made, and who controlled them. If Robeson said that blk boys would not fight for a racist America, Jackie Robinson was hauled before Congress to assure white America we were "all right." Suddenly Robeson wasn't a great singer, a great actor, a football star any longer. His concerts were boycotted; he couldn't get work. No more southern tours to sing for the blk people who had so recently loved him, exalted him, flocked around him as a source of blk strength, talent, and wisdom.

Yet in his decision to become more than an artist by enlisting his body and mind in the fight for freedom of our people against oppression, Robeson became a prophet of the Blk Arts Movement of the sixties and seventies. A prophet because it is this very concept of the blk artist as community mover/builder in a *political as well as cultural sense* that dominates our movement today.

John O'Neal once wrote that he was surprised how many people in the southern civil rights movement considered themselves poets. Out of this potential could come something like the Free Southern Theater, a conscious effort to merge the blk cultural with the fight for political freedom.

In New York blk actors, musicians, painters, dancers can pursue their careers as "careers," but in the South we have learned that this sort of isolated ambition makes no sense. We must work toward the building of the community; the artist has as much obligation to join the fight against racism as anyone else. Both are sides of the same coin.

And this is the legacy of Robeson's lesson. That any "success" achieved at the expense of our people, or at the cost of ignoring our condition in America, is worthless. That the blk artist cannot isolate himself in an Ellisonian cocoon, no matter how important he thinks his work is. That it is senseless to talk about blk artistic development unless we have a concurrent community develop-ment (and vice-versa).

To the furtherance of these ideas and images Paul Robeson gave us the commitment of his life. He was far, far ahead of his time. For those of us working in the South today, we see him, in our mature vision, as an indelible source of blk strength, blk talent, blk wisdom.

Kush (Tom Dent)

JAZZ & HERITAGE FESTIVAL 1976

Tom had served on the board of Directors of the Jazz and Heritage Foundation. Years later, in 1987, Tom Dent became the executive director of the Jazz and Heritage Festival. Here is his 1976 assessment of the strengths and weaknesses of Jazzfest. (Unpublished)

IMPRESSIONS

April 11, 1976

Lightnin Hopkins—the poetic master. He knows what he is doing, what he is perpetuating. He also knows how to belittle the audience for how little they know. His guitar style...the consistent high level of his playing...his ability to stay in pitch no matter what he's doing...impeccable. He's an independent and proud of it. To hear him is to hear the querulous Texas barbecue man who makes the best barbecue but isn't going to give you a toothy smile just because he's black; he's had a hard life & he's not going to let you forget it. Backstage, after his set, a white boy asked Hopkins, "Why do you always look so mean.... And you're my favorite musician." Lightin replied because he didn't believe in no bullshit. End of conversation.

Gospel Tent—hot with flies buzzing & people fanning. A rural setting under the big tent. Sammy Burphy was a jam on the organ

during the brief portion I caught, proving that the distance between blues & gospel is more lyrics & intent than musics. The
Swan Silvertones, a well-known group from Monroe, LA, were
excellent. Mature artists confident of what they can do. Their lead
singer had a flexible voice somewhat similar to that of the master,
James Cleveland, but it was one of the backup singers with an unusually high voice and great control that won the audience.

How the gospel groups use call & response! They work it to
death, the black audiences recognizing the artifice but loving
it all the same. The gestures in Gospel are huge, not only the
hands but the arms: it is a world of electric & theatrical ritual.
The crowning point of gospel ritual is *testimony*: the pain, the
catharsis of public testimony, as psychologically arduous as
group therapy. It's not just confession, but *public* confession, &
the climax of all songs must reach this magic, emotional peak.
The audience/congregation knows it's coming, but the artist has
to make them believe it. The Silvertones made the peak & wrung
it for all it was worth.

It always fascinates me that in Gospel shows the MC (whether he
be radio disc jockey or local minister) has the right to enter the performance at chosen moments, urging the audience, or really congregation, on—or cooling them off, or whatever—as if the professional
performers are merely a choir or quartet, in the minister's church.
The minister has the right to do anything he wants in his church.

Professor Longhair/Gatemouth Brown—Longhair is a very sup-
ple musician with a very firm concept of what he's doing. It's an
ornate, embellished piano, developed with percussionistic counter rhythms, but somehow he achieves a genuine piano lyricism. It
is very difficult to do and most striking.

It is interesting that Longhair's concept enables him to do any kind
of song, though all we ever hear on the radio are the Mardi Gras songs.

Now some white boys have worked their way into his band, which is unpleasant, particularly the drummer, sharing the bandstand with Earl Turbinton, Julius Farmer, and Alfred Uganda Roberts.

But blues great Gatemouth Brown soloed on guitar & violin, as he had at previous Festivals. He is Longhair's perfect partner. Longhair & Gatemouth are basically blues musicians, but they can play anything they want. They could almost make the Star Spangled Banner sound good.

April 14, 1976

Ellis Marsallis/James Rivers/Walter Washington—Ellis and his band of students & family should have had four gigs at least. They are what it's all about. There isn't any more important group—Ellis is perpetuating something vital & crucial.

Rivers was monumental, but the sound system was horrible and too loud. Rivers doesn't need volume: he needs intimacy to sustain his moods. No matter how bluesy. And where the hell did he learn to play the bagpipes? For someone generally not known outside of the black New Orleans musical community, Rivers' kind of versatility is mysterious & wonderful—he had to be seen & heard rather than described.

The greatest injustice was done to Walter Washington & the AFB's. They had the last gig this afternoon, coming on late because the previous group finished late, and were given only a half-hour. The security people chose to close things down rather than give a little leeway to a growing, relaxed, grooving audience digging everything Walter & the band were doing. Yet Walter is another musician who should have had more than one set: he is indigenous New Orleans, he is a blues master (though in his early thirties), he is not commercial, he has a small but strong following that has been loyal to him for a number of years; he probably more than any musician booked into the entire Festival could have made the most of the Fair Grounds exposure.

QUESTIONS

Compared to what happens other places it was, no doubt, an excellent Festival. I don't mean the Municipal Auditorium shows, which are basically the same everywhere, but the Fair Grounds— which is uniquely New Orleans.

There *are* some ominous signs, and some things that left me with a more negative impression than in previous years. I wonder if the Fair Grounds section isn't getting too large—too many crafts, too great a portion of the allotted space—possibly an attempt to do too much. I did not like the increased distances between stages, or the volume of the sound systems, much too loud in almost every case. The increased distances meant it was impossible to hustle over to another stage to hear a second band in a given time slot. There was no excuse for the volume of the speakers, since there were no more people at a particular stage than there were the previous two years. The loudness distorted the value of what was being done musically, whereas in previous years, possibly because the stages were closer, the sound was at an admirable level to produce fidelity.

I did not like the fact that *all* the tech people & MCs (except for the Gospel Tent), that I saw anyway, were white. For a Festival that depends so strongly on black talent, this left an unpleasant taste in my mouth, & it was remarked upon by other black people I talked to.

I also thought there were too many crafts & food concessions. Which created the biggest problem getting from stage to stage. The encouragement and exposure given to crafts is fine, but there was considerable duplication, & some of the people who purchased food concessions apparently had no restaurant or professional food background, & what they sold showed it.

*   *   *

The black community should take a close & critical look at the Festival, since much of the "jazz" & "heritage" is ours. The Festival organizers should be commended for the information, through exposure & printed material, provided on so many black musicians who have been laboring in relative obscurity. Let's hope the musicians get something out of it—not that we can expect them to make a great deal from these gigs—but let's hope they are fully protected financially. In cases where tapes are being made, we should be concerned that musicians have contracts that protect their interests in the release of these tapes—they will constitute a valuable musical library, which will, apparently, be in the possession of the Festival organizers. Or someone.

Certainly we could hope for more input in the future from the black community in planning the Festival. Not just because jazz is our heritage. Because we are 40% of the greater city, and because we have patronized so strongly this Festival, in 1976 & in the past, helping to make it a success.

tom dent

SOUTHERN JOURNEY

Tom wanted to see what changes had been made in the social land-
scape. He wanted to talk to people and not just get news reports.

He got in his car, drove through the deep south and came back
with a report. He knew this was an important task, he quit the Jazz
and Heritage in order to do this. He knew that this was a moment,
and he had to answer the moment. (Unpublished)

My maternal great grandfather, Ben Covington, was an itiner-
ant stagecoach driver who worked a route that took him from
Oklahoma to Mexico and all parts in between. We have only one
photograph of him, in which he stares steadfastly ahead, taken
during that harsh, uncertain period following the Civil War when
ex-slaves were emptied out upon the land.

Of all my ancestors, "Stagecoach Ben" intrigues me the most. I
commune with him often during my travels, feeling his spirit stir
within me, he with his essentials packed in a leather satchel, chasing trails and barely charted roads in quest of his past and future.

*   *   *

During the summer of 1986, I drove from my home in New
Orleans across the breast of the Southland along a network of new
and old highways to New York City.

I chose to drive because I wanted to see the South again in one
sweep, as one can only do slowly, mile by mile. As I drove, the region seemed at casual glance to have acquired a new face—Burger

Kings and McDonalds, new schools of brick and glass, Sheratons and Holiday Inns, suburban shopping centers, racially integrated athletic teams, the black television reporter on every station. It was a hopeful "New South" of economic well-being and, above all, surface racial amity.

The reality was more complex, I suspected. From the accounts I had heard, this smiling face was a facade beneath which lay extreme economic hardship for many, a jostling between the races for hegemony in an entirely new political arena created by unprecedented black enfranchisement, a boiling cauldron of problems that reflected a South in extreme flux. It is a South still attempting to adjust to new economic imperatives caused by the advent of automation, the development of competing world economies, the impact of television and, most of all, a new interracialism for which no adequate parlance has yet been invented.

Many of the towns I passed through were the sites of important civil rights struggles in the 1960s and early 1970s. What, I wondered, do black (and some white) Southerners, especially those who worked to bring about racial change at great personal sacrifice, believe is the real measure of change in the South of today?

My mind flashed back to the journeys from New Orleans to New York that my parents[1] and I had made when I was a child in the late 1940s. From my back seat window, I had watched a South unfold before me that was rich with rolling fields and forests, a vista of great agricultural variety and expanse. The endless flatness of southern Louisiana and coastal Mississippi would give way to the foothills of Alabama as we turned northward toward Atlanta, negotiating the steep hills and winding roads, past the textile mills and tobacco factories of North Carolina, feeding into the swift-paced, grimy greys of the densely-populated Northeast.

On these trips through the segregated South, we were always conscious of our overnight stops. Hotels and motels were out

of the question, so the respites were planned where my parents
had friends who had been forewarned of our arrival. Because all
restaurants on the highways and in towns were closed to us, eating
was an adventurous mobile picnic filled with sandwiches, boiled
eggs (with portions of salt and pepper wrapped in wax paper),
fried chicken (because it can be eaten cold), and bags full of assorted fruit that my mother had prepared meticulously in New
Orleans for the long journey. Locating restrooms required a sixth
sense cultivated over many years by my father. Upon entering a
likely service station, he would ask, just before ordering gasoline,
"By the way, do you have bathrooms for colored?" If the answer
was "No," we moved on. This might go on for several towns. Dad
was aware of every speed limit sign, since the limits were often
arbitrarily enforced by local police. If we were stopped, my father
employed all his diplomacy and tact; he must never contest an
officer's authority too strenuously lest he be perceived as "uppity."
At the same time, he must not surrender his manhood.

Searching a town for the "railroad tracks" brought forth this
wry comment from my father: "If you find the tracks, cross them
and that's where the colored people live." Black communities were
little towns unto themselves, almost all of them separated from the
white commercial and residential districts by natural barriers, like
rivers or creeks, or by such man-made barriers as the legendary
railroad tracks or highways. For me, the approach to the "Colored
downtown" was always tinged with excitement and discovery, for
here—in small restaurants and fish fry joints, bars and nightclubs,
insurance companies, funeral homes and the alluring, full-of-life
barber shops where everything about everyone was known and
wagered upon—here was a repository of secrets, extraordinary
tales, and wondrous knowledge. And there was the ubiquitous
church, usually Baptist, some of them red brick with a cascade
of steps leading to the sanctuary. In church, the community met

to decide its fate, hear about its condition and sing music crafted during black people's long sojourn in this land.

Black college towns usually looked more prosperous: better homes, better streets, a decent restaurant, sometimes a community newspaper. The colleges themselves and the areas around them were considered havens from the racial harassment that could occur anytime, anywhere, for any reason, or for no reason at all. They were havens, that is, as long as no challenge to the racial status quo issued forth from their campuses.

The families residing in these towns spanned a wide range of occupations and interests, their members having come in search of better conditions and good work—a 20th century quest that supplanted the forced, brutal and arbitrary separations wrought by slavery. There were families who, like mine, anchored their lives in the church, who learned to read and write in schools that churches built and supported, education having become the religion of racial advancement after Emancipation. Education was the highway to status, the earliest professions bastions of community service: teaching, preaching, medicine and law. Over time, the mindset of successful blacks had settled into a delicately-balanced accommodation of segregation. Overt challenges to the system were rare, no matter how much the system was deplored. This tacit acceptance was counterbalanced by a strong ethos of sacrifice and hope for the future: "We're here doing the best we can, putting up with hardships and insults so that your situation may be better," the elders reminded the young.

This pattern, with its system of tenuous racial balances, came under momentous siege in the sixties. The sudden appearance of singing, marching, praying demonstrators, the defiance of so much held sacred, burst upon Southern towns like a dreaded plague that was often heralded by militant, "out of control" young blacks. Sometimes the plague followed in the wake of protracted, tactical warfare to overturn local segregation laws; sometimes it was propelled by a growing demand for the ballot in places where black suffrage had been unthinkable. Marching, chanting masses of black youngsters often aided by activist ministers; determined elderly dissidents abetted by a handful of white allies; killings, beatings, threats, burnings of "movement" churches, acts of heroism from the most unlikely individuals; inexplicable islands of humanity in a sea of brutality—such was life in those tumultuous years. The worst aspect of all to those in control was the "outsiders," those feared and hated organizers who arrived to march with, go to jail with and inspire, through their actions and speeches, the defiant protestors, often bringing with them the glare of national publicity—unwanted and invariably unfavorable.

These crises constituted the greatest threat to the "Old South" since Reconstruction, and the tremors of change eventually reverberated far beyond the original target of eliminating segregated and inferior public facilities. New possibilities sprouted for: a new, more open society; a more equitable distribution of political and economic power; new terms of interracial exchange; a new language of human relationships. All this was on the horizon even though ominous clouds were gathering, heavily weighted with attitudes acquired from centuries of slavery, endless violence, an abominable lack of rudimentary education, and a stifling isolation from the culture and ideas of the world at large.

The main attack on the status quo—overwhelmingly approved by all segments of black Southern communities—consisted of constitutional challenges to segregation brought by National Association for the Advancement of Colored People (NAACP) attorneys. These challenges, which were gradual legal steps that sometimes merely asked for better facilities within the "separate but equal" doctrine established by the Supreme Court in 1896, formed a decades-long campaign that charted the course to, and reached its triumphant apex in, the *Supreme Court's Brown v. Board of Education* decision of 1954 declaring school segregation unconstitutional.

Among blacks, *Brown* assumed the proportions of a mythical leap forward, a sort of second Emancipation Proclamation. *Brown* reaffirmed all the hopes for a better future, justified the huge and all-too-often tragic sacrifices. But more than that, *Brown* changed *everything*. The new activism meant not only a new confrontational approach between blacks and whites, but a restructuring of Southern black society, a throwing to the winds of the compromises and gentlemen's agreements that had prevailed in the past.

I experienced much of this firsthand. Working as the public information officer for the NAACP Legal Defense Fund (LDF) in New York, I spent time in Mississippi, Louisiana, Alabama and Georgia dealing with the national press on the important LDF cases—including James Meredith's explosive court-ordered admission to the University of Mississippi and representation of Martin King and his fellow demonstrators in Birmingham. I returned to some of the same areas during 1965-70 as Associate Director of the Free Southern Theater, a cultural wing of the civil rights movement that developed out of the 1964 Mississippi "Freedom Summer."

What are the realities of life in the South of today, particularly the South of small cities and towns; what truths underlie the mask the region appears to wear? How did mostly young black Southerners, in conflict with their elders, press the desegregation drive after *Brown*?

Seeking answers to these and a host of other questions, I propose to take a four to six month journey through the South, conducting interviews with veteran activists and important witnesses to the Civil Rights Movement and recording their stories and assessments. I will follow roughly my old childhood route but in reverse: starting out in Greensboro, North Carolina, where the sit-ins began, working my way slowly southward through the seaboard states (with only a few deviations to broaden contacts), and ending my investigations in my home city of New Orleans. Thus will I pass through several towns that are noteworthy for their historic role in key civil rights conflicts.

And thus will I gauge the extent to which the South has changed as a result of the protests of the sixties.

I will deliberately bypass Atlanta, Montgomery and Birmingham, which were on my childhood route and which are extremely important in civil rights history, because these cities have already been much studied and written about by movement chroniclers. I will focus largely on the smaller, more obscure or forgotten "movement towns" to obtain the testimony of those not previously heard from; those who offered small and unrecognized sacrifices to the struggle; those who were not necessarily leaders but are people the leaders could not do without. From them I hope to gain, not only important information about civil rights history, but a comprehensive "feel" for place, culture and mores, daily life and its costs, a sense of what has been gained and lost during these epochal decades.

Greensboro, North Carolina: A Beginning

The drive from Durham to Greensboro on Interstate 85 is a journey of ever ascending and descending hills and heavy trucks that hog the road. North Carolina is industrial, the trucks being proof of the heavy commerce generated by the state's textile mills and mammoth tobacco factories.

Greensboro in 1960 was the scene of dramatic events that began with a decision by four North Carolina Agricultural and

Technical University students to sit at "white only" lunch counters in downtown stores until they were served or arrested.

This seminal demonstration opened a new phase of the Civil Rights Movement, in which direct, non-violent action was the tactic of choice for battering the walls of segregation. When the first group was arrested, wave after spontaneous wave of enthusiastic and determined students took their places and were themselves arrested. The sit-ins spread to black college towns throughout North Carolina and, within months, throughout the South.

It was fitting that the sit-ins began in North Carolina, where traditionally there has been a strong emphasis on education. The University of North Carolina at Chapel Hill was a bellwether of liberalism in the Old South, and several of the state's private colleges were and are fabulously endowed. North Carolina has also been home to numerous black colleges, as well as to strong black economic institutions like the North Carolina Mutual Life Insurance Company in Durham—the nation's most prosperous African-American business for most of the 20th century. The sit-ins may have been an unanticipated result of North Carolina's progressiveness and prosperity, for here was a state where educated young blacks had every reason to aspire to high civic and economic achievement.

I will especially seek out surviving veterans of those first sit-ins to learn of their motivations for becoming involved, of their memories, of the paths their lives have taken in the intervening decades. I will interview downtown businessmen, particularly those who were owners or managers of stores where sit-ins occurred, to ascertain their attitudes toward the demonstrations and their roles in 1960. I will interview administrators and teachers at North Carolina A&T University who were there in 1960. How do they assess their roles then? In Southern college towns, many teachers and administrators were not supportive of the student

demonstrations; they tried to suppress them for fear that the tumult would endanger the positions of elders.

Out of the sit-ins developed the Student Non-Violent
Coordinating Committee (SNCC), a loose, South-wide alliance
of activist black students. That organization became the cutting
edge of the sixties movement. I will talk to early SNCC leaders
about the rapid spread of the sit-ins and the first efforts to call a
South-wide meeting.

Southward to Orangeburg, South Carolina

I'll head out of Greensboro on Interstate 85, at Charlotte picking
up Interstate 77 to Columbia, South Carolina, then onto Interstate
26 for about four miles into Orangeburg. In the course of this
drive, the land begins to flatten a bit as the terrain becomes more
agricultural. By the time one reaches Orangeburg, the heavy traffic of North Carolina interstates will have slowed considerably.

Orangeburg retains a particularly tragic notoriety in the annals
of Southern civil rights confrontations: It was here in 1968, in
a scene akin to Latin American dictatorships, that state police
opened fire on demonstrating students at South Carolina State
College, killing three and wounding dozens.

I will interview survivors of that violent incident, seeking out
residents who remember the shootings and the events leading
up to them. Was such violence characteristic of race relations in
Orangeburg? Why was the reaction to student protest there different from what it had been in Greensboro, where sit-ins quickly
brought about a decision by store owners to desegregate? Has
Orangeburg seen notable racial progress since the sixties? Were
lessons learned from the traumatic events of 1968? Several SNCC
organizers went to Orangeburg to encourage students there to
adopt more militant attitudes. I'll speak with some of them, and
I'll speak with adult black leaders—those who were supportive

of the students and those who opposed them. How do they now assess their roles in 1968?

Eastward to the Carolina Lowlands and Charleston

I'll take Interstate 26 East out of Orangeburg, heading directly to the Atlantic Coast and the venerable city of Charleston, one of the major capitals of the Confederacy. Charleston was rather quiet during the sixties. Few demonstrations were attempted, possibly because no black college is located there. However, in 1970, some poorly paid, low-level hospital workers at the College of Charleston Hospital attempted to form a union—unheard of in public or quasi-public institutions in the South. Rebuffed by the hospital administrators, the workers launched a strike. The hospital retaliated by firing the strikers. The fired workers, almost all of them middle-aged black women, quickly gained wide support in the black community. Within a short time, the Southern Christian Leadership Conference, with Ralph Abernathy as director, decided to back the strike, creating a rare labor-civil rights partnership. Friendly unions in Charleston and throughout the state threatened to initiate sympathy strikes. Within a few months, the hospital decided to settle, accepting the right of workers to unionize and reinstating the fired workers.

Charleston was the capital of colonial South Carolina, a town that grew and prospered from the surrounding rice, cotton and indigo plantations. Large numbers of African slaves were brought to work the plantations and, by secession in 1860, blacks were clearly in the majority in the lowlands of the state. Whites, in the face of this majority, made justifications of slavery, and the state's right to maintain slavery, central themes in their antebellum affairs. Logically, the first blow for secession from the Union was struck at Charleston.

During early Reconstruction, ex-slaves, who for a brief period gained the ballot and served in the state legislature, were able to hold the state's former slave-holding establishment at bay. The blacks' good fortune was reversed, however, as the old South re-emerged with a vengeance in the late 19th century to enact a maze of segregation laws and racial proscriptions that made South Carolina (along with Mississippi) the leader among Southern states in disenfranchising its black citizens.

The 1970 hospital workers strike was, therefore, a startling deviation from a century of black subservience, all the more remarkable because the action was initiated by extremely vulnerable black women. The strike, which had been preceded by an innovative and determined effort to establish voter and citizenship education as a model for the entire disenfranchised South, was also among the few important campaigns not initiated by college-age youth.

How has Charleston accommodated the forced racial change of the sixties? I will interview veterans of those efforts to hear their memories of the citizenship education leaders, Septima Clark and Esau Jenkins. I will seek out leaders of the hospital workers strike and those who supported them.

Southwestward to Albany, Georgia

From Charleston, I'll head southward along Highway 17, paralleling the Atlantic Coast, until it intersects with Interstate 95, which slices down through the entire United States from Canada to Miami. On 95 I will cross the Georgia-South Carolina line, bypassing Savannah, the original capital of Georgia, and driving twenty miles east to the intersection where Highway 82 begins. Highway 82 is one of those old routes rich in Southern lore because it almost perfectly bissects the heart of the "Black Belt."

The Black Belt describes an area roughly 100 miles wide that begins its arc on the Atlantic Coast in South Carolina and Georgia, sweeping through Alabama, Mississippi and Louisiana, until it ends in eastern Texas where the cotton-producing

farmlands recede. Here were great cotton, sugar and rice plantations with their armies of black slaves. In the sixties, Black
Belt counties were the prime target for civil rights organizing
because of their huge black populations and their long history
of racial oppression and terror.

Following Highway 82, I'll dip southwestward through
Waycross, Georgia, then travel about 100 miles to the town of
Albany, capital of the southwest Georgia region with a population
of about 70,000 people.

Albany, a paragon of Southern small town conservatism,
was the target of a major civil rights campaign in 1961 and '62.
Demonstrations began in November 1961 when a few members
of SNCC decided to test segregated facilities at the Albany bus
station. They were arrested but won the support of a local committee of prominent citizens and ministers, who led daily sympathy marches to City Hall. The marches were soon buttressed by
a mass infusion of students from Albany State College and local
high schools. In early December, the citizens' committee invited
Martin King and his Southern Christian leadership Conference,
headquarted in Atlanta, to lead a march in Albany. He did and was
arrested and jailed, along with fellow minster Ralph Abernathy
and hundreds of others.

In the following months, demonstrations with and without King continued on a sporadic basis, eventually becoming
bogged down in mass jailings and legal obstructions imposed by
the courts. Finally, in the summer of 1962, King abandoned the
Albany effort in favor of launching a campaign in Birmingham,
Alabama. King's change of direction left the Albany campaign
in a state of irresolution and cost it the attention of the national
media.

Though the Albany demonstrations were not considered a success, they did signify a broadening of the movement to include a

much wider spectrum of the black community: youth, religious leaders, elite black professionals, King and his SCLC associates, as well as the increasingly assertive SNCC activists. The issues changed character, too, moving from the initial objective of de-segregating bus facilities to include almost every facet of segregation and, most significantly, the new economic demands of the black poor. Albany represented an important point of transition in movement history: It foretold the multiplicity of directions the movement would embrace in subsequent years. Moreover, it was in Albany that the first stages of a rift between older leaders like King and younger SNCC leaders occurred, a split that widened as the movement grew.

I will interview veterans of the Albany wars, those who were student militants, those who were supportive elders. What spurred them into activity; what suffering did they endure because of their commitment; what do they think of Albany and southwest Georgia today? How do they perceive today the generational split that occurred back then? What are their memories and assessments of King? I will interview teachers and administrators at Albany State College, expanding on the theme of the unique role black schools and their students played in driving the civil rights protests. I will visit the county jails, where King and others were incarcerated, to interview those who shared or have knowledge of those experiences.

Albany was also the first main source of the music associated with the movement; the first Freedom Singers were formed there. I will interview some of them.

Since 1962, considerable community and organizational work has been done in southwest Georgia, led by Rev. Charles Sherrod, who emigrated from Virginia as a volunteer and never left. I will interview Sherrod.

Southeastward to St. Augustine, Florida

Next stop: St. Augustine, Florida, reached via U.S. 19 for 90 miles, across the state border and on to the intersection with Interstate 10, a highway that traverses the southern region of the continental U.S. Along 1-10 are flat, desolate lands up to and beyond the Suwanee River, reaching South below the Okefenokee Swamp. At Jacksonville, I'll pick up U.S. 1 South and, in about 15 miles, arrive at that small, ancient town.

Picturesque St. Augustine, on the Florida Coast, founded as a Spanish settlement in 1565 and claiming, therefore, to be the "oldest American city," was the site of short-lived demonstrations in 1964 that commanded national attention because of the extreme violence with which demonstrators were attacked by police and white onlookers. Marchers were beaten and jailed; the home of the local NAACP leader was bombed. Martin King and SCLC were invited in to help and King was jailed. SCLC joined the local NAACP demonstrations to underscore the pervasiveness of segregation and violence in such a historic town. The resultant embarrassment to the town's officialdom helped pressure Congress into passing the Civil Rights Act of 1964.

The cost of applying the pressure was considerable. In the absence of a local college population, most of the demonstrators were elderly churchgoers who braved nightly marches to the downtown square; there they were met by vigilantes from neighboring counties who rained missiles and invective upon them. Once it was learned that passage of the Civil Rights Act was imminent, the black community called the demonstrations off.

Today St. Augustine features startling political gains by blacks. I will interview several black elected officials about the distance St. Augustine has traveled in 25 years. I will talk with veterans of the marches and prior civil rights efforts for their stories, memories, and assessments of the past and present.

Westward and Northward to Selma, Alabama

From St. Augustine I will double back to Jacksonville, taking 1-10 West across northern Florida to Highway 231, and further northward near the town of Mariana. I'll venture on through Dothan and Troy and Montgomery, Alabama, then turn westward on old Highway 80 for 50 miles to the town of Selma.

Selma, this antebellum "jewel" on the banks of the Alabama River, brings me once again into the heart of the Black Belt, to the very center of cotton-growing, cotton-merchandising country and the very soul of traditional Southern values.

Selma is, of course, the site of the famous voter registration drive of 1965, a campaign led by Martin King and his SCLC staff in an area where black voting was nonexistent. Earlier in the decade, a few brave SNCC workers had attempted such drives with scant success. This time, the larger objective was to call attention to the desperate need for federal voting rights legislation if blacks were ever to vote in such historically repressive locales as Selma.

The Selma campaign featured daily marches to the Dallas County Courthouse by demonstrators who had attained a new level of purpose and organization, greater sophistication in dealing with the national media, and heightened awareness that the eyes of the White House and Congress were upon them.

The campaign, little noticed at first, drew national attention in March 1965 when the marchers were viciously attacked and beaten by state troopers on the Edmond Pettus Bridge. In the wake of the beatings, hundreds of volunteers flooded into Selma to join a massive march on Montgomery. With the world watching, President Lyndon Johnson decided to propose a voting rights bill to Congress. For the Voting Rights Act of 1965 alone, which has dramatically altered the political face of the South, the Selma campaign is considered a signal triumph of the Southern movement and an immense personal triumph for Dr. King.

In Selma, the rift between movement elders and youth that had begun in Albany widened into an irreconcilable dispute. How do Selma's veteran activists interpret the split? What political gains have blacks made in Selma and the neighboring counties during the last two decades? I'll be interested to hear what Mayor Smitherman has to say about this since he was also mayor in 1965. I will interview the black political organizers recently convicted of voting irregularities, most of whom were products of the Selma campaign.

Out of the youth-elder split, SNCC radicals created their own voter project in nearby Lowndes County to elect blacks in a sparsely populated, but majority black, area under the emblem of the Black Panthers. I will travel to Lowndes County to investigate the legacy of that effort.

Northwestward to Greenwood, Mississippi

The drive to Mississippi is magical: through the forests and red-clay foothills of western central Alabama and Mississippi, over 200 miles of land that is flat and black with river silt and largely cultivated with cotton and the alternate crop popular today—soybean; then, just before entering Greenwood, a magnificent descent to the flat basin of the Mississippi River Delta as if one is gliding to earth from the air.

Greenwood was the site of Mississippi's first major voter registration campaign, in 1962. Greenwood was chosen for the opportune presence there of large numbers of unemployed blacks recently driven off the surrounding plantations by automation, and because the Delta provided the movement's first Mississippi native recruits. Mrs. Fannie Lou Hamer, forced off her farm in Ruleville, Mississippi, emerged as the most eloquent spokesperson and leader of this group.

Mississippi had, of course, acquired a reputation as the most racist and repressive of the Southern states, in which blacks (and

many whites) lived in extreme poverty, and whose power structure was determined to maintain segregation in defiance of the
Supreme Court. Thus, the voter registration drives there were as
much an effort to overcome fear as to register black voters. The
daily marches to the courthouse led by a handful of volunteers,
and the nightly song-filled meetings in friendly churches, drew
sharp reprisals from the authorities and national media attention.
The Greenwood campaign helped set the stage for the Freedom
Summer of 1964, when a coalition of civil rights groups brought a
wave of interracial volunteers into the state to conduct a massive
protest campaign.

I will collect stories from Greenwood veterans on how the
demonstrations were organized and what methods were used
to conquer fear. Once again, I will seek out elders, particularly
supportive ministers and members of their congregations. What's
happening in the way of black political activity in Greenwood
and the Delta today? Have economic conditions improved for the
poor? Now, 35 years after the Supreme Court's *Brown* decision,
is there effective school desegregation in Greenwood and its
environs?

Southward to Philadelphia, Mississippi
The way from the Delta flatlands of Greenwood to the infamous
Philadelphia is eastward into the hills of Highway 82 as far as
the junction at Eupora, then southward on Highway 9 through
Choctaw County to the town of Ackerman, where Highway 9
becomes Highway 15. Continuing southward for about 50 miles
through the Tombigbee National Forest, one enters sparsely-popu-
lated, heavily-wooded Neshoba County and isolated Philadelphia,
the county seat.

As preparations for Freedom Summer were underway in Ohio
in 1964, white Mississippi was preparing to resist the anticipated
civil rights "incursion" from the North. In June, no sooner had

the first wave of volunteers entered the state, than one of the most tragic events in the history of the movement occurred: An inter-racial team of CORE workers, Mickey Schwerner and Andrew Goodman of New York, and James Chaney of Meridian, was abducted on its way to investigate a church-bombing. Discovery of the trio's bodies after a long search, as well as disclosures of official complicity in the murders, shocked the nation and fo-cused the world's attention on the horrendous conditions of life in Mississippi. The murders did not, however, deter the subsequent broad-based, state-wide demonstrations and voter registration ef-forts that made 1964 a year of permanent transition in Mississippi racial relations.

I will interview people in Philadelphia and Longdale who re-member those days. Did the backwoods isolation of Philadelphia contribute to the vulnerability of the black community? Is there fear of violent repression in the black community today?

Westward to Canton, Mississippi

Leaving Philadelphia on Highway 16, I will drive west for about 60 miles through the forests to the small town of Canton. In 1963, Canton was the site of voter registration marches to the courthouse of Madison County, which had and still has a 70-30 percent black majority. Blacks had lived in virtual terror in this lumber and cotton mill town since its founding, and they had never voted. The town responded to the sixties' demonstrations with extreme repression and jailing of the protest leaders. Though little progress was achieved, the rarely-noted Canton struggle was a significant precursor of Freedom Summer and produced two leaders of state-wide importance—Annie Devine and C.O. Chinn, a former nightclub owner who lost his business as a result of his movement activities. I will interview Mrs. Devine, Mr. Chinn and other Canton activists. I will also talk to some of the younger white officials for their retrospective impressions of the Canton movement.

Many blacks have migrated north to Chicago from Mississippi towns like Canton because of the lack of economic opportunities. Does this migration exist at the same rate today? Mr. Chinn has noted a recent heavy infusion of drugs into the Canton area. Is this phenomenon widespread in small Mississippi towns that were previously immune to problems associated with the ghettos of large cities?

Northeastward to West Point, Mississippi

Highway 16 leads 20 miles eastward from Canton to the junction with Natchez Trace Parkway. The Trace is a beautiful, winding two-lane federal highway, following roughly old Choctaw and Chickasaw trails that slice across the state from Natchez to Tupelo, revealing the spectacular beauty of Mississippi's deep forests. I will briefly meet Highway 82 again and exit northward a few miles to State Highway 50, then proceed eastward for 30 miles to West Point.

West Point and surrounding Clay County are noteworthy for several innovative economic cooperatives that were established there in the late sixties. Even though a town of only 15,000, West Point is the home of a black college, Mary Holmes, that played a role in the development of the cooperatives. These county-wide projects were affiliated with the visionary Mississippi Poor Peoples Corporation, a legacy of Freedom Summer. The Corporation was formed to manufacture native crafts and sell them through a national chain of retail stores called "Liberty Houses." By the late seventies, the Poor People's Corporation and its economic co-ops were no more.

I will interview veterans of that effort, including founders Jesse Morris and John Buffington, on the history of the PPC organization and the reasons for its failure. What led to the unusual decision by Mary Holmes administrators to identify with and help coordinate the projects? Is there an economic legacy of the PPC in Clay County today?

Westward to the Mississippi River Hamlet of Mayersville
From West Point, which abuts the Alabama border, I'll cross the breadth of the state southward on Highway 45 up to the intersection with 82, and then head westward through the Delta to Greenville, the largest and most important Mississippi River Delta port. From Greenville, I'll descend on Mississippi Highway 1 for about 40 miles to an intersection with Highway 14 near Rolling Fork. A short drive westward will bring me to Mayersville, the county seat of the very sparsely populated Isaquena County and the home of Eunita Blackwell, one of the most fascinating women to emerge from the Southern movement.

In the 19th century, Mayersville thrived as a cotton port, but by the Freedom Summer of 1964, prosperity was only a memory. When a handful of SNCC workers organized in Mayersville, Eunita Blackwell was among those who attempted to register. She was unsuccessful, but once recruited into the statewide effort, she became one of Mississippi's most effective young organizers. Today Mrs. Blackwell is mayor of Mayersville—an assertive, eloquent, and distinguished local and national leader.

I will question Eunita Blackwell about her remarkable personal history of movement activism and success in politics, as well as talk with other black and white townspeople. Can Mayersville and Isaquena County be revived? What have been the consequences of black entry into the political process over the last two decades?

Southward to Plaquemines, Louisiana
I'll depart Mayersville on Highway 1, turning southward at

Rolling Fork on Highway 61, another of the fabled roads of the South that runs parallel to the mighty Mississippi from New Orleans to St. Louis. It will take me past Vicksburg and Natchez, cross the Louisiana state line and down to Baton Rouge. From Baton Rouge, I'll pick up Louisiana Highway 1 South for about 20 miles to Plaquemines, one of the many southern Louisiana sugar plantation towns with large black populations sprinkled along the Mississippi. Blacks in such towns lacked even a modicum of civil or political rights.

In 1963, Plaquemines was a target of voter registration drives mounted by the New York-based Congress of Racial Equality (CORE). It was the only small river town in Louisiana touched by the movement. Police violence reigned. In one instance, officers rode their horses into the sanctuary of a church in an attempt to abduct CORE national leader James Farmer. Locals spirited Farmer away to New Orleans in a hearse, which saved his life according to veteran organizers.

I will interview longtime residents and talk with veterans of Louisiana CORE on why Plaquemines was targeted. Were there abortive attempts in neighboring parishes? Was there community support in Plaquemines? Are blacks politically active in Plaquemines and similar river towns today? I will interview older residents for their perspectives regarding the historical aspects of life on the riverside plantations and pre-movement agitation for civil and political rights.

Eastward to Bogalusa, Louisiana

Returning to Baton Rouge on Louisiana 1, I will then take Interstate 12 eastward to Covington and follow Highway 21 up into the foothills and pine forests. After about 45 miles, I'll come to the isolated lumber town of Bogalusa, situated on the banks of the Pearl River a few miles from the Mississippi state line.

Bogalusa is the birthplace of the Deacons for Defense, the only armed self-defense group to arise amid the overwhelmingly passive resisters of the Southern movement. Whites in Bogalusa and Washington Parish, in their frontier mentality more akin to Mississippians and Texans than to southern Louisiana folk, had long subjected black residents to large doses of Ku Klux Klan repression and violence. Thus, the Deacons' decision to offer armed protection to demonstrators once protests began in 1965 is understandable.

I will interview organizers and members of the Deacons on the group's origins, experiences, tactics and achievements. Did older civil rights leaders try to discourage formation of such a group or disassociate themselves from it? Were branches of the Deacons formed in other towns? Did the armed presence contribute to black pride in the area? How did the white police force respond to the group? Have there been reprisals against former Deacon members?

Southward to Journey's End: New Orleans

Leaving Bogalusa, I will hit Highway 21 going south on the last leg of my journey. At Covington, I'll cross Lake Ponchartrain on the world's longest bridge and enter the fabled city of New Orleans, my hometown.

In the early sixties, student sit-ins at downtown segregated lunch counters kicked off civil rights demonstrations here as they had in other towns where black colleges existed. The first group of demonstrators was a thin legion whose activism had germinated in the NAACP Youth Council and, more pointedly, had been inspired by the bravery and sacrifices of 1961 Freedom Riders whose final destination was New Orleans.

The Freedom Rides were forged by biracial teams to test new Interstate Commerce Commission rulings, routinely ignored in the Deep South, that prohibited segregation on intercity buses and trains. The first Freedom Riders were greeted with vicious beatings by vigilantes when their buses pulled into Alabama and Mississippi depots, then by jailings for violating the old state segregation statutes. The Riders who made it to New Orleans were housed and cared for by young people who often became Riders themselves. Since the Freedom Rides were organized by CORE, most of the younger New Orleans activists joined that organization, eventually making New Orleans the most important base of CORE activity in the South.

Other early demonstrations included boycotts, led by black professionals and Protestant ministers, against white-owned businesses with no black employees in black shopping areas. These boycotts were much like the ones staged during the "Battle of Birmingham" and were equally successful; but unlike Birmingham, they drew virtually no national press.

The initial effort to desegregate New Orleans public schools in 1960, however, did draw attention. In the spotlight were groups of whites that for months harangued the selected black students, and the federal marshals escorting them, who desegregated the Franz School under a court order implementing *Brown*.

In the late sixties, civil rights attorneys and activists established the first well-organized, city-wide black political institutions of the 20th century. This new political clout, enhanced by the Civil Rights Act of 1964 and Voting Rights Act of 1965, made possible unprecedented successful endorsements of a new mayor and governor, thereby accelerating changes in the racial balance of power.

I will focus on movement activities, both CORE veterans and those who occupied positions of leadership when the movement began. How effective is the new black political leadership? Has the election of two black mayors (of Creole heritage) and several black city councilmen made a difference for the majority of black citizens? Have the public schools been largely desegregated during the past three decades? Are the schools perceived as improved in quality? What about the now large population of unskilled, unemployed black poor, those in "the Projects"—have they benefited from the struggles of the sixties and the legacy of the movement?

Finally, how does New Orleans fit into the Southwide context of movement objectives, achievements, and failures discussed during the course of this journey?

*   *   *

From Greensboro to New Orleans, I will have traveled many miles and heard many stories of sacrifice, disappointment and achievement from those who were actors in one of the greatest social dramas of our time. With their words as my guide, I will attempt an honest and illuminating appraisal of the Southern and American present as our nation moves uncertainly toward the 21st century.

Everything I have learned and everyone I have known in my life impels me to make this Southern Journey. And I am impelled by the spirit of Stagecoach Ben, who bids me to drive not only as conducter but as intelligent observer. The journey is sure to be one of discovery and revelation, seasoned now and again with sadness, wonder and joy. I will endeavor to convey to the reader all the colors and shadings of the experience.

Tom Dent
New Orleans

Endnote

1.   Although I share much in common with other black Southerners who came of age during the postwar period, my journey through life has been extremely atypical, as it does not embrace growing up and living in one region or locality, over-coming poverty or a personal history of extreme deprivation of opportunity—all familiar themes in the lives of black Americans.

Though born in New Orleans, I have nevertheless always thought of myself as at home anywhere in the South. My father came to New Orleans from Atlanta, my mother from Houston. We were first generation New Orleanians with roots in Georgia and Texas.

I came of age in a well-defined, extremely insular black Southern world, a world of the mind as well as of locality. We were bred with a strong, generally unstated sense of racial identity, surrounded by negative definitions imposed by the larger society, but also de-termined to counter white allegations of our "inferiority" by the exemplary way we lived our lives.

My father, Albert Dent, was light-skinned, outgoing, attractive, well-spoken, and always conscious of his bearing, which tended to be formal and self-important. His dress, demeanor and speech were intended to contradict the poverty of his early childhood and challenge the image of the downtrodden Negro.

The son of a father he never knew and a mother who was a maid for a wealthy white family, Albert was given by his moth-er in informal adoption to a childless couple, her close friends. These adoptive parents were prominent in one of the oldest black Baptist churches in Atlanta, the "home church" of a thriving early twentieth century Atlanta University educational system. The adoptive father, Will Thomas (for whom I am named) was sexton of his church.

These fortunate circumstances made possible my father's graduation from Morehouse College in the mid-1920s as their first business adminstration student. Hired by the Atlanta Life Insurance Company, he served as a regional salesman, setting up an office in Houston, Texas. John Hope, the patriarchal president of Morehouse, asked him to return to work for the school. As part of his job, my father traveled throughout the South organizing the first Morehouse Alumni Association. Singled out by prominent blacks and a few whites as a man with a future, he was appointed superintendent of the new Flint-Goodrich Hospital in New Orleans at the unlikely age of 27.

Flint-Goodrich was a merger of two 19th century medical facilities affiliated with Strait College and New Orleans University, which were black institutions founded during Reconstruction. Though a novice in the public health field, my father established innovative programs for outpatient care of the impoverished. In 1941, he was chosen president of Dillard University, a merger of Strait and New Orleans Universities. In the space of two decades, my father had risen from poverty into Negro "middle-classness" and a position of influence within the world of Negro leadership.

My mother's beginnings were far more privileged. Medium brown-skinned, soft-spoken, of rather fragile health, Jessie Covington was the only child of a physician. Mother showed an early talent for music and, driven by her determined mother, learned piano from a prominent Houston teacher and went on to study at the Oberlin Conservatory of Music. She returned to Texas in the late 1920s to teach piano between concert tours to black colleges and musical societies throughout the South. She met my father in Houston. In 1931, they were married and departed immediately for New Orleans and Flint-Goodrich Hospital.

My mother continued her musical career while raising her family of three sons, ceasing to perform only when she suffered a serious injury to her hand in the late 1930s.

Mother's mother was the daughter of an Irishman and a black woman from a landowning family in Gonzales, Texas, which is near San Antonio. She was raised in the extended family of her mother, growing into an aggressive, competitive woman. My grandmother met her husband, a medical student, through his sister. She quickly won him, and they were married in 1900. Free to do as she pleased, she created a fine home full of social and church activities and ran several small businesses. She never relinquished her farm in Gonzales, commuting there regularly to raise cattle to sell at the market in San Antonio.

Doctor Covington, as we always called my maternal grandfather, was born and raised on a farm near Marlin, Texas. A bright student, he taught school for a few years, then decided he wanted to become a doctor. Marlin was a hot springs town, with healing and health its only industry. This is how we came to understand my grandfather's aspirations. Somehow, he made his way to Meharry Medical School in Nashville, one of only two medical colleges for blacks in the 1890s. He passed the entrance examination and worked his way through the school as its janitor over a six-year period of stops and restarts. Upon returning to Texas, he married and decided to set up shop in rapidly growing Houston, 200 miles south of Marlin.

ANNIE DEVINE REMEMBERS

The terror of Jim Crow was not an abstraction. Most people who are not from that background have no way of understanding, and no access to how deeply this terror lived in the lives and psyches of those it was meant to terrorize. Some people died, and some survived, and before the people who had witnessed this passed on, Tom wanted to get these stories onto paper.

  Published in Freedomways

Last spring, while driving through Mississippi en route from Memphis to New Orleans, I reflected on the beauty of the rolling green hills, the plethora of fast food restaurants, the similarity of the highway to others in the United States.

As I noted the names on the exit turnoffs—*Hernando, Oxford, Holly Springs, Marks, Cleveland, Greenwood*—it seemed almost unbelievable that a few years ago these names had held so much meaning in the civil rights wars of Mississippi. They were names that brought forth poignant memories, each with its own story. Now, only a few years later, it seemed that nothing had ever happened in these towns: seeing them now was like waking from an especially frightening and intense nightmare—or was the nightmare real and this now lazy, peaceful land a dream?

I reflected that nineteen years had passed since the murder of Medgar Evers and twelve years since the killing of Martin Luther King. These deaths are watermarks by which black southerners mark the passing of years and sometimes progress, or the lack of it. In my case, each of these deaths is tied inextricably to Mississippi. I had known Medgar Evers, while I was working with the Legal Defense Fund, as a man whom I felt safest with, more than any other in Mississippi. How absurd it seemed that someone so unmindful of danger and threats could be killed. My earliest mature memories of driving through Mississippi were with Medgar. The day King was killed I had driven through tornado warnings from New Orleans to Mary Holmes College in West Point, Misssissippi, to teach a class in Afro-American literature. It was an evil day, and I had wondered if keeping an appointment to teach a class was worth the trip. I recalled vividly that community leaders John Buffington and Cliff Whitley had been so involved in the struggle to qualify Whitley as a candidate for political office, the demands and the needs of the Clay County, Mississippi, struggle so pressing, that it had taken a long time for the news that King had been shot to sink in. The Mississippi struggle had its own imperatives.

Now, as I was driving, I wondered whether Mississippi—this strange, forsaken, legendary, fearful place—had *really* changed, could ever really change.

I decided during that drive to return to Mississippi and talk to people who were in Mississippi when the struggle began in the sixties, were intimately involved in the movement and were still in the state. I wondered what *they* thought of Mississippi now.

I mentioned this idea to former SNCC leader Ed Brown, a veteran of the Mississippi wars. Ed Brown works in Atlanta now, but he founded the post-Movement organization MACE, the Mississippi Action for Community Education, a successful economic development project situated in the poverty-stricken Delta. "You couldn't do better," he said, "than to go to Canton and talk with Annie Devine."

*   *   *

I knew that Canton had had a reputation as a bastion of segregation. I knew Mrs. Devine had been one of the leaders of the Freedom Democratic Party. Though I had never met Mrs. Devine, I also knew that she was something of an underground legend of the Mississippi movement. Not as widely known as her close friend and associate, the late Fannie Lou Hamer, she was nonetheless known by everyone who worked in Mississippi, and highly esteemed for her commitment and honesty. I knew, too, that Canton had been a "CORE" town. (The Movement had divided Mississippi into territories which were assigned to the key civil rights groups, SNCC, CORE and the NAACP. However, progressive NAACP state leaders like Medgar Evers, Aaron Henry and Amzie Moore worked with both SNCC and CORE, and by 1964 there was considerable coordination among groups in the state.) New Orleans had also been CORE territory; several of the New Orleans civil rights "family" had received their fiery baptisms in Canton.

"There wouldn't have been no movement in Canton without Mrs. Devine," said Ed Brown. He called her on the telephone, telling her that I was "one of *our* guys."

*   *   *

It takes just an hour to drive from New Orleans to the Mississippi state line and only four hours from there to Canton, but it takes far longer to adjust to the different landscape. For example, in New Orleans the colors of black people are incredibly diverse, ranging from very light to very dark with all variations of hair, and in New Orleans the manifestations of racism are subtle and full of strange contradictions. In Mississippi, there is greater uniformity of skin color among our people, which symbolizes the state's social reality. Matters are more or less black or white.

In New Orleans black culture, a certain *joie de vivre* marks even the most serious matters—funerals, for instance; whereas the unrelenting repression Blacks have experienced in Mississippi has lent to their milieu more the rich pathos of Delta blues. Perceived as "frivolous" by many hard-working, puritanical southern black leaders, life in black New Orleans has permitted imaginative fantasies and dreams about racial identity and life's possibilities; but in Mississippi, life for Blacks has been far more proscribed.

*   *   *

Annie Devine lives in a small brick house on the outskirts of Canton, about twenty-five miles north of Jackson. She is a short woman in her late sixties, deliberate in her motions and direct in her speech. Despite her sense of grace, I could see that she might make some people feel very nervous. Small talk is not one of Mrs. Devine's gifts.

The photographs adorning Annie Devine's home reflect the primary concerns of many Black women her age: they feature her two daughters and two sons, all grown and living elsewhere, and her church. There are no noticeable civil rights mementoes.

When I asked her how she felt about the seventies and eighties, what kind of progress she feels black folk have made in Mississippi, she smiled. "It is a *strange* time," she said. "Of course we *have* made progress, but it's difficult to figure out just where."

Riding through downtown Canton, one sees that black people, especially teenagers, have a strong presence, especially on weekends. The young people shop in the stores, their soft, musical accents rippling the air, as if there had never been a problem; while older people sit and appear to be waiting for something to happen. If the youngsters strolling the streets don't recognize your car, they may look up hopefully, for they lack that look of despair so characteristic of northern ghettos.

Here are young people who have little personal knowledge of the Mississippi movement struggles that were waged on these very streets. For the first time, we have a generation now in school that is for the most part unfamiliar with names like King, Evers, Stokely, Wilkins, Young, Rap, Meredith. They know nothing of Montgomery, Selma, Birmingham, the Mississippi Freedom Summer.

Mrs. Devine comments on the most common measure of southern racial progress—the number of political offices won by Blacks: "Too often the allegiances of these politicians are to the white power structure, not to the black community." We discuss the fact that although a few more Blacks are employed, so many of the jobs came from federal programs. "In a place like Madison County [where Canton is located], 200 or so jobs obviously make a difference," said Mrs. Devine. But she expressed mixed feelings about these jobs: "On the one hand people need the money; on the other hand so many people have become satisfied with the situation as it is now, there's not much drive to better the community. The thinking is 'don't rock the boat.'"

What about the "progress" of school desegregation, one of the strongest objectives of the civil rights struggle? Indeed, the successful legal attack on segregated schools was really the beginning of the end of the segregated South. "The problems have been numerous. Under desegregation black teachers and administrators have lost even the limited controls they maintained under segregation. We can't return to segregation, but in a lot of cases the schools now are worse than they were twenty years ago. Also, many of the best public schools today are the ones that remained all-black. That might go against popular belief, but that's true."

"Throughout Mississippi," Mrs. Devine adds, "black principals from the old black schools were reassigned as assistant principals under desegregation; fine black coaches were made assistant coaches. Whites got the senior authority." As a former school-teacher, Mrs. Devine is particularly interested in what has happened to the public schools. "In the old days there were a few black teachers who cared about what our children learned and how they behaved, though there should have been more. Who cares today? Who makes sure that our students learn? I'm not even sure there's anyone who cares about whether they're actually in school."

All over Mississippi, white children who can afford it go to the private high schools that were set up to avoid desegregation. The result is a depleted tax base for public education, with no interest among wealthy whites in public schools since their children don't attend them. In effect, the public schools have been abandoned to the poor and the Black. Courses in black history, and extra-curricular programs designed to involve the black community, often quite common in the old "black" schools, are now anathema. Many white administrators consider courses or programs exhibiting black consciousness or pride to be detrimental to "racial harmony." "Where," asks Mrs. Devine, "in the black community today do we gather to discuss issues and develop policies about matters that are crucial to our community?"

*   *   *

Annie Devine has lived in Canton since she was a child, raised there by an aunt after her mother died. "We were just among the poorest of the poor," she says. After completing high school she worked briefly for a black printer. She married in the early forties and bore two daughters and two sons. Eventually her husband moved north, leaving her with the task of raising their four children.

She taught elementary school in nearby Flora, which paid thiry-five dollars a week: "It was never a matter of doing something I wanted to do, or felt particularly qualified to do." She taught for eight years. During those years, she took classes at Tougaloo College to upgrade her education. In the middle fifties, she left the school system to sell insurance for a Jackson-based company. Mrs. Devine was struggling as an independent insurance agent and living in a federal housing project when the first CORE workers came to Canton in early 1962.

*   *   *

In the nineteenth century, Canton had developed into a prosperous cotton-marketing center where, as elsewhere in Mississippi, the white owners of the town ruled over the seventy percent black population with absolute authority. And as elsewhere, any black person in Canton who took on the burden of fighting for black rights, or even protesting, was literally courting death and might have to get out of the state by sundown. Blacks owned 40 percent of the land in Madison County, but out of a population of approximately thirty thousand Blacks, only 150 to 200 were registered to vote. Of these, less than half actually voted.

Against this background, it should be noted that the Civil Rights Movement of the sixties also sought to change the psychology engendered by conditions such as the above, which were widespread and historical. A psychological revolution became possible precisely because the Movement was broader in scope than a city or region or state or personal grievance. It offered, for the first time in the twentieth century, a large and basically spiritual unity to those who would challenge the power structure. Growing Movement participation promised that individual and local protests against injustice, previously so isolated and sporadic, could now be part of a bridge that spanned the entire Southland in a new broad-based battle for social change.

The first CORE volunteer to attempt a voter registration drive in the sleepy town of Canton was George Raymond, who was barely in his twenties and a native of New Orleans. His story really needs fuller telling than is possible here for he is a true unsung hero of the Movement. It was Raymond, with a style of bravado and fear-lessness, who captured the imagination of Canton's young people and got the Movement going. It is interesting, however, that as the Movement in Canton blossomed, Raymond's influence decreased: finally, he became sidetracked in the late sixties. He remained in Canton, but Movement activity there and across the state was slowing to a halt. He suffered a serious heart attack in 1969 and died in New Orleans in 1970 from a follow-up attack. He was not yet thirty. In effect, he devoted his entire adult life to the black community of Canton, Mississippi.

Raymond's first task had been to convince Blacks to go to the Canton courthouse to register. The problem there was Foote Campbell, the County Circuit Clerk, who used his multifaceted and imaginative "constitutional interpretation test" to fail Blacks who attempted to register. In addition, after registration drives began through CORE's efforts, the Canton town square was often filled with hostile, armed whites from all over the county. Police harass-ment was constant. In a small town like Canton, special note was taken of any black person who joined the registration struggle.

Since fear was pervasive, Raymond and the early CORE vol-unteers did not receive a warm reception from the adult black community. The first strong adult supporter of CORE was C. O. Chinn, a local cafe owner and businessman, another unsung hero of the Movement. Chinn took the lead in providing CORE work-ers with housing, food and transportation. "When George had to go somewhere, Chinn took him. When he needed protection,

Chinn, who was known to be fearless, protected him. When he and the other workers needed somewhere to sleep, Chinn found beds," remembers Mathew Suarez of New Orleans, who joined Canton CORE soon after Raymond arrived.

The Movement could not have secured a foothold in Canton without Chinn's support, and it is a measure of Chinn's sacrifice that he is said to have suffered the loss of almost all his financial holdings because he aided the CORE volunteers. He was also jailed. Annie Moody, a former Tougaloo student and author of the excellent *Coming of Age in Mississippi,* which deals at length with the Canton struggle during her involvement there, said that at one point Chinn himself had to go on the meager CORE salary of thirty-five dollars a week.

* * *

Annie Devine's decision, very soon after Raymond arrived, to quit her job and commit herself to the freedom struggle as a CORE staff member was extremely important in gaining for CORE another level of black community support. As a mature and soft-spoken woman, mother, former schoolteacher, well-connected insurance agent and churchwoman, Mrs. Devine represented the respectable center of the black community, and must have set a striking example for those adults who were afraid to step forward. In contrast, Chinn was a bar owner, opinionated and regarded as something of an outlaw. Thus, the Chinn/Devine alliance in support of CORE and the Movement symbolized the unification of the black community and provided the Canton Movement with an important and unusual legitimacy in the history of the southern civil rights struggle.

George Raymond and Annie Moody invited Annie Devine to her first Movement meeting. She recalls:

The meeting was at Pleasant Green Holiness Church on Walnut Street. When I arrived there were police cars everywhere. There were cars of roving whites for blocks as far as you could see. About a dozen policemen were milling about the church grounds.

After the meeting the police went to each car to ask questions; they already had our tag numbers. They were taking down names, addresses and jobs. I was in George Raymond's car when one of the six policemen got to me. He asked me my name. I said, "*Mrs.* Devine." He seemed to stiffen. He asked me where I lived. I told him the name of the project where I was living. He said, "Well, you won't be living there tomorrow."

Remembering this incident vividly, she says:

It made me *very* angry, very hurt. I didn't tell the children anything when I got home, but I didn't sleep that night. With four children, where was I supposed to go if I was forced to move?

When it came time to pay the rent I didn't have the money. When I went to tell the woman in the office, who was white, she said something like, "Well, it seems as if you have time for everything else, so I hear." I knew she had been informed I had gone to a Movement meeting.

I think I made a decision right there. If I was going to be harassed, be made to move just because I went to a meeting, then I was already *in* the Movement. I was either going to be a part of it or out of it, and I wanted to be a part of it. Because something had to be done *now*.

After successfully protesting an effort to evict her, Mrs. Devine resigned from her insurance job and went to work for CORE. She was fifty years old. Her friends in church and other people who had known her probably thought she had lost her mind. Her daughter Monique says that Mrs. Devine's friends couldn't understand why she had to become so "personally involved." But Mrs. Devine's decision probably changed the course of the struggle in Madison County.

Matthew Suarez, a CORE activist, states:

> We were young and full of energy...We were trying to bust down brick walls by running our heads through them. We understood very little about Mississippi and how whites and Blacks related to each other. All of us had come from larger towns and cities...[Mrs. Devine] knew her community and understood it. She knew what we could get away with and what we could not, who to talk to, who to trust. Too often we tried to intimidate people into becoming involved. She agreed with our goals, but she believed in approaching people with more subtlety and sensitivity, and she was more successful. She could reach people by saying, "You should do such-and-such because you *know* what has happened around here, you know it better than anyone else."

Attorney Dave Dennis of Lafayette, Louisiana, who was then director of the CORE Mississippi project, notes that "Mrs. Devine's strength was not manifested through words but through actions. She was a catalyst in a quiet but extremely effective way."

It was not long before Mrs. Devine's involvement became statewide. By 1964 she was attending regional meetings throughout the state, and in the spring of that unforgettable year she played a key role in forming the Council of Federated Organizations (COFO), the new supra-organization created to coordinate the efforts of Mississippi civil rights groups.

The objective of COFO was to sharply increase the number of volunteer civil rights workers in the state. A large-scale recruitment was planned for the summer of 1964, to be called Freedom Summer. A two-week recruitment session, held in May at Oxford, Ohio, was attended by Mrs. Devine as the representative from Madison County. More should be written about the intense sessions at Oxford and about Freedom Summer itself, for they were the arenas in which all the future directions and divisions within the Movement surfaced.

Mrs. Devine brought some twenty volunteers back from Oxford to Madison County. June 1964 was a fearsome time because of the disappearances of civil rights workers James Chaney, Andrew Goodman and Mickey Schwerner while on a trip to Neshoba County, just a few miles east of Canton. (Later that summer their bodies were found near Philadelphia, Mississippi. This was the Klan's answer to Freedom Summer!) Dr. Rudy Lombard of New Orleans was one of Mrs. Devine's Canton recruits. He remembers, with amusement:

> I had no intention of working in Mississippi that summer. I went to Oxford on the urging of friends from the New Orleans Movement, but I planned to return to school to work on my degree. Somehow I ended up in Mrs. Devine's sessions. Then just before we left, she looked me in the eye and said, "Rudy, I *know* you won't deny us the benefit of your talents in Canton this summer. I'm depending on you." I knew I was trapped. No way I could turn that woman down.

*   *   *

No Freedom Summer activity was more significant than the creation of the legendary Freedom Democratic Party (FDP). The FDP was an attempt to utilize the black voting strength that was developing out of the statewide voter registration drives. The FDP set as its goal a challenge to the legitimacy of the lily-white, regular Democratic Party of Mississippi at the Democratic National Convention in Atlantic City in August 1964.

Annie Devine was involved in forming the FDP, as were her close friends and co-workers, Fannie Lou Hamer of Sunflower County and Victoria Gray of Forrest County. The attempt to put FDP together was not taken lightly by state officials. Mrs. Devine recalls:

> We were harassed just trying to meet. Meetings were broken up. Workers were followed. Organizers were arrested. And the harassments hurt us. When someone was arrested, for instance, we had to find money to put up bail, which was a problem. In Canton, we were getting so much heat we moved our meetings out in the county where we had a better chance of meeting unmolested.

At the FDP organizing convention in Jackson in July 1964, Mrs. Devine was one of the sixty-eight delegates chosen to travel to Atlantic City for the Democratic Party challenge. Aaron Henry, state NAACP president then and now, was elected chair of the delegation. What happened at Atlantic City that August also deserves a book. Some readers may remember Mrs. Hamer on television speaking at Convention Hall, testifying unforgettably about the brutal racial realities of Mississippi. Then, she was preempted for a statement by President Johnson, designed, many feel, to push Mrs. Hamer's moving appeal off the screen.

The issues at stake in the challenge made by the FDP in Atlantic City were complex. However, briefly, the FDP was offered a compromise by the national party leaders which allowed for only two of the sixty-eight delegates to be seated along with the regular Mississippi Democratic delegation. This offer sparked a bitter debate within the FDP between those who wanted to accept the compromise and those who thought two delegates were far too few. Mrs. Devine, along with Hamer and Gray, were leaders of the faction that voted to reject the compromise; Aaron Henry led the faction that voted to accept. The FDP challenge had received much northern liberal support and was the focus of extensive media coverage. Most of the liberal whites argued for acceptance on the basis that two delegates represented a meaningful victory. But when the vote was taken, the majority voted to reject. "We felt," says Mrs. Devine, "the compromise left us right where we were. It didn't give us any leverage at all."

So the FDP delegates returned to Mississippi determined to continue challenging the credentials of the state party's delegation when Congress convened in January 1965. But the split that developed at Atlantic City continued to widen once people were back in Mississippi. Generally, the contending groups were, on one side, "newcomers" to state activism like Hamer, Mrs. Devine and others who were products of the new civil rights organizations like SNCC and CORE; and on the other side, traditional state civil rights leaders best symbolized by Mr. Henry. Many observers testify to Mrs. Devine's efforts at mediating the dispute, and to her attempts to hold the organization together after most of the traditional leaders had left. She says, smiling:

> There were people who said if they had known what
> they were getting into they wouldn't have become
> involved. I felt I understood what I was getting into.
> If we were going to make any progress, we had to fol-
> low through with political organization, whatever the
> consequences.

During the fall of 1964, a revamped FDP decided to challenge the seats of five Mississippi congressmen. Mrs. Devine was select- ed as challenger from the Fourth Congressional District. Hamer and Gray were chosen as challengers from their districts. A na- tional support committee was organized in Washington to fund and publicize the effort, which was expected to be given a hearing in January 1965 in Washington by the Congressional Credentials Committee.

However, when the FDP challenge was presented in January, Mrs. Devine and company found themselves face to face with the U.S. political establishment and a national Democratic Party that was not at all enthusiastic about removing any of the five incumbent Mississippi Congressmen. Six hundred black Mississippians were bused to Washington in support of the FDPers, but their supporters were not even allowed in the halls of Congress. The FDP was told that it would be "a long time" before the Credentials Committee could get around to hearing them. In fact, they had to wait exactly *eight months*. Devine, Hamer and Gray rented an apartment in Washington as hearing date after hearing date was postponed.

Finally, on September 17, 1965, the FDP challenge was heard and summarily rejected. Mrs. Devine remembers that during the hearing one of the Mississippi Congressmen, whose seat was being challenged, shouted that he "didn't have to sit here and lis- ten to this stuff." At the end of the hearing, Fannie Lou Hamer made a beautiful statement. Mrs. Devine recalls:

She said no matter how the nation looked on this challenge, we weren't there to play. We were there because we wanted the nation to know it was sick. Everything we testified to was true. "I hope," Mrs. Hamer said, "I live long enough to see some changes made, some hearts soften, some people begin to do some right things in Mississippi."

The Freedom Democratic Party was unique among black political movements because it never lost its integrity as a people's movement. The strength and vision of the FDP stand in stark contrast to some of the conservative and compromised-almost-beyond-recognition black elected politicians of the current period. The three great women who helped build FDP and keep it true to the needs of the people were Fannie Lou Hamer, Victoria Gray and Annie Devine. Ed Brown, a SNCC leader in those days, calls Mrs. Hamer "the spokeswoman," Mrs. Gray "the strategist" and Mrs. Devine "the unifier." "Within the specific context of what went on, Mrs. Devine was an unsung heroine because her role was one that did not draw public attention." Rev. Harry Bouie of McComb, formerly a leader of the Delta Ministry, assesses Mrs. Devine's contribution to the struggles of those days by noting: "Too often we view leadership in the black community only in terms of spokesmanship. But there is another kind of leadership that comes from day-to-day, unpublicized and dedicated work. We need to value this quality more in our communities."

*   *   *

Facing the eighties, Mrs. Devine, like many other Movement veterans, sees a falling off of commitment: "Somehow we've been steered away from the objectives of the Movement." There has been progress, "particularly in the minds of youth," but she feels that progress for Blacks in the South has in many ways been more superficial than substantive. "Economically, black people are weak. Politically, there is little that black communities control. Culturally, we are still struggling to find and have confidence in ourselves. There is no unity of direction. Sometimes I fear," she laughs, "that the Movement opened Pandora's box."

She does not idle her time away. She worked in a community program until retiring in 1977 ("I'm a senior citizen, you know") and continues to be active as one of the founding board members of the Greenville-based Delta Foundation. Of the "three great women" of the sixties, only she remains in the state. Mrs. Gray now lives in Virginia, and the unforgettable Fannie Lou Hamer died in her home at Ruleville in March of 1977.

*   *   *

Leaving Mississippi to return to New Orleans, I pondered the nature of the harvest sown by the struggles of black people in Mississippi and the South. For sure, it is difficult to assess current "progress"; things are not, as Mrs. Devine suggested, what they seem. Of course, more Blacks vote; there are more black elected officials; more Blacks are getting higher wages; and much of the racism that was rampant in the South has been pushed to the rear of our collective consciousness. Unquestionably, these conditions represent substantial changes and progress over conditions fifty or even twenty-five years ago.

On the other hand, unemployment among Blacks today is higher than at any time since the Great Depression, particularly in the cities. The greater presence of Blacks in politics has not been able to turn our disastrous economic condition around. Organizational efforts by Blacks to produce change have slowed to a halt, while the U.S. has become increasingly conservative and unwilling to address fundamental economic inequities and social injustice, symbolized by the election and policies of Ronald Reagan.

The deeper meaning of the sacrifices of Annie Devine and others like her, who were not ordained or recognized as national leaders, suggests to us in 1982 that effective leadership can and must come from people who are interested and who care; that a real movement in the future will be forged by committed, knowledgeable individuals, not by some great mythic leader who will descend upon us like a comet from afar. Mrs. Devine's story and the stories of other Mississippians who devoted themselves to the sixties Movement instruct that social progress derives from a sense of personal sacrifice on the part of a dedicated few. Perhaps part of our problem today is that we have lost the sense of how leadership develops, how a movement for social change develops. Everything we know about the sixties tells us that movements emerge when enough people in a society take upon themselves the responsibility of effecting change without being told by someone "above" them that it must be done. In reality, the committed show the leaders where to lead. All great leaders know how to listen to the hearts and voices of the people and synthesize what they hear, as the gifted Martin Luther King did, into a collective, eloquent expression of aspiration and purpose.

Finally, the value of black history lies in its lessons for survival. If we can forget a history so recent as the heroic struggles of our people two decades ago, then no wonder our ship is now rudderless. To know how we can better our condition, we have to know how we did it before. To know in what direction we must move, we have to know the details of our tortuous journey from whence we came to where we are now. History is not in the library; history was, is, and will be our lives.

*   *   *

Nearing New Orleans, which has such a curious spiritual tie to Canton, I felt that what is happening to Mississippi is that it is becoming more like New Orleans—more subtle and contradictory. Mrs. Devine mentioned Pandora's box. A trick bag. It may be that if we don't take on the responsibility of interpreting our journeys in America, we will drown in the glitter of her promises and fantasies, never knowing what happened to us or what we struggled for.

Interviews

A broadening of our vision

In the early 90s, Tom had the opportunity of ghostwriting the autobiography of Andy Young, former U.S. ambassador to the United Nations, and Tom's high school classmate and good friend. The project could have been a breakthrough into a national spotlight; as Tom put it, "for the first time in a long time I was under pressure to produce something that was commercial…for the first time ever." In addition to writing about a friend, Tom was deeply interested in documenting the Civil Rights Movement by chronicling Andy's experiences as a key aide to Martin Luther King. Although Tom worked hard to make the project work, he was eventually replaced. When the book was finally published in 1996, portions of Tom's work were used, but Tom was not credited as a writer.

Following the rejection of his Civil Rights focus for the Andy Young project, that Tom mustered the courage to propose and complete *Southern Journey* is almost miraculous. With the administrative help of his close friend Dr. Jerry Ward, between 1978 and 1985 Tom had been conducting intensive interviews with Mississippi-based veterans of the Civil Rights Movement. Tom had also won a Whitney Young fellowship (1979-1981), and in 1984 interviewed Cajun and zydeco musicians. The book *Southern Journey* is a culmination of these accomplishments, and of Tom's life's work as a writer.

Over the years, while wrestling with the difficulty of finding a commercial outlet for his nuanced and community-based history of the Civil Rights Movement, Tom also had to face down a seemingly never-ending series of personal disasters and disappointments.

Shortly after returning to New Orleans after his Umbra days in New York City, Tom became the associate director of Free Southern Theater [FST] from 1966–1970. Tom and I co-edited nine issues of the journal *Nkombo* between 1968 and 1974, when the final issue was published; FST imploded in the mid-seventies. Although Tom had been the main person holding the theater together, when FST was finally revived, he was not part of the new mix.

In 1976, Tom, Jerry Ward, and Charles Rowell founded the literary journal *Callaloo* with the explicit purpose of showcasing black writers from the South. Within a few years, the trio parted ways, with Charles Rowell taking over sole ownership. And then in the eighties, there was the Andy Young debacle.

How much can a man take? How many times can you go all in on projects that fail and still be ready to give it another go? Tom was sometimes shaken. Most people knew Tom as an easy-going fellow who was a great conversationalist and an even better listener; some even thought he was too nice. I was privy to the private Tom Dent. I knew, admired, and loved the man of steel resolve. I know he had a number of sleepless nights, but all the hardships notwithstanding, through it all, Tom stayed the course.

He could have retired. He could have taken an academic position, graded papers, given lectures, and wrote at his leisure, but that would not have been the Tom I knew, the Tom who was "not so sure [commercial success] would be preferable or more worthwhile" than the cultural work that he was devoted to. Like New Orleans musicians who were proud to die playing on the bandstand or falling out after marching in a street parade, this stalwart Tom Dent was literally continuing to do griot work till the time of his death on June 6, 1998.

Tom's last home was on Treme Street. Following directly in Tom's footsteps, I literally carried on the "plain work" that Tom knew was "so important," for ten years conducting the Nommo

Literary Society (we used to joke, tongue-in-cheek, that the name meant "no mo of that literary shit"). Nommo was terminated a few days before our tenth anniversary by the arrival and subsequent disruption of Hurricane Katrina. But for its last five years or so, Nommo was domiciled in Tom's former residence.

New Orleans is full of spirits, full of legacies built on preceding generations and passed on to emerging generations, the sort of connections that can only occur when you have generation after generation walking the same streets, residing in the same structures, living, working, partying, worshipping, organizing, being born, and yes, dying in the same city—or, as we're fond of saying ourselves: *Like my parents and like my children, I be born, raised and hope to die right here in New Orleans.*

Tom accepted the baton of past generations and carried it forward in his time before passing it on to me. Looking back, I can clearly see the legacy at play, but at the time, I was just doing what we do without thinking too much about the historical value of documenting and passing on our culture—the historical value of griot work.

Unlike me, in the moment of the doing, Tom was extremely clear. In an interview with Dr. Jerry Ward, contained in this section, Tom broke it down:

> You simply cannot just begin writing. You don't know what you're writing about. You're writing about yourself, and that is important. But you have to know how that relates to what has been written, what we've done, from Frederick Douglass through Ellison. You may not like it, you may not agree with it, but you've got to know it exists. Then you can begin to progress.

As Dr. Ward points out in his headnote, the interview focuses on Tom's "recent thinking about New Orleans as a matrix for

new orleans griot: the tom dent reader

creativity." In it, Tom offers an unsentimental autopsy of the successes, failures, potentials, and limitations of the decades of cultural work he undertook after returning to New Orleans in 1965. This work included the FST as well as the Congo Square Writers Union, which Tom saw as "a descendent of the FST in establishing and inculcating the kind of black cultural traditions and institutions" that he found critical.

In addition to this interview, this last section offers an overview of the Tom Dent archives housed at the Amistad Research Center on Tulane University's campus. Through significant financial support from his brothers Ben and Walter, Tom's voluminous collection of papers, manuscripts, journals, tape recordings, and memorabilia, along with his personal library and a miscellany of paraphernalia, have all been catalogued and are available for scholarly research.

And there is much to investigate, given both Tom's prolificness and his rich theoretical underpinnings. Some of us have argued that our blackness consists of three elements: color (biology), culture (behavior), and consciousness (personal and social identity). Tom and I agreed that consciousness—that is, how we identify ourselves and how we identify with others—is the key element. Throughout his work, Tom displays a critical consciousness that is *a sine qua non* of revolution. Anybody can rebel when oppressed. Not just anyone can envision overthrowing the dominating system and instituting a more progressive, more humane social order, within which plurality, rather than hierarchy, constitutes culture, as Tom describes of his experience in the Lower East Side.

In the final two interviews in this section, Tom and I were consciously addressing questions of legacy. One is an exploration of Tom's Umbra years and includes some surprising background material detailing Tom's experiences in New York. In the concluding interview, Tom once again assesses his achievements and points to potentials yet to be developed. The interview, titled "Establishing

The Paper Trail," stands as a very important this-is-who-I-am-and-what-I-did statement for Tom Dent.

Tom had no children. His work—all the writing, and journaling, and chronicling, and recording, and interviewing, all of that plus the books and other physical objects he collected, in aggregate—comprised Tom's contribution to the future. In 1986, a full dozen years before his death, Tom was already assessing the future impact of his life's work. In his interview with Jerry Ward, the final question was "where is Tom Dent the writer going now?" Tom did not hesitate to conclude with a prophetic statement:

> Progress requires a critical dimension toward our struggle to establish and authenticate our culture, a critical dimension toward the political progress that we have hoped for through our elected officials but have not always seen materialize, a critical dimension toward our mad dash for improved economic opportunity while we forget the people in the projects and the poorest among us...I hope my work will be considered part of that effort.

This book is proof that Tom's work was not in vain. But to be totally truthful, doing this work came at a high cost. There was one more major disappointment that Tom and I shared: both of us had failed marriages. After his divorce, Tom remained single the rest of his life.

Living with a serious writer is a serious challenge. Making a marriage work is hard enough without the competition of one (or both) of the partners making meaningful art, which has its own serious demands of time, resources, and emotional investment. As some of my friends say about living with jazz musicians: *Don't ever challenge the music because ninety-nine times out of a hundred, you're going to lose.* Ditto for writers; we can't help ourselves. In most cases, we commit to writing long before uttering a nuptial "I do."

I knew Tom's wife, Roberta "Bobbi" Yancey, and was genuinely hurt that they didn't make it. In later years, when Bobbi was on staff at the Schomburg Center in New York, we worked together on various projects, but we never talked too much about Tom. In the archives are letters between Tom and Bobbi—I have never been tempted to read them. I leave all of that for a later generation of scholars to excavate; I was present at the burial.

While working on *New Orleans Griot*, I went up to Amistad one afternoon to pick up a CD of my interviews with Tom, converted from the cassette recordings he'd retained. I pushed the CD into my car's player. Before I could start the drive back home, I sat transfixed for a number of minutes. I hadn't been prepared for the impact of Tom's deliberate, baritone voice embracing me. It wasn't just sounds, just words: it was Tom, close enough to touch. Over the course of our thirty-year relationship, I had spent many an hour driving and talking with Tom. Although on this particular trip he could not hear me as we drove home across the Mississippi River, I heard him. My ears, my heart, my spirit, we all heard Tom.

And thus, over a decade and half after his physical transition, Tom's visionary griot work lives, providing both foundation for the present and inspiration for the future. His mining of our history is the gift of all our people have done, and a guarantee of all that future generations can do, if we so choose.

Kalamu ya Salaam

TOM DENT TALKING: New Orleans as a Resource of Genius

For *Xavier Review*
by Jerry W. Ward, Jr.

Since 1965 when he returned to New Orleans and became an associate director of the Free Southern Theater, Thomas C. Dent has been one of the most creative forces in his uniquely creative hometown. In the early 1960s, Dent was a member of the now legendary Umbra group.[1] He is widely known for his work with the FST and the Southern Black Cultural Alliance, as an oral historian, and as founder of the Congo Square Writers Union. His poems, reviews, and essays have been published in numerous magazines. His two collections of poetry are *Magnolia Street* (1976) and *Blue Lights and River Songs* (1982). Dent also co-edited the landmark book *The Free Southern Theater* by the Free Southern Theater (Bobbs-Merrill, 1969). This interview, which focuses on his recent thinking about New Orleans as a matrix for creativity, was taped on March 3 and 13, 1986 at Tougaloo College.

Jerry Ward: Can we begin with the present state of the Congo Square Writers Union? The November 1985 program "The Role of the Arts in the Process of Social Change," which included a reunion and a symbolic funeral, marked a definite end for the

Free Southern Theater. Congo Square is not dead as a workshop, but it seems to be hibernating.

Tom Dent: I feel bad about it. I guess what happened to it was that I happened to it. First of all, when the Andy Young autobiography came about as something I was working on in 1980, for the first time in a long time I was under pressure to produce something that was commercial…for the first time ever. So I had to give that priority over projects like the Congo Square Writers Union, which I always considered a descendent of the Free Southern Theater in establishing and inculcating the kind of black cultural traditions and institutions I thought were important. But I had to make a choice. If I kept the workshop going and put energy into it, I couldn't go into a major writing project where there's not only a priority on commerce, but the axis was taking me away from New Orleans. In other words, I had to be in Atlanta to work with Andy, and the book was operating out of New York. So if it was a question of meeting with Andy, or going to New York for meetings at Random House or Bantam, then I couldn't say "I can't go because I have a workshop." I mean I could have, but I had to make a choice. It was a not a pleasant choice, because even if it had worked out so that the Andy Young book would have brought me a lot of credit and a lot of money (or if any other writing I do brings me the recognition I don't have now as a writer), I'm not so sure that would be preferable or more worthwhile than the kind of hard, difficult teaching and just plain work we were doing before and that I felt was so important.

JW: It probably still is very important.

TD: Yeah, I don't feel that I've progressed past that work, because I don't think that's the way to look at it.

JW: The writers union was founded in 1974?

TD: No, 1973. It was just a descendent of the writing workshop I had with the Free Southern Theater, which was a descendent of the Umbra workshop. But it was more than a writing workshop, obviously. It was a fellowship of people who had the same artistic yearnings, if not artistic production. It was a fellowship of friends. More importantly, I look upon it as a fellowship of broader cultural and artistic consciousness and interrelationships than is ordinarily possible in a place like New Orleans. See, by having been in New York and Umbra and experiences like the Free Southern Theater, I knew most of the key people or a lot of them who were doing the important writing, both in theater and in literature. If I didn't know them, I knew about them. I knew the world of jazz through having learned it and experienced it in New York where it was really happening in the early sixties. And the key thing that younger black people need in a place in the South—whether it is in Mississippi or New Orleans or Atlanta or Houston—is a way to hook into the language and knowledge of the world that literature and culture operate in.

You simply cannot just begin writing. You don't know what you're writing about. You're writing about yourself, and that is important. But you have to know how that relates to what has been written, what we've done, from Frederick Douglass through Ellison. You may not like it, you may not agree with it, but you've got to know it exists. Then you can begin to process. For instance, I'll give you an analogy. In analyzing the history of jazz, somebody said that all of the stages of progression had come from cities. Just think of the history of jazz in terms of place. Not artists but place… in places where all of the previous influences have coalesced or can coalesce so that something new can happen. In other words, you can't have a new development, you can't have a new cultural development in a place that is isolated from all the other developments. If jazz, as we think of it, began to take off from New Orleans, it was because between 1890 and 1920 all of the influences of black music coalesced in New Orleans during that period. You had the African tradition in Congo Square of drumming, dance and African harmonics. You had the European tradition of marching bands and brass instruments, which the whites brought in but which the Creoles mastered and taught to the people of the African tradition. You also had one of the few places in the South where there was an opera. You had an orchestra. So you had the European classical tradition, the European brass band tradition, you had the West African cultural remnants in drumming and dance and music and intonation and scale. And you had black Creoles who had mastered the instruments, plus you had a little of the tradition which is so germane to Mississippi, the field tradition or the blues tradition, which some scholars now relate to the northwest African tradition of the old griot and the kora and string instruments. And you had a freedom for the music to actually happen and develop in an air of competitiveness. Then you can have a cultural advance. Now, in terms of literature…it can't really happen for us except in places where there are enough people of talent who are familiar with all traditions germane to them. Then they can know where to go next, making a literary progression. In the history of jazz, it has been New Orleans, then Chicago, and then for a while places like Kansas City, and then New York. Now, because of teachers who have brought what happened in Chicago, Kansas City, and New York back to contemporary New Orleans, teachers like Ellis Marsalis, it can help happen again in New Orleans. I knew, without ever having to explain it to younger people, that you can say "writing workshop," but what they really needed to do was read. And what you need to do is expose them to the Brathwaites, the Killens's, the Baldwins. So getting our people to go to the writers' conference at Howard, or the African Literature Association meetings, simply to hear and get into the world of where we are now and the course we have come...this is really the key to artistic production.

JW: I think you're right about the need to know the antecedents of any art form if you're going to be in it. There's something else that perhaps you tried in starting Congo Square. There's more than just exposing would-be writers to writers and the literature. You also have to build a writer's way of seeing. You can get a Ph.D. in literature and know a lot about writing and tradition, but that does not make you a writer. I'm trying to get at what some people think is a secret ingredient for writing (and it doesn't exist). But what is it that makes the writer, in addition to the knowledge of the tradition in which he works or she's working?

TD: Well, a kind of attitude toward creativity, toward writing really, would have started for me with Umbra. Umbra was the incubating experience for me in terms of the workshop and the interaction among creative people. It represented a very high amount of creative energy over a two or three year period. So I wasn't bringing anything new there to something like Congo Square. I think that one of the ideas I was able to get over with some of the New Orleans people was that New Orleans and our own experiences and history were worth writing about, were fit subjects for literature. I was really the first one to start trying to do that, and it came to a kind of fruition in pieces like *Magnolia Street* and *Ritual Murder*. But if we did not look at it in that way, we would have been only a minor wave of the national black consciousness or black literature movement, whose headquarters were in New York and in Chicago when *Black World* was going. So part of my argument with Kalamu ya Salaam, for instance, who was probably the most energetic and creative person to come out of that whole FST-Congo Square experience, was that it's all right to admire what Baraka is doing, what Haki Madhubuti is doing, but real creativity is to use our own experience to do the things they can't do. That took a while, because they were getting all the publicity.

JW: I think Kalamu was very successful in being the New Orleans wing of the Black Arts Movement. He got more material out than anyone else. But then there's a change in his work. Perhaps it's a coming back to the New Orleans bit. I don't know if it continues in his new book *Banana Republic*, which I have not seen, or in his recent endeavour, the writing of 90 haiku. But some of the other writers I met through Congo Square and become interested in are people like Tony Bolden and Sharon Adams, a young woman who had a fantastic future; James Borders, of course, went in a different direction because he had his own Brown University writing experiences…

TD: He's a good writer, though.

JW: Yes, a very good writer. So what I'm getting around to is that you got off into the project in 1980. That is already seven years from the time you started the workshop. Why couldn't someone have kept the workshop going since you could only be there as a consultant, a peripheral figure?

TD: Well, I was disappointed that there was nobody to pick it up and keep it going apparently, except Chakula cha Jua. Chakula is primarily a theater person and convener, not a writer. But what happened, what really happened, is that the difficult years in terms of young black writers trying to continue to write are the years after they get married and begin to have children. Then the time and the kind of career gambles necessary to produce and maximize your talent are harder to sustain. I mean, economic necessities become paramount. You must take care of your children. You must have a job. You don't have the kind of time and energy you have when you're in school or just out of school, or when you're single. So that group that began with Felipe Smith and Sharon Adams, Lloyd Medley, Quo Vadis Gex, Raymond Breaux, and a few other people like that...I've come to believe that they've pretty much stopped writing, though they keep talking about trying to get back to it. What has been gained for them, what has been retained in them, is a heightened sense of consciousness, a heightened sensitivity, a heightened knowledge of the culture. It means that even though they may not be published writers, they are the kind of people who will continue to support continued creative effort in the city, and maybe their children will be the ones to do the writing. But when I realized the workshop would not be as productive as I had hoped in terms of published material, I thought it important for me to go ahead and get done what I have to do as a writer. Maybe if I can produce work that reaches a wider audience, that in itself will be an inspiration to a still younger generation, even if I'm gone or even if I don't have personal contact with them.

JW: Well, you'll be the local model. They'll be able to point to the work of Tom Dent and say he was from New Orleans and he was able to do it, so maybe we can do it too.

TD: Yes, that's what I would hope. The workshop still meets, but I can' t meet with them on a regular basis. And making a workshop work is trailblazing work. You can't just sit there and say, "Well here I am. Everybody should show up and tune into this." You really have to go out and recruit. You have to find some way to discern and discover talent and where it's coming from, and to try to encourage young people. You've got to have programs like readings and journals, so that younger people can have an awareness that certain kinds of activities are occurring. In other words, to have a workshop you have to have more than a workshop. Somebody reads something or they see one of your programs and they say "I want to be part of that."

JW: Tom, I want to share something you might or might not have seen, the new history of Southern literature from LSU Press.[2] One of the first things I looked for was what was said about Black South writers, and there's an interesting paragraph on page 576, following the discussion of the Southern Black Cultural Alliance. It reads:

> The Congo Square Writers Workshop in New Orleans introduced many young black writers in its first anthology of poems, *Bamboula*, which appeared in 1976. Although no writer included in that volume has become well known, the volume was nevertheless significant in marking a time in history when black writers once again found their own outlets for publication, as they had done in the 1920s. Tom Dent, a member of that workshop, is perhaps the best known of its participants. His *Magnolia Street* (1976), poems focusing on black New Orleans, received favorable reviews, and his play *Ritual Murder* was performed in 1978 by the Ethiopian Theater in New Orleans.

TD: Well, what about it?

JW: It's an interesting paragraph. It say [sic] you were a participant. It does not say you were the founder. I think it is a necessary matter in literary history to distinguish founders from participants.

TD: Yes, the paragraph is not necessarily misinformed. It's half-informed, because for the record the Congo Square Writers Union was a descendent of the writers' workshop that we had in the Free Southern Theater. There's a rationale behind that, the rationale being that the kind of theater we had and the kind of direct communications with black communities we were trying to make functional within the theater required new work. And we began trying to write it. *Ritual Murder* was a direct result of that concept. Kalamu's plays were also and so forth and so on. So, you cannot start with the Congo Square Writers Union. It really starts with Free Southern Theater, and a lot of my ideas about writing start with Umbra. So that's why I say it's half-informed. *Bamboula* was the anthology that Raymond Breaux got out in '76, but I was not in the anthology. So whoever wrote that just tied together some pieces of information.

JW: It is good to have that small correction for the record. Now, *Black River Journal* (1977) was not a part of the Congo Square Writers Union projects?

TD: Yes, it was a separate project, but the idea in *Black River Journal* was to get one piece by almost every person who was writing up to a certain level in New Orleans at that time. There were pieces by several people in the workshop, but I wanted it to be broader than just those people, and to include people like Norbert Davidson and Akinshiju Chinua Ola, who had started out in New Orleans with a small theater group called the Nat Turner Theater in 1967 or 1968. Akinshiju was arrested for an alleged weapons violation in Mississippi in 1968 or 1969 as an offshoot of the arrests of people in the Republic of New Africa, and he served time in a federal prison for almost four or five years. We were not very close friends, but he began to write me while he was in prison. He became a Marxist in prison, and I much enjoyed replying to his letters, because he was, and is, unusually brilliant. That sort of correspondence was important to him and important to me. When he was released in the mid-seventies, he returned to New Orleans and became editor of a small weekly, *Data*, subsidized by one of the liquor industries. But the chief editor was an old New Orleans newspaperman who I knew as a boy and who has plenty good sense by the name of Scoop Jones. Scoop hired Akinshiju to be editor, which was unusual because Scoop Jones is not a Marxist, or a radical, he just has good sense. And Akinshiju did a very fine job with *Data Magazine* for the year or two he was there. His "Prison Letters, Prison Writings" in *Black River Journal* was an edited compilation of some of his letters to me. He also wrote the best review of *Ritual Murder* in 1976 for another small journal he was editing.

JW: Tom, there's another group I'd like to ask you about, a family group that has been responsible for promoting a great deal of theater in New Orleans, the Bean brothers. What connection did those brothers have with FST or Congo Square?

TD: None. But New Orleans is a small enough place, so that all of the people who were involved in black theater knew each other, and were to some extent involved in each other's productions, the FST being the forerunner of those theaters. With Congo Square there was always a relationship, with Chakula being the key theater connection between what we were doing as writers and

theater, because of our common FST involvements (The original
Congo Square members had all to various extents been participants in FST workshops and productions). Monroe Bean and his
brothers Anthony and Floyd quickly became known and accepted
by all the theater people when they began Ethiopian Theater in
the early seventies. I see that as evidence of an advanced cultural community that was trying to establish and maintain new
institutions—FST, Dashiki Project Theater, Nat Turner Theater,
Ethiopian Theater, Act I, Congo Square, and so forth—all these
groups knew each other, related to each other, and were kind of
supportive of each other.

JW: That relating to each other...I had the privilege of knowing
people in most of those groups...I can't call "relating" a Southern
phenomenon because it happens in other places, but it seems one
of the things that in a more expanded way we had in Southern
Black Cultural Alliance, in Jackson with the Mississippi Cultural
Arts Coalition... these institutions are more than just cultural
institutions. As you said before, Tom, they're communities. They
are communities of people who are trying to build cultural forms.
Perhaps that will be the great strength in the South. Perhaps they
will keep our efforts alive. They wither away, new people come in,
they disband, but they seem always to reshape in another way.

TD: Once again the concept of communication with artists,
younger artists, who are attempting to do the same kind of black
cultural work, be it writing, theater, or visual arts, throughout the
South. That idea originates for me with the Free Southern Theater,
because FST was travelling, and became a vehicle for communi-
cating, encouraging, and serving as a model for people in other
localities to establish their own institutions. FST can't take all the
credit. Many black communities in the South were establishing

their own theaters, their own black bookstores, their poets and small journals. Southern Black Cultural Alliance was an attempt to formalize that and coordinate it, only SBCA itself never had any money. SBCA began to run into real trouble in the late seventies and early eighties when so many of these local efforts fell by the wayside for lack of funding. For the same reasons I stated before... people getting older and not being able to sustain creative efforts. Younger people coming along take their models now from what they see on television or the big screen. They just aren't the kinds of models that we built around.

JW: Tom, I'd like to end with two questions. The first has to do with music. You wrote the album notes for the first LP the Dirty Dozen Brass Band produced.[3] I know you've been a faithful recorder, even if not in words, of the work that Walter Washington is doing. I'd like for you to comment on the Dirty Dozens and Washington.

TD: I guess Walter Washington, who is a blues singer and guitarist in New Orleans, represented to me, when I first began to discover him, what I think is a unique phenomenon in New Orleans and in the South. Let's say New Orleans. I saw Walter as a self-taught, natural genius, who, number one, was not conscious of the extent of his own phenomenal talent, and number two, for reasons that have everything to do with the way New Orleans is, laced the professional know-how and the economic substructure to be able to become "commercial," to bring his genius through the recording and performing industry to a wider audience than small clubs in New Orleans. Now, there are a lot of Walters in the history of black music. There have been other Walters in New Orleans. A prototype for Walter would be Professor Longhair. Longhair was a genius as a writer and as a performer of a particular type of rhythm and blues which is germane to New Orleans, who lived and worked in the old Rampart Street area all his life. That area, which produced many great performers of rhythm and blues, was destroyed in the late forties when the city decided to convert the area into the new City Center. Longhair hardly made a cent and would have died forgotten except that later in his life some young whites became interested in him and began to record him, push him, and obtain performances for him. The kind of genius Longhair represents takes on mythic proportion when we realize that his carnival music has, almost like a magical folk revolution, overturned the carnival music that was in vogue when we grew up. The song "If I Ever Cease to Love" is never played any more at carnival. Longhair's "Mardi Gras in New Orleans" became popular, first in the black community, then spread like wildfire in the white community, first with younger whites, then with all whites. No other music is now so identified with the city as Longhair's. Yet, he died in poverty. His wife is still having benefits to try to support herself. Larry McKinley, a DJ in New Orleans, told me that Longhair had to support himself for a while delivering records and sandwiches and stuff on a bicycle on Rampart Street. The man was almost fifty years old, and this was the kind of economic impotence he had been reduced to, despite his genius and the growing influence of his music. Walter is the kind of genius who fits into that category, though I would hope he can escape that fate. But I think Walter brought home to me the extreme irony and contradiction and realization of the vast resource of genius, particularly musical genius, in our city lacking the recognition it deserves. That fact bespeaks a truth about our musical genius as community and as artists that we have to deal with. It's not only the talent but *which* talents can be used or can get out, which might have to do with luck. Or who gets exploited. Calvin Hernton, who was in Umbra and one of my close friends, said one time, "Listen, there were a lot of Marian Andersons where I came from, but only one Marian Anderson got to the concert hall." What he meant was that that talent, that extreme talent, particularly in music, is there in so many black artists, but there's a long, tricky road between the genius and recognition, with its attendant commercial benefits. If this truth exists anywhere, it exists in abundance in New Orleans.

I have been fascinated by the Dozens, which is a band of eight young musicians with traditional music backgrounds. They have integrated the major historical phases of jazz, beginning with traditional and culminating with the modern sound of Parker, Monk, Coltrane into one music, retaining the New Orleans rhythmic structure. I see this as not a peak they've arrived at but as a level they are striving for. This music is exciting because it retains that sense of discovery germane to all innovative art; they have a sense of freedom which alarms purists but excites audiences, whether the audiences are jazz connoisseurs or the plain, rhythmic-loving "blues people" of New Orleans. I see them in the progression of New Orleans music phases as very important. Equal in importance, for instance, to the precocious "phenom" soloists developed by Ellis Marsalis over at NOCCA: his sons, Wynton and Branford, Terrence Blanchard, Donald Harrison, Kent Jordan, Elton Heron, and so forth. The Dozens are one of the most beautiful products of New Orleans culture today; they are in the grand tradition of innovative New Orleans music.

JW: And the final question. Where is Tom Dent the writer going now?

TD: Where I want to go now is to begin, through subjective essays, some fiction, and other kinds of non-fictional material which uses imaginative devices, to really render New Orleans—which I see as far more important than just one city in the South, but as a microcosm of black communities throughout the African Diaspora. To really render it as it has never been rendered before. And as a black Southerner with perspectives, through my ancestry and through travels with Free Southern Theater and work with Andrew Young in Atlanta, through experiences in Texas and Mississippi as well as New Orleans, to write an honest, revealing, imaginative portrait of the South. Such a perspective is pretty much ignored now in the rush to homogenize and smooth over the sharp edges of racial history and conflict.

JW: So you want to give us back the jagged edges?

TD: We have to, because if we don't there will be no progress. Progress requires a critical dimension toward our struggle to establish and authenticate our culture, a critical dimension toward the political progress that we have hoped for through our elected officials but have not always seen materialize, a critical dimension toward our mad dash for improved economic opportunity while we forget the people in the projects and the poorest among us. A broadening of our vision to include what is happening, first, in Africa, then in the Afro-Caribbean, and, finally, with people throughout the world who have been oppressed and exploited. We, as blacks, are in the best position, having suffered as we have in America, to provide such a critical and widening vision. I hope my work will be considered part of that effort.

NOTES

1. See Dent's essay "Umbra Days," *Black American Literature Forum*, 14 (Fall 1980), 105-108; Lorenzo Thomas, "The Shadow World: New York's Umbra Workshop & Origins of the Black Arts Movement," *Callaloo* #4 (October 1978), 53-72; Michel Oren, "A '60s Saga: The Life and Death of Umbra," *Freedomways*, 24 (Third Quarter 1984), 167-181 and *Freedomways*, 24 (Fourth Quarter, 1984), 237-254

2. *The History of Southern Literature*, ed. Louis D. Rubin, Jr. et al. (Baton Rogue: LSU Press, 1985).

3. *My Feet Can't Fail Me Now*, Concord Jazz, Inc. GW-300S-C (1984)

NEW YORK DAYS INTERVIEW UMBRA DAYS INTERVIEW

Kalamu ya Salaam: We'll talk about Umbra but also about the circumstances that gave birth to Umbra and the influence that Umbra exerts on your life, to a large degree especially .on your particular philosophy about your art work.

Tom Dent: Did you know that I did not want to get so much on Umbra, but around it?

KYS: So basically there are more aspects to talk about. One is the condition and the context which gives rise to Umbra. Two is some of the—if you will, what Umbra did in the social sense. Just publishing a publication is one thing which people away from here might see, but there's a dynamic that happens in the process. Third is the lessons that you not only draw from Umbra, but the influences that it exerted on your own outlook on what it means to be a writer and how one goes about doing that. You left New Orleans, went to school away from here, Morehouse and then up to Syracuse. You also had a desire to be a writer and I don't know if I'm phrasing it correctly to say it was a more or less general

402 new orleans griot: the tom dent reader

desire, not a specific one. I don't think you desired to be a novelist

desire, not a specific one. I don't think you desired to be a novelist or a poet, or did you? Maybe we should ask that question first, and then when you left you didn't come immediately back to New Orleans. Why not, and what was the aspiration?

TD: You asked me a lot, so let's try and break it down. Whenever I think of Umbra, I think of it as the result, for me personally, of a desire to meet and share with other blacks in my age group who are interested in becoming writers. Not that we didn't know what that involved but it's just a very lonely kind of aspiration unless you're in a situation where there's a structure through which you can do that or there is some kind of model. For me, when I began reading and writing, that writing was basically journalism in college, and my first job in New York was with a newspaper, the *New York Age*. From my generation coming out of Morehouse College, one of the most esteemed black schools, I'm the only person who ended up doing that. The only other person in any class who ended up writing that I came in contact within four years was Laron Bennett, who was ahead of me. So it made me feel very good and very uncertain about whether I could ever publish a book. Whatever it was. Now two things happened when I left the Army and went back to New York in '57...

KYS: You said back to New York: you had been in Syracuse, right?

TD: Yeah—I had been in Syracuse four years. Go through the business of trying to get a piece doing International Relations. I left and moved to New York for a few months and got a job as a copyboy on the *New York Post* and I did that for about four months. I was drafted on January 1, 1957, then I came back in '59. I'd already arranged through a furlough trip to New York to get a job with the *New York Age* as a reporter, which was edited by Al Duckett and then Chuck Stone. I was living in Harlem in '59, and I went to a poetry reading at 7th Avenue and 135th Street where I heard, over a series of months, Calvin Hernton's work and read Roscoe Lee Brown's work, Phil Petrie's work, Lloyd Addison's work.

KYS: Petrie the editor?

TD: Phil Petrie became an editor, Lloyd Addison a poet. There were also readings by Langston Hughes—

KYS: Before you go on with that—you left the city, went to Morehouse, Morehouse to Syracuse—when we say you left the city of New Orleans?
TD: Right.

KYS: When you decided to leave Syracuse you didn't come back to New Orleans, you went back to New York. At that point, had you written New Orleans off?

TD: Yeah, oh yeah. There was nothing here for me as far as I could see, and the decision to leave school was of course very painful for my parents, who thought I would just go on and get this Ph.D. and end up teaching or something. But it was the first real, conscious, independent decision about the course of my life that I ever made. I've never regretted it.

KYS: So a part of not coming back to New Orleans was the fact of a symbolic leaving of home.

TD: Well, I had left home. I really had left by the time I was sixteen to pursue—I think subconsciously—working on a newspaper like the *New York Post*. And I had done a little poetry and some writing, and there was no opportunity to really do that in New Orleans. The whole idea of writing—particularly in New York City—was very liberating at that time, and it was a way to discover the world out there.

KYS: So I hear things. There was an attraction of the place in terms of the freedom and opportunity it offered that New Orleans didn't have.

TD: That's right.

KYS: There was an opportunity in a field you were interested in. That direction of your own choosing was very different from what your parents would have had in mind.

TD: That's right, all those things were at play, and they all had to do with knowingness on my part in returning to New Orleans.

KYS: So you end up in New York, go to the army, return to New York. I'm interested in one other aspect—many people in the late forties, well mid forties/early fifties, ended up going to California or had some friends that went that route. Had you ever given thought to going to California?

TD: No. Never. Now California rivals New York as a mecca for art and some sorts of opportunity but not then. We're talking about the late fifties, early sixties. New York was in a class by itself, and I had visited New York often from Syracuse on vacations, weekends, so forth and so on.

KYS: Had you ever visited California?

TD: No.

KYS: And had you no desire to go?

TD: Well, I wouldn't say I didn't have any desire. I didn't know anybody—family I had never met, but the whole idea of say, the Bay area and the development of Berkeley, this really didn't happen until the sixties when Berkeley and the anti-establishments really emerged in California. No, I wanted to go to New York because it represented something in terms of the arts, in terms of freedom. I'd been raised in a situation here where as a child/young boy I was high profiled for no reasons of my own.

KYS: You were high profiled?

TD: High profiled. Right, and that was more of a burden than any kind of benefit. And New York, it's so large that you can be there, and no one knows who you are, even in graduate school. I was in that situation at the Maxwell School of Citizenship at Syracuse University. I was the only Afro-American student in the entire department. In this school encompassing political science and history—I'm talking about the graduate school—there were one or two African students. There was Charles B. Willie who was teaching and working on his Ph. D.—and me in political science. So it was a chance to get into a place where I could discover—I felt that I needed my freedom to try and formulate what I wanted to be before I could bring someone else to freedom. If I came back south I would get trapped into the same image contradictions and it would just be very difficult for me. I had friends in SNICK, I was asked several times by Andrew Young to come back and work as public relations person for the SCLC, but Atlanta was this high borgeois black thing, I felt like I would have just been swallowed up.

KYS: So it was not just New Orleans that you were leaving, it was in effect a whole network of people, some of whom were friends, but all of whom were interrelated in terms…

TD: Of my family and my father's image. That's right, I felt that I needed to get away from that.

KYS: So Atlanta, with all the schools, would have just been the same?

TD: Of course, because I had been to school. My father was Atlanta. Even though I had worked for Martin Luther King it would have not freed me up from all those restrictions that I felt, imagined or real. That I would be subjected to.

KYS: So in a real sense then it wasn't simply that there were no opportunities in New Orleans or in the South, it was that some of those opportunities came with strings attached that you felt you didn't want to be bound by?

TD: The opportunities in New Orleans and in the South were limited if I were interested in writing and journalism or the arts generally. New York offered a whole world to learn about many diverse peoples.

KYS: Yeah, but it was for lack of…and Andy offered you the opportunity.

TD: Oh yeah, I could have come back south, but I felt that I would not have broadened myself. I mean, I would be a different person than I am now because I wouldn't have had the opportunities that New York afforded in terms of broadening myself culturally and through some of the job experiences I had.

KYS: So for you this was a very conscious decision?

TD: No, some of it would have been subconscious, but I knew that I didn't want to come back.

KYS: That's what I mean. You were aware that there was a direction you wanted to head in and there were some things you were trying to get at, however undefined and unclear they may have been in your mind. But you knew you couldn't accomplish that in New Orleans or the South in general and that New York offered that opportunity.

TD: Yeah, for instance when I went back I worked for a Harlem newspaper and I really wanted to live in Harlem. It may not have been a big thing for all blacks my age, but it was for me because I'd been raised a little bit protected from the black community, and in some ways I was afraid. I realized I had to get over that, that fear. I enjoyed living in Harlem. It was an incredible community at that time.

KYS: Tell me how, after you got out of the army—you went back, got a job at the newspaper—how did you find your first apartment? And what was that like?

TD: Did I ever tell you that story?

KYS: No, that what's I'm saying.

TD: Well I lived in two or three places before I ended up in Harlem. I had no place so I arranged to stay with Andy Young. Andy Young had just moved from Georgia. They were staying in Jamaica, Queens. So I lived in their house for about three or four months beginning in January '59 and then Andy was working at the National Council of Churches and he knew somebody who had an apartment they wanted to rent out around 85th street between Amsterdam and Columbus. I was sharing that apartment with a young person working in the church, this young white boy. We stayed there about two months and then it was funny because I was trying to locate a place in Harlem. I told the other writers at the *New York Age*, and these were classy people. The society editor gossiped and knew everybody and everything, though she was not of society. So it was just funny, because when I was younger, I was very good looking. And she said, "Honey, you don't have to pay for an apartment. Just tell me what block you want to live on." There was a woman who owned an art gallery on 135th street, and she also owned an apartment on 139th between 7th and 8th. And I ended up getting that apartment and sharing it with another guy from New Orleans, Parnell Collins, who also had stayed with Andrew Young and was going to Xavier. He was a visual artist. So that's how I found my first apartment, and from there I could walk to work. It was a short walk. The *New York Age* was 125th near 5th.

KYS: To me this was interesting: you had already made the decision. For instance, Leroy Jones talked about in his book *Home…* you had made that decision to go home to Harlem, as it were—it was there that you worked with the newspaper.

TD: It was while I was living on 139th street, the *New York Age* job didn't last more than eight or nine months because it went out of business, but all that was coalesced into that period of time. It was an art gallery somebody was attempting. I think Carmen exhibited there and that's where I also met Tom Fieldings. He did one of his first exhibits at the gallery. The *Age*, however, was more than just a newspaper; it was also a coalition or a meeting place for writers and intellectuals. I met Calvin Hicks there, Tom Felix did some work there, and it lead directly to how I got headed to the Lower East Side.

KYS: So at this point, essentially working on your dream. Working as a writer, you were meeting others who were interested in the arts and interested in writing who were actually writers. You were living in Harlem, and then you moved to the Lower East Side, explain this.
TD: Well, I wouldn't say that I was satisfied or that happy 'cause it was a quest. I was trying to meet other writers who were poets, who wanted to be creative writers, not just journalists, not that I shoo journalism. Calvin Hicks, who was from Boston and who came from excellent Communist Party Lean—was living on the Lower East Side down around Henry Street Settlement Center. He was married to Nora, who was white, and I think she came from a similar background on the white side. And so Calvin was part of an interracial group; he was trying to do some writing for the *Age*, and we became friends. He was interested in putting together another paper or journal, but it would be done by a group that met on the Lower East Side and came to be called On Guard for Freedom. This was sort of a Black Nationalist, early Black Nationalist group interested in African Liberation and so forth and so on.

KYS: Did this have any relationship to the *Liberator*?

TD: No, and it preceded it. I began to go to On Guard meetings. I traveled all the way down there from Harlem to the Lower East Side. It took an hour to get down there.

KYS: Did you take the A train or the One?

TD: No, you had to take the D train as it cuts over to Brooklyn. It was over by the East River. And I liked it. Once again it opened up a new group of people for me, new ideas. My first exposure, for instance, to West Indians. There were a couple of West Indian writers on the *Age*.

Since we worked on 5th Avenue—I mean on 125th—we were always going up and down the street. It was a magnificent street. You could walk it for three hours on Saturday, but it was a very politicized street because of the speeches on 7th Avenue and 125th. This was during the time that Castro stayed at Hotel Theresa, this was during the time Malcolm X was speaking a lot, but not just Malcolm. There were Black Nationalists, and I didn't know what it was at the time, but now I would assume people were descendents of Garvey, and these were West Indians. So the West Indian background and the Black Nationalist idea were tied in my mind, and I always felt Malcolm was a descendant of that, though he added a couple of other things. I was very interested in all of that, though certainly not one of the leaders. I began to go down and work with Calvin. We had meetings. We also opened an office in Harlem on 125th street.

KYS: Why did you open your office in Harlem when you were having all of your meetings on the Lower East Side?

TD: We didn't have a place on the Lower East Side. We wanted to have an office. Somehow we got some money and we wanted to open the office in Harlem, but there is a more complicated answer to that question.

There were a lot of problems because when we put out one issue of the journal, there was an indecision within the organization about whether it would be some sort of activist community group or a publication, or writer's group. We actually never had a writer's workshop, and some people wanted a more activist situation where they would actually do something. For instance, we were all up in arms about the death of Lamomba and we were going to picket or demonstrate on 125th Street at the subway stop where the A train comes, and we couldn't quite pull that off. We had cultural events; we had support from Mack Roach and Abbey Lincoln. There was that indecision. There were also problems. There were white women involved from the very get go, including Calvin's wife, Joe Johnson the poet, Roland Snellings.

KYS: So it was a recipe book complex?

TD: Well, it was quite a group of people, and I think the decision to have the office in Harlem and not on the Lower East Side was a result of the fact that, very consciously, the group wanted to be Uptown. Finally there was some kind of crazy resolution/a white woman problem. By the summer of '62, those of us who were really interested in writing decided we needed to develop another organization. On Guard wouldn't do it.

KYS: During the later sixties and throughout the seventies, that would become one of the defining conflicts of most of the culturally based movements—whether it should be more activist-oriented or whether it should focus on the development of the art, whatever the form.

TD: You put your finger right on it. That conflict also ran through Umbra. We consciously started Umbra out of On Guard for those people who were more interested in writing. Even so it wasn't enough for some people. They felt that somehow we should be doing more in a situation where so much was going on, and particularly there were all kinds of developments in the Civil Rights Movement in the South. In fact, some people did go South.

KYS: So in a sense, you had already solved the problem of home-ness—that is, making Harlem your home solved that issue of commitment and the social-political problem of black identity. You wanted to go to Harlem because you hadn't had that sort of experience dealing with the black community, not as a sheltered member of the upper crust of the community, but as just another person.

TD: Just learning the community.

KYS: You had that, so now you were struggling to develop your-self as a writer. And the people who you felt were interested—and the people who you were interested in going in that direction with—were actually located on the Lower East Side.

TD: The Lower East Side which also attracted me because of the kind of community it was. It let me go back and say something about my Harlem experience.

KYS: So here you were having this experience, you were at-tempting to develop one of your main interests at that time, and that was to develop yourself as a writer. You intuitively, perhaps somewhat consciously, understood that it was the group of peo-ple living on the Lower East Side who were not necessarily serv-ing as role models, but who were certainly from a peer group you could work out of.

TD: Yeah, no question about it, though I wanted to go back and say something about my Harlem experience. When the *Age* went out of business, it was owned by S.B. Fuller, a Chicago black cos-metics man who was very successful, but also uneducated. He bought a newspaper because he always wanted a newspaper. He quickly killed the paper 'cause it didn't make any money. He didn't understand the value, that you should support it, sustain it. The *Amsterdam News* was the other paper in Harlem, and it was doing pretty well, but he decided he didn't want the *Age* anymore. As part of Fuller's strange concept of how things should operate, the reporters and other employees of the newspaper were required to go to the cosmetic meetings. He had meetings and he ran the company like a church. There was singing of a gospel type, only the hymns and songs were songs about cosmetics, and the company and those salesmen who had done well that week door-to-door—this was door-to-door salesmanship—got up, and they testified, and those who had done very well would almost do a shout. We had to go to these meetings. When the paper died, one of the women who was quite well known for working for the *Age* was Anna Arnold Hedgeman. Anna had been in New York since the thirties with the YWCA, and she was active in the campaigns to open up jobs for blacks at the 125th Street businesses that were owned by all whites just about. She worked on that with Adam Clayton Powell and other blacks—it was quite a campaign. She was quite a figure in Harlem and had some national reputation, and she also ended up with a job on the *Age*. She decided to go work for the cosmetics company, working for an office on 8th Avenue and 155th Street near the Paul Dunbar homes. So she asked me about selling cosmetics, and I decided to try it, and I was the world's worst salesman. I'd never done anything like this in my life. It required somehow getting through my own shyness to knock on people's doors and try to get them to open the door and somehow buy what we had. Deodorants, colognes—little of this, a little of that.

KYS: Tom Dent going through Harlem, knocking on doors, selling cologne.

TD: Yep. I'm afraid so. This I did. We had little black briefcases, plastic ones to put the stuff in, and it got to be that everyone in Harlem got to know us by those briefcases. A lot of time I worked at night—that was when people were home—going in apartment buildings, walking up to the fifth floor, knocking on people's doors or the doors of people who had previously bought. That took me into a place where I had never been. I wouldn't do that now, but it helped me overcome my fear of Harlem. One of the loves that I have for black people comes from that experience because people were not harsh to us. There were some people who would ask you to come in and have a cup of coffee or tea or Coke; they weren't buying anything.

KYS: This brings us to a point. A point I relate to in two ways, one poetical and one personal. When I was in high school, during the Civil Rights Movement here in New Orleans, one of the major things we did was voter registration. We actually went door to door. And at the time there was a Voter Registration test you had to pass, and we would sit down with people and help school them on how to pass this test, which included figuring out your age to the date that you went down there to register. There were some other things you had to do, and I don't have memories of any specific person, but I do have memories of going from house to house early in the mornings on the weekends and particularly Saturday mornings—9, 10, 11 o'clock in the morning—literally going from house to house, knocking on doors, asking if people were registered and if they weren't registered, did they want to learn how to register, so forth and so on. It's interesting what I remember about that experience is not the Voter Registration Act, but the process itself—the different music coming out of the houses and on the street. It's just one of those kinds of things. On a philosophical level, I think of Ama Caulkal Brown, who lead the movement in Cape Verde and Guinea

Bissau. He went to school and was educated in Portugal and was sent back as a civil servant to Guinea Bissau, and he was required to go around the countryside to do surveys, and he was surveying the country. And so I think there is a certain appreciation for people you develop when you go out amongst the people almost randomly, but at the same time systematically.

TD: That's right. You can't just get it from ideology; that's what I got out of that job. I was terrible as a salesman, but I met people. I just had a warmth. This was supposed to be a bad community with a lot of crime. I was never robbed, even though people knew you were coming, dark hallways…all that.

KYS: It was the same thing when we were going to register people who couldn't even read or write. These were considered the "worst" neighborhoods, and I think there were groups—people who came into the Black Arts Movement and other movements purely from an ideological perspective, who didn't have the grounding of actually touching people or working with people on a person-to-person basis.

TD: Right, and also I found that in dealing with our people, from all our diverse backgrounds, I could finally relax and just be myself. I could say I'm from the South, I'm New Orleans. You didn't have to put on a pretense or an artificial personality. I didn't try to be like what I was not. I certainly was not a salesman or businessperson, and that made me feel real good, but by the time I moved to the Lower East Side, I was fascinated by that now extremely diverse community.

KYS: My point is that you could move on to the Lower East Side because you had already gotten the foundation in the community. In a sense what you brought to that experience that you got on the Lower East Side was something qualitatively different from somebody who just came to it with new ideas.

TD: Yeah, well I think you put your finger on it when you said that in terms of fellow artists, the Lower East Side offered opportunities and friendships and connections that did not exist in Harlem for whatever reason. During the time of the Harlem Renaissance, they might have, but by 1960 they did not. Therefore if I really wanted to pursue that, I had to leave. It was a long trip on the subway, so I couldn't keep going backwards and forwards.

KYS: So can you remember when you decided to move to the Lower East Side?

TD: I met a girlfriend on the Lower East Side who lived in a building I ended up moving into, 242 E. 2nd Street. So I was not only going down for On Guard, but also to see her. I think she decided to leave and go elsewhere, and I took her apartment. I think by the time I actually moved in to the building, she had left, but that's how I found that apartment. Other than that, I was just developing friendships on the Lower East Side that were different than what I had in Harlem. That's what it amounted to.

KYS: So the job base was gone in Harlem?

TD: The job base was gone. By that time, I had gone through two more jobs. One of the people who I met on the cosmetic group was Lena Payne. She was a lady who had worked since the thirties for the Welfare Department, one of the top blacks in the department, and she was also interested in writing. So just out of sheer interest, she opened her doors to me and also my roommate, Parnell Collins. So one day she said, you are the worst salesman in the world, you're never going to sell anything, you're not interested, why don't you come on down and let me get you a job in the Welfare Department.

So I had to take the test for investigator, and Parnell also ended up working for the Welfare Department. I was assigned to the Melrose Center in the Bronx, near Yankee Stadium. The Bronx was really going bad. It was on its way to what it has become. I had ninety cases, almost all Puerto Ricans, one or two elderly Jewish women whose families had abandoned them—before it became Puerto Rican, the Bronx had been mostly Jewish. It was a very painful kind of job. I had friends on the job who I was close to, and we talked about that pain. The longer you stayed there, the more you made yourself immune to suffering and just treated people like a case.

I found myself internally rebellious against that, so I ended up working for the NAACP Legal Defense Fund after I went to interview Thurgood Marshall for an article for *Jet*. I was moonlighting some articles for *Jet* while I was working for the Welfare Department. So by the time I moved to the Lower East Side, I was working for the Legal Defense Fund on 59th Street.

KYS: So how did you get that offer for that job?

TD: After our interview, Mr. Marshall asked what I was doing, and I said I was working for the Welfare Department. He said just come work for me if you're interested because things are getting busy now. This was the spring of '61, right around the time of the Freedom Rides. He said, "We've had a part-time pressperson, Arnold Demill, who comes in and writes releases on our cases, but things are getting busy. We need a full-time person." And of course I accepted right away. So that's how I got out of the Welfare Department. They were probably going to fire me from the Welfare Department.

KYS: So now you end up being a publicist.

TD: No, it wasn't that grand at all. It was more like a press attaché. Legal Defense had quite a few cases, so my first job was to write releases in some kind of intelligible, everyday language—not Legal Eagle—that could be mailed out to a press list, to all the black papers plus the main white papers on the wire services, and also to reporters who'd called in wanting to interview attorneys. So it wasn't like I was PR—Mr. Marshall was the PR person for LDF—it was really more like a press thing, but there was getting to be a lot of press because all the action with the Sit In, with the Freedom Riders, with all that coming to the Supreme Court...

KYS: So it was more like a Press Secretary. And so here you are doing this—did you feel you were making a living doing something that involved writing yet not making it as a writer?

TD: Well yeah, in no way did the LDF job satisfy my desire to develop my creative writing. It was, however, a very interesting job. I had to make myself write the press releases and learn how to do that and develop a kind of a skill at it, but as soon as I got to the Lower East Side, I began to seek out other writers, specifically Calvin Hernton, whose work I'd heard. And I knew Joe Johnson and Rollin Snellings, and with On Guard falling apart, we began talking of putting together another group. I think I met David Henderson through Hernton. We became almost instantaneous friends, particularly the three of us, and so we put together the first meeting of Umbra in the fall of '61, then I moved there early '62.

KYS: How did you choose the name Umbra?

TD: One of the things we did—let me just expand out a little bit. One of the new things about the Lower East Side was that there were several cafés, basically coffee shops, that I had never before experienced, and they hosted poetry readings every Tuesday night and Thursday night. These were basically open readings. Also at that time, the Lower East Side was attracting the alternative artists, those people who were not made. The Village was unbelievably expensive, but on the Lower East Side my apartment was fifty-five or sixty dollars a month, and so you live cheaply...

KYS: An apartment in Manhattan for fifty-five dollars a month?

TD: Fifty-five dollars a month. It was a small apartment, but it was affordable. So beginning around 1960, there was this coalescing of what would have earlier been called beat writers: counterculture people, dancers, theater people, actors, and writers. So the coffee scene was something a lot of people came to and a few black writers read at. That's where I met Calvin Hernton. He was reading one night. I was afraid to read, but he was reading. So the first thing we did toward the organization of Umbra was to have it at my apartment on 2nd Street—we all read, we just sat around in a circle and we read. One of the poets whose work I'd heard who did actually show up for that reading was Lloyd Addison. A sort of surrealist Black Poet. And he had a line in one of his poems that went Pumbra the Umbra blah blah blah blah—and that sounds fantastic; what does it mean? And it just blew our minds. Addison had this cold bass voice: *the Umbra*. We looked it up, and it meant the dark side of the moon during an eclipse. Someone else said it was another way of saying "black." Before we named ourselves consciously the Umbra poets, we were being called "that Umbra gang" always talking about the Umbra and Pumbra, so we just took it as our name, knowing that as soon as people heard it, people would ask what's that suppose to mean, and we'd tell them look it up.

KYS: So there was sort of a gang peer group at work?

TD: We were finding each other, which was beautiful. Sheerly one of the more beautiful experiences of my life.

We were all from diverse backgrounds. Almost none of us were . from New York. We had all come to New York for the same reason: looking for somebody else just like us. So a lot of the commune-like friendships that developed were a sharing of where we had come from and what we aspired to do. Roland Snelling was a painter who started writing poetry, and Hernton had taught sociology at Southern and come back to New York. David said he was part of a singing group in Harlem, and Joe Johnson was from Brooklyn, and Ishmel was from Chattanooga. So everybody was from somewhere else, and that sharing of backgrounds and aspirations and hopes—that was a beautiful thing, I want to tell you.

KYS: Why do you think the Lower East Side became the focus of it?

TD: The neighborhood was inexpensive and where you have a power center, others are attracted to that. I imagine that there was a point for white artists when it was Greenwich Village, and there was a point for black artists when it was Harlem. Now it might be Brooklyn, but at that time it just happened to be the Lower East Side. This was before canonizing the East Village; we did not call it "East Village." It was a place of Eastern European immigrants of all types, of bakeries and restaurants and bars and cafés. Of all Eastern European and Jewish ethnicities. It was a place of the old left and the Communist Party, and many of their organizations and meeting halls were still there, though they had kind of died out. That scene left just before we got there. It was a strong Jewish area, so there were a lot of Jewish and Yiddish remnants, delis and stuff, with new Puerto Rican immigrants having moved in towards the East River. You could walk down the street for days and never hear the English language.

KYS: So to use a Baldwin phrase, it was another country, but it was at the same time in New York.

TD: It was another country, but at the same time in New York, which made it utterly fascinating. It didn't melt; none of these people melted, but you could sense that you were in New York. Of all the sections or areas in the city, I internalized the Lower East Side the most. I think that may have to do with the fact that we were kind of accepted as blacks on the Earth. There was a very small black community— only scattered people on the Lower East Side— and most of the people were artists.

KYS: So are you saying that you physically felt comfortable in the whole neighborhood—and not just in your peer group—because within such great diversity, being different is not a stigma?

TD: No, it wasn't a stigma, and the discovery of the area and its uniqueness—especially the shops, going to the market and so forth where you could buy all these ethnic foods and fifty different kinds of breads—was an adventure. To walk out on the streets was an adventure. Harlem was much more monolithic.

KYS: I would say monocultural.

TD: Oh, monocultured. The Lower East Side was extremely varied and...

KYS: It must have been very stimulating to the senses, to the psyche, to the...

TD: It was. But there were places where we would not have been welcomed—bars, so forth and so on. So we finally developed our own bar, and I'll tell you about that. But yeah, I was a walker, and I would walk at night, maybe two hours. I walk over to the Village, walk back, walk down to Chinatown. Each avenue was different. I lived between Avenues B and C, and from C on over was kind of Puerto Rican. I wasn't afraid. A few years later the area was devastated by drugs and became a very bad area, but this hadn't quite happened by the time we got there.

KYS: So when you all became the Umbra gang, what was the first decision?

TD: To have a magazine, but we also decided to set up a weekly workshop on Friday nights. So we started meeting at my house, and people wrote material for the workshop. None of us were published, except for Hernton.

KYS: So you decided to do a publication?
TD: That was our objective, a magazine.

KYS: A literary magazine was the objective, and how did you decide to do the workshops? Was it that you didn't have enough materials or what?

TD: No, I'm sure the workshops developed out of the need to commune and to share, to share criticism. The only other writers' workshop for blacks in New York was John Killen's Harlem Writers Guild, but it was fiction writers, and most of us were writing some poetry. Don't forget that the Lower East Side was this scene of readings and so forth. The workshop was a way for us to share as black writers. Eventually of course it drew blacks who were not living on the Lower East Side, who would just come down for the workshops from Brooklyn or whatever. That's how Lorenzo Thomas got there, and two or three other people.

KYS: Question, was there a conscious decision to make Umbra a black-oriented group?

TD: Yes, oh yes, there wasn't anything like it. Even though we had friends who were white women.

KYS: Were the white women in Umbra, or were they just associated with the men in Umbra?

TD: They were associated with the men in Umbra, but they felt like they were in Umbra even though they weren't writing. Don't forget that we were coming from the political lineage of On Guard for Freedom and the Black Nationalists. Quite consciously it was a black group. There was one white writer of the old labor leftist type who begged us to come in, and we voted him in. That was Art Berger.

KYS: Why did you vote him in?

TD: We knew that what we were doing should be—and was— a black artistic thrust, but we didn't have an iron-clad rule. Don't forget there were white women involved, and there were guests who were not black, but who were interested in what we were doing. I mean, we didn't tell anyone they couldn't come in.

KYS: So consciously you decided to establish this country, but others could be voted in.

TD: In terms of writers in the group, we voted on Art Berger at Calvin's urging. And Art was a friend; he'd been around. He was on the Lower East Side. He was older than we were. He wrote the first article on Umbra in *Masses and Mainstream*.

KYS: A leftist publication?

TD: A leftist publication, and the first piece done just a few months after he came. And it wasn't one of those things where there had been a lot of whites who wanted to become members of Umbra—then we would have had to deal with that. But Art being there didn't change anything.

KYS: It's interesting you say that you consciously vote on people. How many?

TD: Just one. Just him.

KYS: Oh, that's the only one that you consciously voted on?

TD: Just him because he was white.

KYS: So how did other people become members?

TD: By basically coming to the workshop and continuing to come. We had no membership requirements.

KYS: So in that sense, it wasn't a movement—it was a family, a community.

TD: It was more like a community.

KYS: You became part of it by being part of it.

TD: By being part of it, by participating and by sharing, and it was also a social group. For instance, in trying to find a hangout we ended up going to what had been a Polish bar on Avenue B and 12th Street. Stanley's Bar. Stanley had about three ole Polish customers in there, and when one or two of us went in there he was receptive. Finally he just opened it up, and we would all go there and then many other blacks came. Black artists, and many of the whites who hung out from all over the Lower East Side, made his bar such a success he had to open up the basement and renovate it. It still couldn't handle all of the people after a couple of years, and so he opened a second bar, which became one of the celebrity spots in New York called the DON on St. Mark's Place. It was unbelievable, but I think at that time the word was spreading that there were revolutionary, crazy black writers and artists on the Lower East Side who hung out at Stanley's, and people would start coming down on weekends who were tourists.
KYS: To see if it was really a thing?

TD: Yeah, to see what it was. I ran into Martin Luther King's brother one night. I said what are you doing, and he said somebody told him this is where they at. The police went after Stanley after he opened this bar up for blacks and the way they came. Stanley told me this story, and it was so funny. He said the police came and said, "You know you're running prostitution." Stanley said, "Don't you know how far behind the times you are? They give it away." Because there were so many interracial contacts.

Stanley's was sort of like a hangout. I could go by Stanley's on a Tuesday night, and I could get over there about 9:30 or 10:00 and find out where everybody was. Usually somebody was there when we weren't having a workshop that night. Nor was there, David's there, Calvin went, so and so, I hadn't heard from Rollin yet. It was amazing. It was like the headquarters, and I think we went more or less every night to check in. Particularly when we started making sandwiches.

KYS: So this then becomes another point of distinction—that the purpose of the group was not just the development of artistic activity. It was much more of an extended family than a political organization, and it was not driven by any particular ideology.

TD: Absolutely. Even though we had splits. The reason why it was so painful was because it was like an extended family and because most of us felt dispossessed. We had all left home—or else our home situations offered us little—in order to explore New York and to explore all the issues.

KYS: And to a certain extent, all of you had at one level or another rejected the straitjacket of one particular ideology, and then you were not interested in getting hooked into another one, whether it was your own choosing or not.

TD: Well, we had rejected what we had been offered at home, so to speak, whatever ideology we had grown up with, to search for something. There was a group that were writers, then there was a group surrounding us who were not writing, but felt very close to us. Many of them went on to do other things. Alvin Simon was a photographer who would come to the Umbra workshop—he never wrote anything, never read anything— but he became later one of the top blacks in the Communist Party in New York. This guy by the name of Churchwell, who started an alternative school like you did in Philadelphia, went back home after coming South. And there was people like Archie Shepherd who were into music who would show up at the workshop, but Archie was also a writer. There was a photographer, Leroy McLucas, who did a film. He would come around. So there were a lot of people around and this was sort of like an extended family.

KYS: I'm just suggesting that there are patterns that are established. Like the blues said, "burnt child afraid of fire." There's a certain reluctance to get into something you fought hard to escape.

TD: Well it was for me. Because ideology is not the number one thing for me as a writer or as a thinker. However, for some of the other people, without going into detail, I think they did feel maybe we needed an ideology and a more rigid kind of ethos or ethic or something. Those pressures helped tear the group. Once again I think a division was made between those people who were to be activists and organizers, and people who would go on with their writing careers. That's what happened in Umbra too, but it wasn't apparent in the beginning. But you're right—for me, I wasn't interested in ideology that much, or setting a style. By that time, by the mid-sixties, we did have people who were beginning to form ideals of a black aesthetic that didn't feel that important.

KYS: Well for some people it's not, and for some people it is. And it's difficult for those people—the people for whom ideology is important—to live with the others. In other words, you could personally be much more tolerant of diversity than someone who was looking for something very specific.

TD: I think I was. I'd never been ideologically rigid. As I developed, I was politically concerned and committed, but the group's ideologies could come from several different avenues as far as I was concerned. We tried to preserve that openness, but by the time '65 came, if we had kept the group and the magazine going, then certain people would have dropped out or been forced out and other people would have kept it going as a literary magazine.

KYS: All I'm saying is that all of the major issues would have happened time and time again, whether we talk about our particular circumstances here in New Orleans with black arts, or on the national scene or even the international scene. It seems to me that there are certain patterns, and a lot of the patterns have to do with one's basic orientation in life. When you find people who are ideology-driven, it is very, very difficult for them to deal with diversity.

TD: I would agree. In our situation, I would say when we first came together, all from extremely diverse backgrounds and interests, we were persons in an extreme state of flux. In the course of two years—in the course of workshops or whatever we were going through—people began to solidify and to become more defined in terms of the direction they wanted to move in. By '65 we dissolved basically because of that and began to move off in different directions. However, I do feel that even though people did not go in my direction and vice versa, we did share a family-like closeness for that period of time. That fact still remains. That good feeling still remains. It was strong enough that it sustained us—when we had the reunion two years ago, that was one of the beauties that we could remember, what we had shared. Some of the people who went off in their own direction really developed on their own. Like Ishmel, he developed his own thing. I would say some of the other writers in the group had a big problem with it as he developed his message and his way of delivering it, but Ishmel made beautiful statements. He said it was my way of learning, and for someone like me coming from a sheltered Southern background, even though I had been in New York for two years, it was an education. It was an education of exposing myself to varieties of black experience and what other people felt and what other people had read—exposing myself with a high level of criticism and involvement, intense involvement. I had read some Richard Wright, but you couldn't come near Calvin Hernton unless you read a lot of Richard Wright. As far as *Invisible Man* was concerned, you better master it because in the discussions of people's work, it was going to come up as an allusion. If you didn't know what they were talking about, you were just lost. As far as the poetry was concerned, I had to get with it. It made me, and I imagine that happened with a lot of other people. I think what it taught in terms of the workshop is that you don't criticize people's work just based on the way you feel or what you like or what you don't like, what sounds good. It has to have some context of literature that it refers to, and that was a real education for me—even though in a lot of ways, I was leading the workshop.

KYS: How were you leading the workshop?

TD: As a convener. I figured that as an experienced writer and as a critic who people listened to, Hernton was the leader.

KYS: You also say you served the function of the social group leader.

TD: Yeah, and because I didn't have any ideological constraints about how I dealt with people, I felt it was easier for me to deal with everybody and invite new people in.

KYS: That's a function you did when you came back to New Orleans?

TD: Yeah. I could do that without really working on it. I never knew why, but it was a great benefit to me too because of what I was personally searching for. That community with others helped me define my role, what I would do. I mean, it wasn't just a self-sacrifice on my part.

KYS: No, I didn't mean that. But people have desires, and they also need skills. Some skills are learned, and some are a result of the coincidence of psychology and personality.

TD: That's right. I have many mixed feelings about that skill. I wasn't altogether happy that I could do that. Something both drew me to that role and at the same time made me resent it.

KYS: What did you resent about that?

TD: Maybe I would have preferred to be more clear about known workers and artists, to have spent more time developing that and less time as the center of activities. Once you put yourself out there as kind of leader, people keeping looking to you in that kind of a role, and it was just a tricky little problem somebody else might have to explain. I remember I just wouldn't show up at my old house for the workshop just to see what would happen. One of the reasons I've been successful in that kind of role is because people sense that I don't have to have it. It's not necessary for me as an ego thing. There's no power in it that I want. I think people refer to me a little easier than to somebody who's trying to do it that way.

KYS: Always let somebody hold the money who doesn't need the money.

TD: He doesn't need to steal the money. Precisely. I didn't know enough about myself at that time, but I did feel that because we had such diversity, there were going to be factions. And I knew that to hold the group together, somebody had to make all of the factions work together. Finally I couldn't do that either. I had to make decisions that put me at odds with Ishmel and Charles Patterson, Al Haines and somebody else and Rollins, and for most of that year I had to make a decision. Sometimes you have to make a decision. There is a time to be able to compromise and work with everybody; there's also a time you can't compromise. You must stand your ground on whatever you feel is right, and when it came to that point, I made the decision, along with Calvin and David, that broke up the group. It was weird. Apparently among some of the people, there was a resentment of Calvin's role as leader, and also Calvin was beginning to move out. And I think he had gotten a contract for *Sex and Racism in America*, and people resented that. Some people. David and Calvin were very close, and it was a feeling that whatever Calvin wanted, David was with it, and I was close to them so I was leading that in a way too.

But this didn't bubble to the top as a real problem until we were getting the material together for the second issue and Kennedy was shot, which created a weird situation. One of the poems was from a writer in California who we didn't know. Now people were sending us stuff. We were getting stuff from all over. The mailbox was full.

Ray Durham was the name of the poet who had a genius for writing bitter racial ironies. I think his work was sent to us by another black poet in the L.A. area. It was most strange. One of the poems was about the bombing of Havana and the Bay of Pigs, saying someone should send the Kennedys the fingers that had been cut off the

hands of children. I may be forgetting the poem, but it had something to do with that. When Kennedy was shot, Calvin said that
we should take out that poem because you don't dance on people's
graves, and David agreed, and so did I. I felt as long as he was alive
and bombing people you could use the poem, but this happened
in the wake of the assassination, and there was a lot of grief. If
somebody wrote something like that now about Kennedy, we might
include it, but at that time there was a lot of grief. Nothing like that
had ever happened before, and that was also a time of extreme racial
conflict in the South. That was '63; the bombing of a church where
the children were killed was in September. Medgar Evers had been
shot in June, and that upset me because I knew Medgar. Kennedy
was shot in November, and so an argument developed between the
three of us on one side, and Ishmel, Alvin and Rollin, Al Haines
and Charles Patterson on the other side. They were arguing that
the poem should not be take out, and if it was taken out, they didn't
want their work published.

It went on and developed into kind of a nasty confrontation. I
don't know what they wanted to do, but the extreme hostilities
were over with in about two weeks. And we went on and published
the magazine with their poems and without the Ray Durham
poem. In an effort to try to resolve it without having a conflict, I
was going to call Ray Durham and see what he wanted to do, if he
wanted to have the poem included. I was willing to go along with
what he wanted. We finally got in touch with someone out there
and found out that he had just died. We also did not know—and
this may have changed a lot of things—that Ray Durham was
white. We thought he was black. He wrote like a black person,
but he was white. You won't find him in any anthology of Black
American poetry.

KYS: Yes, you will. There's one he's in.

TD: There's one he's in.

KYS: I remember reading his work. It was very concise.

TDt: Very concise, beautifully concise.

KYS: There's the one thing about the FBI agent and the lil' girl.

TD: It had a wicked twist to it. Which everybody liked.

KYS: So the compromise position was undercut by Durham's death and then the fact that he was white.

TD: We didn't know he was white. Nobody told us. If we would have known, that might have changed the way they felt about it. Now my interpretation of that story is not so much about Durham's poem. It was just about Rollin, that Rollin was ready to go in a different direction in terms of his work and his interest.

KYS: The poem was the occasion, not the cause.

TD: Ishmel envied Hernton's dominance in the group and was about ready to go off in his own direction.

ENRICHING THE PAPER TRAIL INTERVIEW

Kalamu ya Salaam: In hindsight, under your leadership, we discovered what I now view as a jazz paradigm for artistic development, i.e. individual development within a collective context. That was the model that was responsible for the greatest outpouring of black literacy activity that has ever happened in New Orleans specifically and the South in general. I'm not saying greatest in terms of the quality of the work, but rather in terms of the democratization of intellectual activity, i.e. having it happen across the broadest spectrum of people. We in the South did a lot of this intuitively. We had some successes; we also had some failures and made a lot of mistakes. Nevertheless this opened up a way for people to participate in intellectual activity on a level of exchange with an audience, and also on a level of respect from peers and others, without having to go the route of formal education, especially formal higher education.

You played a major role in a lot of that activity. You did the hard work of maintaining the collective base out of which people did what they wanted to do. You were sort of like an Art Blakey or a Miles Davis: you didn't tell anybody what notes to play when they soloed, but you tried your best to keep the band together so that young people would have an opportunity to play and to learn the music. In that context you were always introducing us to other folk, broadening our horizons without being didactic about it in the sense that you get an "A" if you know this and you get a "B" if you only x, etc. You emphasized us meeting people, so we met a lot of people we otherwise would not have met. It seems to me that is a paradigm for producing a qualitatively different kind of literature than the formal programs produce. I'm not saying that there is no value in going through a formal program in college, but I am saying that we demonstrated there was another way.

You came out of the Umbra experience in New York, moved back south and joined the Free Southern Theater, and set up a workshop which eventually led to the development of BLKARTSOUTH and the Southern Black Cultural Alliance. That set a paradigm that fit comfortably both within the context of the way our music is made *and* within the context of Southern culture as a whole. That is my basic thesis.

Tom Dent: Yes. OK, let me talk some about that. Maybe I can say some things that I didn't say before because I didn't think people would understand them. I wish you could have been at the Umbra reunion in November 1991. In Calvin Hernton's remarks, almost everyone's remarks, we talked about what the Umbra-Lower East Side concentration of artists meant. In addition to writers, there was the visual artist Arturo Cruz; two great musicians who were both on the scene then, Archie Shepp and Randy Weston; LaMama Theatre—it was just one of the most extraordinary confluences of modern artists, for us as black people. This was what today might be called counterculture in its thematic direction, but anyway, after a few years we all dispersed. What Hernton pointed out was that wherever we relocated, we tried to keep a sense of what we had been doing in New York alive.

Now, as you were talking, I was reflecting. First of all, I felt a lot of my motivation came from the realization that I grew up here in New Orleans as a reading child, and I began to do some kind of writing early. In a more literary society, I would have been encouraged to write seriously. But at that time there was no nurturing ground.

I was a reading child, but not "bookish" in the sense that I was overly studious; rather, I was attracted to books of my own choosing. I felt at home in the library. But even that was considered an abnormality, for the most part. And even at Morehouse College, I didn't get any sense of direction. I continued my literary interests—editing of the student newspaper, winning a short story prize, finishing second in my class academically. However, not once did one of my teachers say, "Hey, you ought to get interested in writing." The whole module of black success we were programmed toward was doctor, lawyer, preacher, teacher, and that was it. There was just no concept of doing anything else. They didn't know anything else.

I had an anger and bitterness toward Morehouse for a long time because I felt that that kind of one-sided education was a deprivation. I realized that even the teachers of English literature and the humanities did not write, and they didn't know anybody who wrote. Gwendolyn Brooks came to read after she won the Pulitzer Prize, and that was a very unusual event. I went. It was at Atlanta University. I was the only student from Morehouse there.

There was this lack of a nurturing community, no matter how small. Even little pieces of suggestions, of direction, I cherished. They came from people like Marcus Christian, who had read books and who worked at the library at Dillard, where I worked as a child during the summers. He would point me out books to read. Around the same time, there was Benjamin Quarles, who taught history and was then writing his first book on Frederick

Douglass. He was at Dillard. And I could see him working and working in the library, and I was expecting that this was going to be a bestseller. And then I realized you could work for years on a book but that didn't mean it would make you famous. Anyway Quarles for me became a model of what the work was like. It was silent work. It was lonely work. And you never knew what you were going to get out of it.

So, in coming back here and becoming involved with you all, I felt no matter what happened to me and my career as a writer, at the very least we could begin to provide a nurturing community. That took the form of a workshop and some of our other activities. It expanded into social activities, relationships, everything, because you can't write in social or cultural isolation. Writing goes with reading, the exchange of ideas, and the excitement that comes from being part of something that is bigger than you. That was one of the personal motivations. If I was going to be back here, I wanted to see something develop, so that when interested younger people came along, they wouldn't face the same isolation and alienation I felt, that drove me away.

My Umbra experience came from a search to find other black writers my age in New York. Most of my reading in college, in the Army, and even afterwards, most of it was European and white American writing. On one hand, I realized that it would be impossible for me to make a statement as a writer without relating to my reality as a black American. On the other hand, I didn't quite know how to put that together, and I certainly wasn't sure where I fit into the racial story. Because there was no system I could dip into automatically, I tried other things. Anything. In the Army, I took a correspondence course from *Writer's Digest*. You'd write off for lessons and send them back in the mail, fifteen dollars a lesson. In New York, after I was there for about a year, I came across an ad in the *New York Post* for a writer's class run by Lajos Egri. I went down to see him in his little office on 57th Street and signed up for his weekly course in creative writing. I was just trying to find a way.

Egri was around sixty years old, an immigrant from Hungary who had come over here in the twenties or thirties and done some dramatic writing. He worked with theaters and made some movies but nothing prominent. Then he wrote a book you can still find today called *The Art of Dramatic Writing*. It became a classic and a kind of textbook. He was giving this course; it was about twenty dollars a week. We would bring our lessons in prose or drama, but never poetry. The class would criticize with a strict rule, which I introduced into Umbra and later in our workshop. The rule was that after you read your work, you cannot argue or try to explain what you had written. Everyone else had their say first—you had to sit there and take it until they were done, and then and only then could you comment. That took much more discipline than we first thought because you always wanted to explain or disclaim—you know, "I'm not finished with this"—but Egri would disallow all of that. What was really interesting about his class, which turned out to be only twelve people or so, was that at least five or six of the people were black. The first black writers I met in New York, relative beginners like me, I met in Egri's class.

The blacks became friends. We would go out after class and talk. I became particularly close to Walter Myers, who was as serious as I thought I was. He was from New Jersey. He has now published a tremendous amount of excellent juvenile literature under the name of Walter Dean Myers. It was probably no accident that so many blacks were in Egri's class because one of the theaters he had been involved with was the old Lafayette in Harlem. He knew a lot of those people, knew the writers, and because he was Hungarian, his attitude toward blacks was distinctly not-American.

There were a couple of other things that came out of that experience that fascinated me. I had never met a Hungarian before, but with every Hungarian I've met since, I've been struck by the fact that they cannot speak English. There's no way that you can grow up in Hungary and speak English without an accent because the languages are so strikingly different. I wondered how in the world Egri wrote such a lucid book as *The Art of Dramatic Writing*. Finally, we found out the truth: he didn't write it. I mean he wrote it in Hungarian, and somebody translated it into English, rewrote it for him. This taught me something about the process of writing and being published. Here is a man who comes from Hungary, who can't speak English, and he ends up getting a reputation not only for being an expert, but for also being good at fixing plays, fixing cinema scripts. And even though he's generally considered an expert at what he does, he's really not wealthy. He's just eking out a living.

The other thing, which goes back to my childhood, was that I read black weeklies, newspapers. At that time in the forties, there were several very good papers: *Pittsburgh Courier*, *The Chicago Defender*, *Baltimore Afro-American*, Norfolk's *New Journal and Guide*, Oklahoma's *Black Dispatch*. My father subscribed to all these papers, including the *Atlanta Daily World*, which was the only black daily in the country. When I would pick up the mail for him at Dillard, I would get four or five papers. At that time white dailies did not cover what could be considered black news unless it was some sensational crime. Reading these papers opened me to what was going on in the world, and it was also my first reading of black writers. I mean, not just Hughes or Wright, but columnists, sports writers, political writers and commentators. So my sense of what writers wrote was not limited to the literary. It was also journalistic, on a high level; blacks could perform that role just like whites.

And then the world of black papers died; it went the way of the Negro Leagues. I think, however, what my reading of the papers imbued in me was a sense that you could be a very fine writer, with fundamental ties to the community, through journalism. Through this highly functional and important instrument, you could focus on the fundamental questions that affected you, your community, and the larger society.

I guess I was always looking for that. It just so happened that by the time I came of age and was ready to play a role in black journalism on that level—which I would have loved to do—the world died. It died because of television and because of the expansion of the white dailies into news that affected race, beginning with the civil rights movement. Nevertheless, I tried. The first job I had in New York was in Harlem with a black newspaper, *The New York Age*, a weekly which was fifty years old and had been founded by Thomas Fortune.

KYS: What was your position?

TD: I was a reporter, but the newspaper failed within one year after I started. I knew about the paper because when I came out of graduate school at Syracuse University I lived in New York for about six months. I read the *Age*. When I was at Fort Knox I wrote a letter to the editor, Al Duckett, to tell him I was coming to New York to visit, and I wanted to talk to him about a job. We had the interview and he promised me a job. Very soon after I started in May 1959 Al quit. Chuck Stone became the editor. While working at the *Age* I met Tom Feelings, who was just beginning his career as an artist; Calvin Hicks, who became very important in our subsequent organizational activities, such as "On Guard For Freedom," and to whom I was always very close; a Jamaican writer, Lancelot Evans, who was familiar with Black Nationalism and Garveyism;

a religion editor who had been there at least a hundred years and knew the history of all the churches up there; a society editor who knew Langston Hughes and knew how Harlem was organized; a city editor, Charlie Herndon, who had tough standards of manuscript propriety I had never experienced with any English teacher. I found this whole environment invigorating. Chuck in particular had a tremendous education at Eastern schools, plus he had a political sense that was advanced. He became one of the foremost black journalists of his time. I met Malcolm X on 125th street as his career as an important spokesman was beginning to take off.

At that time, Harlem was a vibrant community. Through contacts such as Calvin Hicks, I got into political activities that were Black Nationalist. I was a part of a group that produced a journal called *On Guard for Freedom*. It was really an early Black Nationalist artists' group: Max Roach, Abbey Lincoln, Archie Shepp, LeRoi Jones, Harold Cruse, Calvin Hicks, among others, and—well, that's a story in itself—several white women. We invited the Africanist, John Henrik Clarke, to speak to us. We met in Harlem, and we met on the Lower East Side.

All of these branching-out activities were a means of discovery for me, leading to the writing workshop that became Umbra. So in terms of what we were trying to do here in New Orleans—and you give me too much credit because we all contributed—I brought the philosophical belief that we could not develop a substantive literature without new ideas, and an openness to the wider world. You knew because you had been away in the service, and I knew, that New Orleans could be stultifyingly provincial. The more we could attack that provinciality through readings, through our own writings, through political ideas and contacts, the more we would have a chance to achieve something meaningful. I believe nothing much happens in a place anyway unless it is a crossroads of goods and ideas. We had to open New Orleans up. We knew

New Orleans had been open in that way for music. But in terms of literature, there had been no opening.

KYS: So what made you come back to New Orleans?

TD: Nothing. I had no desire whatsoever to come back to New Orleans. However, in 1965 there was a point when I was not working and was having a hard time—I was working part time at the NAACP Legal Defense Fund where I formerly had been working full time. I didn't know what I was going to do. At that point I was robbed. Everybody was robbed. The Lower East Side was becoming the center of drug street sales in New York City, maybe in America. People were coming from all over to buy heroin, particularly on Saturdays. People nodding and laid out on the street; Avenue C looked like a horror movie: *The Neighborhood of the Living Dead*.

There were about forty apartments in my building. I think everybody's apartment was broken into at one time or another. I lived on the first floor, and somebody just came in one day and took what I had—it wasn't much, a typewriter and a couple of other things, but I was hysterical.

I tried to do something which I don't advise anybody to ever do: go out on the street and tell people what happened, in the hopes of buying back my typewriter. This led me to two black guys who pulled a knife on me, marched me back to my apartment, and took whatever else they could find. Really, I thought they might kill me. I finally talked them out of the apartment, promising that I would get them more money. They had already taken whatever little money I had.

Well, we had just had an Umbra reading. On 2nd Avenue there was a big poster with all our names on it, including mine. One of the robbers looked at the poster and said, "Is that you?" I said, "Yeah, that's me, I'm a writer." That might have saved my life, simply because they realized I was known and if they did something to

new orleans griot: the tom dent reader

me somebody might really come after them. So we went through a surreal song and dance walking through the Lower East Side with them threatening me. Finally, when we reached 2nd Avenue, I just darted through some traffic to the other side, and then they ran. I was able to get away, but I was terrified. It seemed the entire area was disintegrating—in fact, the Lower East Side became worse as a drug area and still hasn't recovered... I didn't know what to do, but I knew I wanted to get out of there.

At that time my father was in New York for a meeting. I went down to his hotel and told him what happened. He said, "Maybe you better come home to New Orleans for a while." I spent a few days giving away everything I couldn't carry. I had a Puerto Rican friend who had a pistol, and he hung around as my "security." We were going to shoot these two guys if we found them—it sounds bizarre, I know.

Anyway, that's how I came back to New Orleans. I decided I would get a job here and just make a go of it, but it wasn't so easy. I wanted to work as a stringer for *Jet* or *Ebony*, but that didn't work out. At the same time, during those first few weeks, April of 1965, I discovered many things in this city I felt I might like. The racial climate was changing a little, not a lot. But it certainly wasn't the city I grew up in and left ten or twelve years earlier, only returning to visit my parents.

My most meaningful discovery was the Free Southern Theater [FST] troupe, which was rehearsing daily in the horribly mis-named Pentagon Building on London Avenue and Galvez Street. I met John O'Neal in New York in February 1965 when he came up for a fundraiser. One of the FST founders was Doris Derby, whom I had gone out with in New York. Doris Derby was an artist who in the early sixties became fascinated with the South, spending half her time in New York and the other half in Mississippi. In the course of her Southern sojourn, she met Andrew Young, and Andrew introduced me to Doris. He actually set up a blind date—he's never done anything before or since like that, I don't believe—he took us out to an Italian restaurant. At that time we were really poor so this dinner was a three or four dollar plate meal at a place with candles in Chianti bottles. It turned out that Doris lived virtually in Connecticut. Taking her home usually meant I arrived back on the Lower East Side at daybreak. So, although our relationship never went anywhere, the fact was that I knew Doris and had met O'Neal and I was somewhat familiar with the concept of the FST.

I fell in love with the FST people immediately. I was living in my parents' house on Dillard's campus where my father was the president. After all I had been through in New York, I was feeling useless and would have returned to New York if I could've gotten a job there. Meanwhile, I had to do something, so I went to the Pentagon Building every day. John and I became quick friends. I met Gilbert Moses, Denise Nichols, Roscoe Oman, and Bob Costley. After about three weeks I said, wait a minute, they're doing the kind of thing that's desperately needed and it can mesh with the experience I just left.

I didn't know a thing about the theater, though I had several friends in New York who were actors. In New Orleans I realized right away that the concept of liberation theater transcended ideas of "drama" or "theater" as we knew them—or at least it had that potential. Of course, the FST had virtually no money, so there was no question of my working there—members were making fifteen dollars a week, if that. But, at that point, I began seriously looking for a job in New Orleans. My entire circle of friends—other than those few people who were still around from when I was growing up— were FST members, or New Orleans Civil Rights activists, who constituted a small social set in themselves. When I left New Orleans to go to college, fifteen years earlier, no group like this had existed.

I think I saw very clearly that the presence of the FST could be a source of new cultural possibilities in New Orleans, and I had a sense of how to use theater as an instrument, despite the fact that I knew little about theater technique per se.

KYS: Your work outside of New Orleans gave you a perspective so that when you returned here you could see what needed to be done and what would work.

TD: No question about it. Also, I came to realize that for me New York had played itself out. It was time for me, at thirty, to come to terms with myself as a Black Southerner and New Orleanian, whatever that might mean, and try to understand it. There was a great poet, I forgot whom, who said, "You can really do no important work until you master your own terrain." Having left New Orleans at fifteen, I hardly knew it—yet, there was a tremendous culture here, there was a complexity here, there was this rich history of music. I didn't know it, but I knew I had to learn it, and that was something to strive for in terms of mastery of both writing and knowledge of my origins.

KYS: In one sense then you had the two elements necessary for anyone to do something significant here: you had the awareness that comes from being outside of New Orleans as well as all the contacts and experiences that go along with that, and you also had a very deep and developing appreciation for what was here.

TD: The key word is *developing*. When I left and even when I returned in 1965, I had a contempt for this place, a contempt heard from many people who have lived all their lives here. You know: we're backwards, we're slow, etc.

interviews   447

My whole view of the city, its potential and its complexities, changed. That goes for the South as a whole, not just New Orleans. My views changed primarily because of the opportunities afforded me by FST experiences. I don't find that you learn or produce abstractly or unrelatedly. There must be some combustion, moving...

KYS: Some social envelope.

TD: Some sense of moving forward, even if you don't accomplish everything you want to. It's like a boat moving, speeding through a lake, creating waves—something has to create waves. That's an image I associate with the sixties, and with our projects.

KYS: Thinking back when I first joined and some of the things and some of the people you introduced to me, for example Ralph Featherstone on that tractor up in West Point, Mississippi, digging a hole in the ground, which became a pond for the catfish farming co-op. I remember going to Danny Barker's house and being introduced to Danny Barker. So while you were developing this new appreciation for the city that led you to reevaluate your thoughts and feelings, you also transmitted this to many of us who otherwise would not have gotten it at that early age, and would not have seen the value of digging into the city.

TD: For material to write about.

KYS: Right. And at the same time you also turned our eyes outside of New Orleans so that we didn't become insular in our self-development.

TD: That was based on my experiences with the Umbra workshop. We didn't know it at the time because we were all just beginning, but it was a very unusual collaboration of writers: Ishamel Reed, Calvin Hernton, David Henderson, Oliver Pritcher, writers of vastly different styles. I got used to the idea that you could have a very wide range of disagreement, discussion and even argumentation; that such fermentation or agitation is in harmony with creativity. So many people were afraid of that, but if you were afraid you just had to leave.

KYS: That broad style was one of the things that was different about BLKARTSOUTH.

TD: Not only in terms of ideas but also in terms of lifestyles. You just cannot tell people what kind of lifestyle they ought to have or go around trying to be a model. My belief on that stemmed from being exposed to the Lower East Side of New York. It was an area of Eastern European immigrants, strong ethnic constituencies, and later a heavy influx of Puerto Ricans, and some blacks. Everybody was there. You could walk down the street listening to the voices around you and never know you were in America. This gave me a heightened appreciation for the value of diversity. I knew that to come back here and try to work in an atmosphere of conformity would kill us. Also, in terms of breaking out of the provinciality of New Orleans, it was of immense value for us to relate to struggles of people in movements for liberation of oppressed peoples, whoever they were.

For example, I saw Mississippi as being very different from us, and I didn't really know Mississippi until our FST tours, and later, when I taught in West Point. The New Orleans black community was widely divergent, ranging from "passing" Creoles at one extreme to people directly from West Africa at the other. In Mississippi were forged into a unity through a common culture, background, and history of deprivation. We could learn a lot from their unity and sacrifice, I thought.

KYS: That's the point I'm making: you knew, on the one hand, that we had to know more about New Orleans than just growing up and passing through here would allow us to get. On the other hand, we had to know about more than New Orleans at the same time.

TD: Let's go into "knowing more about New Orleans". I felt that was really kind of a battle within the workshop, and, for a while, I was battling you.

The Umbra experience preceded the canonization of Black Nationalism politically—I mean, the formalization of theories of what is Blackness which characterized the Black Arts Movement. I never liked the rigidity that came from *Black World* and from Hoyt Fuller's friend, Addison Gayle, and the Black Aesthetic Movement. For example, knowing personally and being very familiar with the work of LeRoi Jones, who became Baraka, I felt he was a beautiful writer of his experience, but his experience wasn't mine. For one thing, he wasn't from the South, whatever that means, but it is a different feeling from what you get in Newark. Or New York. By the late sixties, I had become convinced that if we became mere adjuncts of a national canonization of writing in Baraka's style or Don L. Lee's style, we could only go but so far because we were really imitating. There was something right here, and it was Black. We had to use that. It was ours.

KYS: I think the music was so strong that there was no way around it, and if we did nothing else, we used music to a much higher degree in our work than other people did. We didn't know it at the time.

TD: We were ahead of our time because the national perception was that the music had left New Orleans. But we could go out on the weekends, every weekend, and hear brilliant music. I said to myself, "Wait a minute, there's a contradiction. If all the music is in New York, what are we listening to?" Not only that, our suspicions that there was a tremendous musical survivalist strength here was strengthened when friends visited us from New York or wherever, and we took them out. They would say, "This is amazing." So, when the new generation of musicians appeared who went out and made it in New York, it was a proof of what we had already seen. There was a power in the music as it relates to community and ritual function that doesn't exist in New York, but nobody here was talking about it. At that time, white New Orleans critics were not especially interested in our music, and they gave it no play.

KYS: On another front, as I remember it, there was that fateful union of the drama workshop and the writing workshop which significantly sped up our development.

TD: Yes, born of necessity and one of the best accidents that ever happened. 1967 was a low point in the theater's history. Bob Costley was one of those people who came here to join the 1965 company and decided to stay. He was a native of Buffalo. Bob, or "Big Daddy" as we called him, was working as news director at radio station WYLD in 1967. I was commuting to teach in Mississippi. What little season we had in the summer of 1967 was over with, and in the fall we decided to try to get some workshops going. Actually, that was our second set of community workshops. We began the first ones in the summer of 1966 before you came out of the army. In 1967, as I remember it, there was nobody attending the workshops except you and maybe one or two others. You would come to Big Daddy's workshop and come to my writing workshop, and finally we decided since Val, a.k.a. Kalamu ya Salaam, is coming to both workshops along with just a few others, why not combine the two. You were just beginning to write little sketches. They weren't really plays yet, one-act sketches.

What Big Daddy did was have all of us present actually walk through your scripts, instead of just reading them as a piece of literature. The writer could see what was happening. This really started me writing plays, and several others too. From that point, the workshop grew. A lot of the recruits to us were younger people you knew, and then people from Lord knows where found their way to us.

KYS: Part of that was because we began to need actors to do the scripts—I mean more people than we had in the workshop. But it also had to do with the fact that we had begun to dramatize the poetry in a very free and innovative way.

TD: Well, first of all, we began to get a lot of poetry. Hardly anyone was writing stories. So we tried to figure out how to use the poems.

KYS: Part of that had do with the fact that most of these writers were not coming out of college, and didn't have a writing background. They just had these emotions and these ideas which they wanted to express.

TD: One of the big problems was even the colleges weren't offering courses in creative writing or black literature. Before people can write effectively they have to have some context for what they're doing. That's why we were always using Wright, Ellison, the new poetry, the new movements in jazz as reference points. You know, it's ignorance if you have an idea for a poem and you think you're the only person to ever think of that.

KYS: The other thing was that whatever it was that we had and to whatever degree that it worked, its biggest success was in inspiring people throughout the Deep South to do their thing where they were. I remember going to Houston and that whole development there.

TD: As the workshops developed, we came up with some pretty good material, a lot of poetry and a few short plays. Gilbert Moses, Denise Nicholas, Roscoe Orman, the original core group, had all returned to New York to pursue their careers. John O'Neal was doing alternate military service in New York. The theater had run out of funding. This was the fall of 1967. The workshops were the only thing we had going. So we began to stage readings of our best poems in the city, and very soon after that I believe Big Daddy directed one of your new plays. This is how some of the more serious people in the workshops began performing. Since it was the only performing unit we had, we called it the Free Southern Theater, though it was composed entirely differently than the original FST troup. Almost all of the original FST members were not from the South. By 1965 we began receiving out-of-town invitations. We were invited to quite a few towns in Mississippi, and I believe two or three towns in Texas. In Houston we were hosted by a post-Movement community organization called HOPE.

KYS: And there was the Southern Christian Leadership Conference's* annual convention in Charleston.

TD: Thanks to Andy Young. That was a great experience. We performed for their "cultural night" at the Charleston Municipal

----

*   One of the major civil rights organizations in the South.

Auditorium. But we stood out like a sore thumb because our work was more militant and realistic than that audience was accustomed to. Andy might have gotten a little flak over inviting us. As I remember it, generally when we performed in those situations, the older, settled, respectable blacks who thought they were coming to a pleasant "cultural evening" were shocked and turned off—but the younger people were turned on and wanted to hang out with us afterwards.

At the time some of the things we were doing were just out, but it was also original in the sense that each of us felt free enough to do something in our own way without having to hew to any one particular stylistic or ideological line. I remember when we would do the "hair pieces." We had three or four different hair poems. The theme was the hair, but we did it all in different ways. I guess subconsciously this came from growing up here in New Orleans and seeing the folk culture. With Mardi Gras Indians, for example, everyone had their own distinctive suit, and you even had two very different styles of making suits. This culture taught us to value individuality, and at the same time there was a collective spirit about it. You had the collectivity without the rigid uniformity.

KYS: Some of those places began doing things after we left.

TD: In Houston that was the case. I guess they said, "If they can do it, why can't we?" They started a group like ours: Sudan Arts Southwest. Then there was a more structured group, the Urban Theater directed by Barbara Marshall. That was a time of high aspirations for black independent cultural efforts, right around 1970. I don't know if we'll ever see that again.

KYS: What do you mean by that?

TD: Well, almost everything up to then had been done in cooperation with or with the strong support of whites, particularly in terms of money. I'm saying "white," but I mean the gamut of formal structures: community arts centers, educational institutions; often whites were crucial participants behind the scenes in those organizations. Then we tried to organize from a black community base, solely. Though a lot of people rejected our independent efforts and still do, we felt this was needed, not only in terms of dramatic presentation, but as an example of what blacks in theater could do.

The point was brought home to me by Reverend Milton Upton, who was a key board member of the Free Southern Theater. One day I might have said something critical about "Big Daddy" Costley. Milton replied, "Well, you don't understand. Big Daddy is more than an actor in a play. Many people in our community have never see a black male on the stage who represents strength in his presence and voice. He opens up a whole new world for them."

We became very aware of that sort of thing. We wanted our cultural activities to be in the black community. Those were conscious decisions, not accidents. For instance, we decided to put our theater in the Desire Project Area, what was considered a very bad area, and interact with people and organizations out there. Today that wouldn't be considered "smart," but we wanted to positively interact with the black community. Our critics said we were too militant, too political, anti-white. We said we were only trying to accentuate black cultural strengths, and there's no such thing as non-political literature and theater, at least not for us. Those blacks who wanted to have "careers" ducked, and started looking for white folks to line up behind.

Then the funding agencies began to pull out the money, not just from us but from every independent black cultural group in the country that didn't have whites intricately involved with it, if it was the least bit political. Thus all those efforts we remember as trying to bring new life in the late sixties and early seventies—small community theaters, small black bookstores, poetry readings, music, non-academic lectures—fell into decline and now they are about dead. In their place we have endless talk and criticisms of technique.

KYS: Talk a bit about the Southern Black Cultural Alliance[SBCA] because this was an attempt to go one step beyond what we could do on our own.

TD: It was...

KYS: Actually, it was a natural next step but the climate in the country was going the other way.

TD: Yes. For me personally, SBCA came out of a great dissatisfaction with the situation in the early seventies because I knew what they were doing in New York, and I knew what we were doing was about on the same level, but we just didn't have any money. I knew that some of the productions of the Free Southern Theater were better than what was being done in New York. But the Black cultural media establishment, to the extent that it existed, particularly *Negro Digest/Black World*, was as based in northern cities, especially New York, in their appraisals as the White newspapers and critical journals were. This came as a shock to me at first.

No matter how many good short stories or poems we might publish in our literary magazine *Nkombo*, or might be published in other small, community literary magazines, that didn't mean as much as one book published by McMillian, which the Black journals reviewed, and then those writers became known. As far as theater was concerned, anything New Lafayette or NEC, Negro

Ensemble Company, did received an attention which dwarfed anything we did. That was just a reality, without taking anything on the value of their work.

I also felt that we in the South, no matter how faithful we were to our community mission or how important the work we were doing was, needed to do something to more aggressively present ourselves, or we would never get any recognition. Not that we wanted to be famous, but we had to have some recognition if we were going to survive in terms of funding, or whatever rewards you need to keep going. Otherwise we would very soon be back to the situation where a young actor or writer in New Orleans did not feel they had arrived until they left here.

The idea of trying to have a regional association of the Southern groups which sprung up between '69 and '72 was based on a need for a substantive exchange of ideas, which could give us a better definition and assessment of what we were doing, firstly, but also on the hope that we could expose our work to a broader audience. I hoped through sponsoring a major festival, we could lure down Hoyt Fuller, or somebody who would say "this work is in the game and worthy of attention." But we never reached that point.

KYS: We did get some recognition. Remember that Hoyt began to include us and the South in his annual theater roundup issue.

TD: Yes, but we were writing the plays, organizing the tours, and then writing the criticism. The idea was to get him down here or somebody other than us to assess what we were doing.

KYS: When I look back over some of the *Nkombo*s, I end up going back to my jazz paradigm. We did a number of regional issues. We did a theater issue that had plays from all over the South in it. The poetry came from Florida, Birmingham, Jackson, Houston, wherever we could find folk. It was almost as if we knew that we couldn't survive isolated but at the same time we didn't want to be *not Southern.*

TD: I may have made a mistake, though. We had a policy that we would reserve the magazine pretty much for our writers and other writers from the South. At one point Ishmael Reed asked if he could submit a piece, and I told him that the magazine was not for him. The other way to have done it would have been to use some national writers, but when you do that, there's always the chance you choke off beginning writers. The tendency is to publish more national writers and less developing writers.

This very conflict came up a few years later when Charles Rowell, Jerry Ward and I talked about the concept of *Callaloo.* My vision of it was that it would be an extension of *Nkombo,* and that we would develop writers. I think Jerry to some extent agreed with me. But Charles wanted to develop a national, high quality journal with a heavy emphasis on scholarly works, which he did.

But you know, Umbra—which was dedicated to publishing new, unpublished writers—eventually produced over forty books. I believed if you were going to build writers, you had to provide a publishing vehicle. The objective was not to build the magazine to a profile that would become nationally renowned, but to build writers. Of course, as the writers developed, if you had the means to keep the magazine going, then the magazine might take on more importance. We also encouraged everybody to publish in other journals, but *Nkombo* was reserved for our Southern focus.

Many of the people who started off *Nkombo* stopped writing. Others like yourself kept writing.

KYS: One important aspect of the whole Southern thing is that we were more concerned about the people than about any abstract ideal of literature. I can remember us having a discussion as editors and saying that everybody who participated in the workshop would have at least one piece in the book. Although we wanted to have quality pieces, we also wanted to make sure that everybody participated.

TD: That was an important value for us, which we felt encouraged people to write. If they knew they were going to get published, they would write. To this day, there's not much writing being done by young people in the South because they have no vehicles. Not even black newspapers. They're not going to go get published. Who wants to submit a poem fifty times to the academic literary journals before you are able to publish one piece? You cannot develop literature like that.

We may have been romantic about what could happen. I think in my mind, I felt we were on a mission to see theater, and to some extent literature and journalism, develop in New Orleans, never equal to, but like our music. I say "never equal to" because music here is so advanced, hyper-developed to the extent that it produces geniuses. It's like comparing gardens. You have this one garden with a lot of weeds and just a few flowers, which is literature. And you have this extensive, varied and rich garden of music. I felt we were trying to find a way to make theater work so that it would be considered useful to the black community, in the way we use our music.

Those ideas were behind the concept I tried to use in *Ritual Murder*. Your plays also. They were designed to impact the audience in a way that would create questions and suggest a sense of direction. They certainly were not designed for commercial audiences.

KYS: That to me suggests an analysis. It's not simply that "we failed, or our vision was lacking." Rather it's that we were actually swimming against the tide. At the time, we felt that this was the way it all should be going, not realizing that many of the people on a national level we thought of as role models were actually playing the game of the individual artist. They were actually aiming to go through the steps of making a name from themselves. It's much clearer now that the two major avenues were the academic, scholarly pursuit and the commercial route.

You're right about much of what we were doing. We didn't care whether it was commercial or not; we did care whether it reached the intended audience of black people in our community. When you are not writing to impress critics but rather to reach a specific audience that you know, the work comes out different.

Looking back, all these things are clear, but at the time we were just doing what we thought was right and figured that other people were doing the same.

TD: Eventually I became very depressed though. I felt we were swimming so much against the tide we couldn't get the message to those for whom we thought it was intended, which is why I gave up the workshop. I felt if what we were doing was not commercial in the sense that it was not in the bookstores, not on TV, and not in *The New York Times*, younger people would look at it and say, "if it's so great why isn't it getting a lot of play." By 1980, the definition of success was back to where it was before the sixties. We were considered antiquated, or I was.

KYS: The eighties were a rough time for all of us.

TD: Yes. I felt that I couldn't get anybody to listen to me anymore or take seriously what I was saying about literature or creativity. The models became Toni Morrison, Alice Walker, Alex Haley. I didn't have any problem with that. It was just very difficult to tell young people that you have to go through certain steps to get to where those established writers are, if that's where you want to go. For one thing, you can begin by mastering stories of your people and their struggles. And that doesn't come easy.

I think now that I was too romantic. I have come to believe that no matter what you are doing and what it means, there is contempt for it unless people can see in it what is defined by others as success.

KYS: One of my views is that there is an element of New Orleans that provides an alternative vision for that. I always use the example of these brass bands. There are people who don't own even one record by a brass band, but if a brass band passes outside they will go out and dance. They will go to the clubs at night and support it.

TD: Oh, I agree. I didn't have any doubt about that. I never questioned the value of my own work because there were people who knew what it was. I've been richly rewarded on that level. I'm talking about something else. Look at the example of the music. We knew fifteen years ago that what Ellis Marsalis was doing was valid. We knew when Danny Barker got the kids interested in traditional brass bands that it was valid. We knew that what Kidd Jordan was doing with his musical experiments was valid. But the payoff in terms of the popular image of success did not come until Wynton made it. And now because of the New York success of his sons and others, there is some attention being given to Ellis.

I've come to accept this reality, but it's not that it doesn't depress me. Ellis could still be here doing what he is doing, and it would be just as valid, and just as important, but until Wynton happens— which had to do with Wynton but also with the times and the need for a new figure in jazz—until then, Ellis was ignored.

KYS: Part of what we're dealing with is the choice between finding commercial validation for an existing identity or finding the root of that identity outside of the mainstream. You're talking about the depressing fact that in order for there to be mass acceptance, what we do has to be validated through the New York—

TD: Through the New York machine, which doesn't really validate it—it just puts a stamp of "success" on it. That's just one vision of success. I have a problem with it, but I recognize it as a reality.

There's another thing that I feel is there. As writers, to the extent that we give expression to the valid aspirations and experiences of our people, there will eventually be a readership, but it may not be in New York, it may not be in America, and it may not be until long after we are dead. As African and Caribbean literature and scholarship becomes a much more active force in the next century, there will probably be a reassessment of what African-American writers have done and are doing.

I was listening to Toni Morrison one time, and she said something about the publishing industry that I've never forgotten. She said that eighty percent of the books sold in the United States were sold within a three hundred mile radius of New York City. As far as black readership is concerned, our readership means nothing to the New York Publishers. There are not enough blacks buying books to mean anything to any major publisher in New York City. The only time it may have ever happened was during the peak of the Black Studies programs when schools ordered so many copies of *Invisible Man* or *Souls of Black Folk*, so those books were republished.

This means almost any book by a black writer is evaluated in terms of salability, by how many books will it sell to whites. And this necessarily impacts, one way or another, the structure and substance of what we write as black writers.

KYS: The same thing is happening with rap. The majority of the people who *buy* rap recordings are white.

TD: Okay. But I was going to say, eventually economic and critical evaluations of Afro-American literature will be impacted by the emergence of Africa and the so-called Third World from colonialism. They'll develop a greater control over their own cultures and self-images. What we're witnessing now, as I see it, is a slow shift, or maybe drift is a better term, away from the dominance of the "first world," which overwhelmingly controls how Africans and other peoples of the world are depicted through absolute control of media, including what is sold in bookstores.

African and disaporan, particularly Caribbean, literature is becoming more assertive. And hopefully, as literacy develops, new standards of image and criticism will emerge, with a healthier and more balanced respect for the diversity and cultural resources of our peoples. In fact, this is beginning to happen now in the poetry and criticism of, for example, Kamau Brathwaite, who stands perfectly positioned at the center of the African diaspora experience. In fact, we can anticipate that a hundred years from now, the most important creative and critical diasporan ideas will be coming from the Caribbean. This can already be detected, I think. Caribbean music is influencing African music, which in turn is beginning to impact Afro-American musics. In terms of musical shifts, the basic innovations revolve around the influence and use of percussion.

KYS: Yes, but diasporic literature has not yet come to power, in terms of diaspora writers controlling the media and presenting their own image without having to appeal to white audiences. I can remember that one issue of *Nkombo* where we talked about *not being about explaining our literature to white folks!*

TD: But so much of our literature does exactly that. You could read almost all of black literature, from slave narratives right up to contemporary works, in these terms—ways of explaining who we are to white readers. Also, to the extent whites can hook into a piece of literature and identify with it, that has a large impact on readership and book buyership.

The other thing to think about is that because of the low level of literacy even in the western worlds and with the advances of technology, two or three hundred years from now there might not be many readers at all. Most material written in terms of stories or drama may eventually become fodder for television, cinema, recordings, or some new form of technical dissemination. Some books are being recorded now. But that doesn't mean that it's not important to write. Somebody has to write the material for these projects.

KYS: This explains, to a large degree, what I consider to be the failure in much of the current wave of black cinema, which is not rooted in a vision of blackness that progresses beyond voyeurism.

TD: And sensationalism. Yes, I agree. On the National Geographic brass bands film you and I worked on, directed by, we decided that the commentators on the music, as well as the profiled musicians themselves, would be black. It's very subtle, but it provides a different feel to have a Danny Barker or a Michael White comment on the music. They come from the culture that we were portraying, and they know it. But opportunities like the brass band film have been rare. For a while there, I felt quite a bit of despair over the fact there was little understanding of what we were trying to do.

KYS: But you know, as I travel around, it is amazing. I continue to run into people who relate to me from that era. I was in Los

Angeles doing a poetry performance, and a young lady came up and had a copy of one of my first books. Just recently I was in Houston, and my friend's brother who teaches drama in the Houston school system said to me, "I remember you as Val Ferdinand from the Free Southern Theater. I went to school at Woodson, and y'all came over and performed." And so forth and so on. I think that the impact of what we had and have is valid for the audience that we reach. It may never be popular in this time period, but the strength of it is undeniable.

TD: Yeah. Okay. When that happens it makes me feel good, too. But you can't rest on that. In this work, you just keep struggling along, searching for new connections and discoveries. Unfortunately, there's no time to rest and be satisfied with what you did yesterday.

AFTERWORD: tom dent and imperatives of history

Thomas Covington Dent
(March 20, 1932-June 6, 1998)

In the twenty-first century, it seems appropriate to think of traces of having been in this world as "visible histories" and "invisible" ones. If the idea of an imperative has meaning as both a command and a plea, it is reasonable to propose that narratives we call history involve ideas about what is seen and unseen. Those stories have sounds, recorded with the help of technology; they also possess sounds that are archived and heard only in the privacy of memory. People who lived meaningful lives remind us of such complexities. If like, Thomas Covington Dent (Tom Dent, as he preferred to be known), those people only provide fragmented autobiographies, the imperatives of their life histories demand special research and remembering. In short, making sense of their lives and works compels us to deal with imperatives.

When we read published histories, we expect story. We want plots and interpretation of verifiable facts. But we ought not be overmuch surprised if the truth is improved and made dramatic by incorporation of fiction. These are some conventions of visible history or written stories of duration. On the other hand, the invisible histories that deepen our understanding of people who are at once creators of history and also its objects are more fascinating. Those valuable versions of history lose some (but not all) of their invisibility in forms of oral histories. You can't understand why Tom Dent is a New Orleans icon unless you can deal with the imperatives of history.

During twenty-four years of friendship with Dent, I came to know a few things about what he valued in life. I truly appreciated the delight he took in linking his friends in conversations that constituted the stuff of culture and history. Unlike writers and scholars who value distance, postures of being remote or downright obtuse, Dent valued what could be derived from immediacy, personal contact, or self-consciousness in confronting difficult changes in cultures and societies.

Of his youth, Dent wrote in *Southern Journey*: "For me and others like me, those dream roads—fueled by books, movies, and legends—led to a nonracial world, where we would find solace from the exclusively black world we were confined to, where the color of our skin, our racial heritage did not matter. But then, that was truly a dream world—a world, I have come to believe, that does not exist."

Those racialized dreams, which matured into critical perspectives, inform his legacy of work in poetry, teaching and active participation in organizations and movements, drama, journalism, and nonfiction writing. Embracing his legacy makes iconoclasm a tool for freeing oneself from traps and delusions.

Like love and life, history is strange and mysterious. At least, the operational definition I use of history is mysterious and strange. History is a narrative arrangement of chronology, the serial ordering of time and duration, designed to find reason and make sense of the actuality we inhabit. We create grids and configurations to assure ourselves that reality exists. Our sense of what is real is determined as well as compromised, in part, by the languages and words we use. History consists of present stories of what we deem to be past as we anticipate the probability of a future. This storytelling is necessary for documenting change as well as for making change.

I can even at this moment hear Tom Dent laughing at my academic definition of how people deal with what in the domain of physics is called entanglement. Dent's early poem "Love," included in the 1964 anthology *New Negro Poets: USA*, edited by Langston Hughes, is a stark, indirect description of historical process:

the gold of heaven
the blue of hell
the sun of day
the tomb of night—
the golden sun
anchoring my
spinning heart
while a blue tomb
lurks icily in
the dark.

The metaphors of lines 1-4 are traditional, focused on oppositions that are complements, while lines 5-10 add motion to stasis in the verbals—*anchoring, spinning, lurks*. The verbs are in the present tense and increase attentiveness to finitude and possible recurrence. In another early poem, "Time Is A Motor," Dent was specific about how time can lock us into stereotypes and effect our dehumanization: "Time is a motor, you know / that never unwinds / never unwinds / and we who worship Time / never unwind...until we become automatic...like a motor" (*Blue Lights*).

Dent did not romanticize history. He exploited its brutal and absurd potentials. Read through the prism of history, Dent's poems in *Magnolia Street* (1976) and *Blue Lights and River Songs* (1982) are lucid constructs which associate people, time, place or geography, and actions in plain language that does not invite obtuse, trash-talking criticism. "Just as rivers determine the shape of land masses (and to a lesser degree the configurations of history)," I wrote in my introduction for *Blue Lights*, "Dent's poet practice gives palpable shape to history, musical response, heroic lives. That is to say, his accessible lyrics and narratives organize felt-through experiences in precise language. It is never his intention to be obscure. The complexity of his work is not on the surface. It exists in the poetic structures of Pan-African vision and the African-American humanistic tradition. It exists, indeed, in our thoughtful engagements of each poem."

From his early articles in *The Maroon Tiger* in the 1950s, which I have commented on in "The Art of Tom Dent: Notes on Early Evidence," to his major achievement in *Southern Journey: A Return to the Civil Rights Movement* (1997), Dent's playful use of history was an analytic weapon. Dent was very much in the black tradition, a tradition that is accorded little respect now. Step by painstaking step, he used language to unify his artistic and political concerns, to certify his active participation in organizations and movements, and to influence thinking about wise or foolish choices in the unfolding of history and change.

By birth, innate intelligence, and educational advantage, Dent was a legitimate member of what W. E. B. DuBois in "The Talented Tenth," published in *The Negro Problem*, was echoing from Henry Lyman Morehouse's article of the same title in the April 1896 issue of *Independence* magazine: Tom belonged to a class that bordered on being a caste. It is myopic to believe that Dent renounced or rejected his elitist heritage in some dramatic, pseudo-revolutionary gesture of identification with the so-called disadvantaged black American. He understood cultural work and history far too well to so cheapen himself. He used his privileges to achieve ends his heritage often misunderstood, disdained, or dismissed. He understood writing, especially writing grounded in a sense of history, to be the articulation of human obligation and responsibility. Or, as he wrote in his editorial for *Nkombo*, vol. 2, no. 3 (1969): "Now we have some beautiful blk people who have come together here to blast away all that deadness & ennui and broaden their individual forces into a concerted, creative effort. I say blast because to do something where little or nothing has been done takes an explosion, and no one cat no matter how brilliant can do it. I say blast because we have tried to make possible these offerings [the contents of the magazine] without the hang-ups of ego, slipping under all the depressing shit of the 'literary' world and even giving a hip, then quick dash around the stone monuments of blk ideological schools to get to another place. It's all amazing & beautiful to me that this should happen here [New Orleans], because these are the people, each of them in their own way, who would have been long gone, or if not gone longing to go, and who would have died on the muscatel vine, consuming their own genius in frustration, producing nothing. If this is what all the stupid little copper pennies we have hustled for FST have come to, and even if we never send another company to Mississippi hell I'm happy because if it hadn't come to this sometime it wouldn't have been worth those five years we've been here anyway."

These are the words of a writer who knew history and change in quite intimate ways, who wanted to share his vision. These are the words of a writer whose insights can still benefit people in the twenty-first century who are having a deadly love affair with the fantasy of the post-racial, and who may not take to heart what Esther Phillips was singing in "Disposable Society" and

"The Performance is Over," what Curtis Mayfield was preaching in "Underground," what Roberta Flack was truth-telling in "Compared to What?" In the final pages of *The Free Southern Theater by the Free Southern Theater* (1969), Dent was uncanny and historically accurate. People do not need culture delivered in acts of benevolence that ignore the conditions of their community location. Blacks already have, according to Dent, "the richest, most viable, most complex and rewarding culture in this potpourri of America. The battle is not one of bringing culture to black people, but of us learning to value, and affirm, the culture we already have—and, as far as the performing company is concerned, to adapt that culture, that strength, to the stage.

"What are these cultural strengths?" Dent continued, "They are those aspects and institutions of black culture which have not been totally absorbed by mass white American culture: our church, our music, our dance, our communal forms of protest against racial injustice. Otis Redding, James Brown, the black Baptist Church, the Movement demonstrations, are theater. We don't call them theater, but they are."

And finally, as if he were speaking history and change to fragmented communities of the present century, Dent wrote: "To bring Broadway, off-Broadway, even radical white theater as it exists today in America, to the black community is most irrelevant. It is a statement of negation, if taken too seriously. It means, it is saying to this community, which already has its own thing, refined past the point where whites in American can even understand its subtleties, it is saying, "What you have ain't shit. If you want to be 'cultured' you got to dig Godot." Well, I say goodbye Godot, we'll stick with Otis. We'll expand and develop from that. And the hell with what the white critics say or expect. It's as simple as that."

But Dent was fully aware that nothing is simple. People live complex lives. Duration or history conceived as a process of

enduring has innate demands. We must make life-sustaining gestures each day in the face of thousands of rituals, including rituals
that belong to the phenomenon of benign genocide in the United
States. Dent made that remarkably clear in his widely known and
most frequently performed play *Ritual Murder*.

Dent's one-act *Ritual Murder* (1967), first performed in 1976, is
a classic of Black South drama. Dent minimized plot and depended on the Narrator's investigation and the individual testimonials
of type-cast characters (the wife, the public school teacher, the
boss, the anti-poverty program administrator, the mother and
father, the chief of police, a black psychiatrist, the victim and
the murderer) to sketch a communal story. His verbal economy
is effective. The only action is focused speech. Spectators can experience the play as an investigative tool, a device for analyzing
a familiar event in modern life: African American men killing
African American men. *Ritual Murder* figuratively incorporates
its audience. It provokes them to speak at the end of the performance. Even spectators who refuse to speak become characters in
a theatrical ritual. Ultimately, *Ritual Murder* is metadrama, i.e., a
play that explains how a play may have a socially engaged purpose.

It is judicious that Dent remixed of some elements of tragedy as
described in Aristotle's *Poetics* with some of the dark, biting humor
Bertolt Brecht used in writing the libretto for *The Threepenny Opera*
(1928), for which Kurt Weill wrote the atonal music. The aesthetic
effect of *Ritual Murder* is cool and unsettling. It does not provoke
fear and pity; its performance does not lead spectators to have any
feeling of catharsis, of being purged and cleansed. On the contrary,
because one witnesses the collection of opinions about the crime
rather than lurid details about Joe Brown's knifing his friend James
Roberts on a Saturday night, one feels moved to have compassionate
disinterest. One experiences the frustration of the need to clarify a
recurring social problem that defies resolution.

If the play is performed as Dent wrote it, music is crucial in governing the actors' timing of delivery and in manipulating the spectators' moods. The play opens with the black-inflected sounds of
George Gershwin's "Summertime," followed midway by Gil Evans'
"Barbara Song" (from the album *The Individualism of Gil Evans*,
Verve Jazz Master 23) The poignant exchange between the living
Joe Brown and the dead James Roberts begins with a repetition
of "Summertime," followed by Otis Redding's "Satisfaction" (from
the album *Otis Redding Live*), reaches an apex with James Roberts'
making a reference to "Groovin'" by Booker T. and the M.G.s, and
ends with a return to a very funky "Summertime." The odd item
is "The Barbara Song," but some quick research turns oddity into a
recognition of how cleverly Dent buried a musical clue in the text
of his play. "Barbara" isn't a woman's name; it is a failure to translate
the German word *Barbar* (barbarian) into English. Gil Evans's com-
position is derived from one of the songs in a German translation
of John Gay's *The Beggar's Opera*, the source for *The Threepenny
Opera*. Given Dent's profound knowledge about music, it is not un-
reasonable to think he deliberately used Evans' music to show how
beautiful jazz may be associated with negative aspects of American
urban life and to signify on Weill's distortion of American jazz.

Even if this idea is sheer fantasy or some contemporary version
of what Richard Iton argued is a property of blackness, the fact
remains that Dent made excellent selections of music to reinforce
the thematics of *Ritual Murder*.

Similar thematics color the totality of Dent's life and writings.
Dent engaged the imperatives of history in a fashion that illumi-
nates Iton's convoluted suggestion that "analyses of black politics,
and by extension the 'generic' political, require that the exhaustion with politics itself that structures so much of contemporary
discourse not delimit our own investigations of the ways certain
things are kept together and others kept apart, and the capacity of

the substances and processes associated with the cultural realm to deepen our understanding of those operations" (290).

Yes, Tom Dent was a major thinker and writer, a man who still bids us to do battle with the complexity of what is simple. It is as simple as that when the past speaks invisible histories to a present and a future in New Orleans. Imperatives of history are unpredictable. And Dent knew it.

JERRY W. WARD, JR

THOMAS C. DENT:
a preliminary
bibliography

Compiled by Jerry W. Ward, Jr.

Thomas Covington Dent, or Tom Dent as he prefers, is a poet, oral historian, essayist, fiction writer, playwright, and critic. He is best known for his involvement with Umbra Poets' Workshop (1962-65), his work with the Free Southern Theater, and as a mentor to many younger writers, performers, and activists who have been inspired by his steadfast, imaginative probing of African-American culture. To understand the literary and cultural history of the contemporary Black South, one must give attention to his significant work.

This bibliography is designed as a guide for those wishing to discover more about Dent's contributions to African-American literature and thought. Arranged chronologically, the bibliography is divided into nine sections. Section I lists Dent's books; Section II includes his poems published in periodicals and anthologies; Section III identifies his short stories, and Section IV, his published and unpublished plays; Section V includes all articles and essays published up to May 1988; Section VI lists his reviews; Section VII consists of works Dent edited; Section VIII lists introductions and miscellaneous pieces; Section IX provides citations for co-authored works.

I wish to thank Tom Dent for his generous help during the several years this bibliography has been in progress.

I. BOOKS

Magnolia Street. New Orleans: Privately Printed, 1976.

Magnolia Street. 2nd ed. North Bergen, NJ: Book Mark Press, 1988.
Blue Lights and River Songs. Detroit: Lotus Press, 1982.

II. POETRY IN PERIODICALS AND ANTHOLOGIES

"Nightdreams (Black)"
"Ode to Miles Davis"
Umbra 1.1 (1963): 7-9, 23-24.

"Love"
"Come Visit My Garden"
New Negro Poets: USA. Ed. Langston Hughes. Bloomington: Indiana University Press, 1964. 71, 80.

"Die Zeit ist ein Motor"
"Bitterer Neger"
Schwarzer Orepheus. Ed. Janheinz Jahn. Munich: Carl Hanser Verlag, 1964. 274, 275.

"Come Visit My Garden"
Introduction to Black Literature in America from 1746 to the Present. Ed. Lindsay Patterson. New York: Publishers Co., 1968. 274.

"The Trial of Rap Brown"
Nkombo 2.1 (1969): 16.

"American Skyarama"
"Natural Haircuts"
"Nigger Teachers"
"For the Southern University in New Orleans Students Arrested Attempting to Raise the Blk Flag of Liberation"
Nkombo 2.2 (1969): 30, 40, 43, 46.

"To Gil Moses:"
"For Walter Washington:"
"Ray Charles at Mississippi State"
Nkombo 2.3 (1969): 37, 41, 46.
"Zulu Parade"
"A Message for Langston"
Nkombo 2.4 (1969): 29, 33.

"Delta Journey"
Nkombo 3.1 (1971): 41-42.

"For Walter Washington:"
"Ray Charles at Mississippi State"
"A Message for Langston"
New Black Voices. Ed. Abraham Chapman. New York: New American Library, 1972. 372-373, 373-374, 380-381.

"Garvey"
Black Culture: Reading and Writing Black. Ed. Gloria M. Simmons and Helene D. Hutchinson. New York: Holt, Rinehart and Winston, 1972. 233.

"For Brother Lawrence Sly on His Wedding Day."
Nkombo N9 (1974): 58.

"Magnolia Street"
Black World 23.11 (1974): 63.

"For Lil Louis"
Black World 24.11 (1975): 64-65.

"For the Southern University in New Orleans Students Arrested Attempting to Raise the Blk Flag of Liberation."
South and West 14.2 (1977): 14.

"Ships Horns Sound"
Black River Journal (Summer 1977): 24.

"Mississippi Mornings'"
"The Blue Light"
"On Dreams and Mexican Songs"
Black American Literature Forum 11.4 (1977): 154.
"Running & Dipping Poem No. 1"
"St. Thomas Island"
Nimrod 21.2/22.1 (1977): 63, 68.

"Return to English Turn"
Callaloo #4 (October 1978): 10-14.

"Secret Messages"
The American Rag 1.1 (1978): 70.

"Viewing Robeson's Body"
South and West 15.2-3 (1976/1979): 13.

"Magnolia Street"
"Secret Messages"
Maple Leaf Rag: An Anthology of New Orleans Poetry.
New Orleans: The New Orleans Poetry Journal Press, 1980. 30-33.

"A Message for Langston"
"Coltrane's Alabama"
"Mississippi Mornings"
"Ray Charles at Mississippi State"
"The Seventies: A Poem for Blacks of the Sixties"
Jackson Advocate. March 4-10, 1982, p. 3B.

"The Seventies: A Poem for Blacks of the Sixties"
"Slipping Through the City"
Each Other's Dreams. Ed. L. E. Scott. Hamilton, New Zealand:
Outrigger Publishers, 1982. 16-21.

"Easter Night"
Black River Journal: 9. Special section of the *New Orleans Jazz &*
Heritage Festival Program Book. 1988.

"The Blue Light"
"Running & Dipping Poem No. 1"
"For Kgositsile"
A Milestone Sampler: 15th Anniversary Anthology. Ed. Naomi
Long Madgett. Detroit: Lotus Press, 1988. 29-33.

III. FICTION

"The Death of Martin Luther King." *Nkombo* 1 (1966): n.p.

"Inner Peace: For Slow Drag Pavageau." *Nkombo* N9 (June 1974): 38-40.

"No. 6." *Hoo-Doo* #III (1975): n.p.

"A Radio for Jim." *OBSIDIAN* 4.2 (1978): 37-48.

"Inner Peace." *Pacific Quarterly Moana* 4.2 (1979): 64-68.

"The Subway." *Pacific Quarterly Moana* 5.2 (1980): 119-127.

"Sun Story." *Callaloo* 3.1-3 (1980): 9-14.

IV. DRAMA

PUBLISHED DRAMA

Snapshot. *Nkombo* 2.4 (1969): 85-90.

Song of Survival. *Nkombo* 2.4 (1969): 91 -96.
Co-authored with Val Ferdinand (Kalamu ya Salaam).

Inner Blk Blues (A poem/play for black bros. & sisters). *Nkombo* N8 (August 1972): 26-42.

Ritual Murder. *Callaloo* #2 (February 1978): 67-81. Play written 1967, FST; produced Fall 1967.

UNPUBLISHED DRAMA

Negro Study No. 34A. 1969.

Riot Duty. 1969. FST, Winter 1969.

Feathers and Stuff. 1970. FST Workshop.

V. ARTICLES AND ESSAYS

"Strange Bedfellows." *On Guard* 1.1 (February 1961): 2.

"Portrait of Three Heroes." *Freedomways* 5 (Spring 1965): 250-262.

"The Free Southern Theater: An Evaluation." *Freedomways* 6 (Winter 1966): 26-30. Reprinted in *Anthology of the American Negro in the Theater.* Ed. Lindsay Patterson. New York: Publishers Co., 1969. 117-119.

"Blues for the Negro College." *Freedomways* 8.4 (1968): 385-394. Also published in 1968 as a mimeographed FST pamphlet under the title *Blues for the Negro College or Should I Ask You What Your Name Is?*

"The Free Southern Theater." *Negro Digest* 16.6 (1967): 40-44.

"Black Theater in America: New Orleans." *Negro Digest* 18.6 (1969): 24-26.

"Beyond Rhetoric Toward a Black Southern Theater." *Black World* 20.6 (1971): 14-24.

"Tribute to Paul Robeson." *Freedomways* 11.1 (1971): 11-14.

"Embattled Education." *The Black Collegian* 2.1(1971): 24.
"The Great White Hope." *Colloquy* 4.10 (1971): 44.

"A Spirit in the Dark: New Black Cultural Groups in the South." *The Black Collegian* 2.3 (1972): 20-21, 42.

"Black Culture: New Theatre, Poetry Reveal Black Identity." *South Today* 3 (Jan/Feb 1972): 3.

"Black Theater in America: New Orleans—New Theater in the South Join Hands." *Black World* 22.6 (1973): 92-95.

"Black Theater in the South: Report and Reflections." *Freedomways* 14.3 (1974): 247-54.

"Arts Organizations in the Deep South: A Report." *Black Creation* 6 (Annual 1974-75): 77-78.

"Arthur Ashe and the Emergence of Black Tennis." *The Black Collegian* 7.2 (1976): 50.

"Octave Lilly, Jr.: In Memoriam." *The Crisis* 83(Aug./Sept. 1976): 243-244.

"Theater: Southern Black Cultural Alliance Festival." *First World* 1.2 (1977): 42-43.

"Design for Claiborne Avenue." *Black River Journal* (Summer 1977): 10-11.

"Octave Lilly, Jr. In Memoriam." *Black River Journal* (Summer 1977): 11.

"New Orleans, Atlanta & Politics: Some Thoughts." *Black River Journal* (Summer 1977): 5.

"Sam Cook & Academic Excellence at Dillard." *Black River Journal* (Summer 1977): 9.

"Tribute to Paul Robeson." *Paul Robeson: The Great Forerunner.* Editors of *Freedomways*. New York: Dodd, Mead, 1978. 280-283. "1978 Howard Writers Conference and SBCA." *Callaloo* #4 (October 1978): 161-163.

"New Orleans Versus Atlanta." *Southern Exposure* 7.1 (1979): 64-68.

"Black Theater in the South: Report and Reflections." *The Theater of Black Americans*. Vol. II. Ed. Errol Hill. Englewood Cliffs, NJ: Prentice-Hall, 1980. 63-71.

"Listening for Longhair." New Orleans Jazz & Heritage Festival *Program Book.* 1980. 8-10.

"The Third Hoo-Doo Poetry and Culture Festival and Bookfair." *The Black Scholar* 11.4 (1980): 88-89.

"Umbra Days." *Black American Literature Forum* 14.3 (1980): 105-108.

"Marcus B. Christian: An Appreciation." *Perspectives on Ethnicity in New Orleans*. Ed. John Cooke. New Orleans: The Committee on Ethnicity in New Orleans, 1980. 2-6.

"Race for the '80's." *Southern Exposure* 8.4 (1980): 29.

"Annie Devine Remembers." *Freedomways* 22.2 (1982): 81-92.

"A Critical Look at Mardi Gras." *Jackson Advocate*, February 18-24, 1982, pp. 1B, 8B.

"Annie Devine, Canton and a Quality of Committment (sic)." *Jackson Advocate*, February 25-March 3, 1982, pp. 1-2B, 7B.

"Strong Spirits in the Carolina Low Country." *Jackson Advocate*, July 14-22, 1982, p. 2A; July 23-28, 1982, pp. 3A, 8A.

"5th Annual Delta Blues Festival." *Jackson Advocate*, November 11-17, 1982, p. 8A.

"A Perspective on the March on Washington 1983." *Jackson Advocate*, September 15-21, 1983, p. 4A.

"Opelousas Holds First Zydeco Festival in Heart of Louisiana Cajun Country." *Jackson Advocate*, September 22-28, 1983, p. 1B.

"Autobiography, History and Black Literature." *SAGALA* No. 4 (1984): 38-42.

"The Martin I Remember: An Oral History." *The Black Collegian* 14.3 (1984): 60-61, 64-65.

"Marcus B. Christian: A Reminiscence and an Appreciation." *Black American Literature Forum* 18.1(1984): 22-26.

"Racial Equality." *Jackson Advocate.* January 16-22, 1986, p. 4A.
"St. Joseph's Day Celebrations or the Origins of Super Sunday." *The New Orleans Tribune* 2.3 (1986): 14-15.

"African Notes: Goree Island." *Jackson Advocate*, March 17-25, 1988, p. 2A.

"A Memoir of Mardi Gras, 1968." *Black River Journal*: 14, 16. Special section of the *New Orleans Jazz & Heritage Festival Program Book.* 1988.

"African Notes." *Catalyst* #4 (Summer 1988): 10-11.

VI. REVIEWS

"Some Facts—No Revelations." Rev. of *Negro Politics* by James Q. Wilson. *Freedomways* 6.3 (1966): 270-271.

"Once More, Without Feeling." Rev. of *Go Up For Glory* by Bill Russell. *Freedomways* 6.4 (1966): 385-386.

"You Can See It, You Can Feel It." Rev. of *De Mayor of Harlem* by David Henderson. *Freedomways* 12.4 (1972): 343-345.

"The Hidden Poet." Rev. of *Cathedral in the Ghetto and Other Poems* by Octave Lilly, Jr. *Freedomways* 12.4 (1972): 345-346.

Rev. of *Black New Orleans, 1860-1880* by John Blassingame. *Freedomways* 15.1 (1975): 57-59.

"New Books of Poetry from the Deep South." *Callaloo* #1 (1976): 66. Annotated checklist of ten books.

"Interviews with Civil Rights Activists." Rev. of *My Soul Is Rested* by Howell Raines. *Freedomways* 18.2 (1978): 164-169.

"Alternative Literatures of Afro-Americans." Rev. of *The Third World Writer* by Peter Nazareth, *Revolutionary Love* by Kalamu ya Salaam, and *Born Into a Felony* edited by Stewart Brisby and Walt Sheppard. *Freedomways* 19.2 (1979): 103-106.

"A Voice from a Tumultuous Time." Rev. of *Medicine Man* by Calvin Hernton. *OBSIDIAN* 6.1-2 (1980): 244-250.

"Two Collections of Unusual Strength." Rev. of *Snake-Back Solos* by Quincy Troupe and *Chances Are Few* by Lorenzo Thomas. *Freedomways* 20.2 (1980): 104-107A.

"A Collection of Poems." *Jackson Advocate*, September 2-8, 1982, p. 3A.

"New from Lotus Press." Rev. of *Exits and Entrances* by Naomi Long Madget, *Lock This Man Up* by David L. Rice, *The Antioch-Suite Jazz* by Abba Elethea (James W. Thompson), and *Season of Hunger/Cry of Rain* by E. Ethelbert Miller. *Freedomways* 23.1 (1983): 42-49.

"Plantation University." Rev. of *Exit 13* by Monte Piliawsky. *Southern Exposure* 11 (Sept/Oct 1983): 67-68.
"Hell in Vietnam." Rev. of *Bloods: An Oral History of the Vietnam War* by Wallace Terry. *Freedomways* 25.1 (1985): 53-55. Also in *Jackson Advocate*, February 28-March 6, 1985, p. 9A.

"A Life in Jazz." Rev. of *A Life in Jazz* by Danny Barker. *Jackson Advocate*, December 18-24, 1986, p. 1B.

Rev. of *Wolf Tracks* by Walter "Wolfman" Washington and *Glazed* by Earl King & Roomful of Blues. *Living Blues* No. 74 (1987): 42.

Rev. of *South Louisiana: New and Selected Poems* by Alvin Aubert. *Black American Literature Forum* 22.1 (1988): 127-129.

VII. EDITOR

Umbra. Vol. 1, No. 1 and Vol. 1, No. 2 (1963).

The Free Southern Theater by the Free Southern Theater. Indianapolis: Bobbs-Merrill, 1969. With Gilbert Moses and Richard Schechner.

"Umbra Poets, 1980." *BALF* 14.3 (1980): 109-114.

Southern Black Cultural Newsletter. Vol. I, No. 1 (November 1980) and Vol. II, No. 1 (May 1981).

VIII. PERIODICAL INTRODUCTIONS/ MISCELLANEOUS

"Foreword." *Umbra* 1.1 (1963): 1-2.

"A Word About the Material in Gumbo/Nkombo II." *Nkombo*, Vol. II, Issue 1 (March 1969): 3.

"From the Kitchen." *Nkombo* 2.3 (1969): 2-3.

"From the Kitchen." *Nkombo* 2.4 (1969): 2.

"From the Kitchen." *Nkombo* 3.1 (1971): 2-3.

"From the Kitchen." *Nkombo* 3.2 (1971): 2.

"From the Kitchen." *Nkombo* N8 (August 1972), n. p.

"From the Kitchen/For the Last Time." *Nkombo* N9 (June 1974): 2-3.

"Preface." *Callaloo* #1 (December 1976): v-vi.
[Dent also wrote "Update on SBCA Member Groups - 11/76," pp. 53-54, for this issue]

"Liner Notes." The Dirty Dozen Brass Band. *My Feet Can't Fail Me Now*. GW-3005-C. 1984.

IX. CO-AUTHORED WORKS

With Keorapetse Kgositsile. "Interview with Octave Lilly, Jr." *Nkombo* N9 (June 1974): 27-36.

With Andrew Young. "Can One Man Make A Difference." *The Black Collegian* 7.4 (March-April 1977): 40, 42-43.

With Jerry W. Ward, Jr. "After the Free Southern Theater: A Dialog." *TDR* 31.3 (1987): 120-125.

ACKNOWLEDGEMENTS

New Orleans Griot, as a collection of writings, owes its existence to a coterie of Tom's supporters. Upon his death, that group, which was chiefly responsible for preparing Tom's life's work for deposit at the Amistad Research Center, included Quo Vadis Gex Breaux and Raymond Breaux, Jerry Ward, Lolis Eric Elie, and Tom's brothers, Walter and Benjamin. This team was augmented by a staff of friends and colleagues at Amistad, including Dr. Kara Tucina Olidge, Executive Director, and Christopher Harter, Director of Library and Reference Services. The Amistad crew was led by Brenda B. Square, and consisted of Wayne Coleman, Rebeca Hankins, and Shannon Burrell. Like midwives, who too often go unsung, this cohort ensured that Tom Dent's oeuvre is preserved and properly catalogued at Amistad, which is currently located on the campus of Tulane University in New Orleans, and which previously had a long residence at Dillard University, also in New Orleans.

The UNO Press staff was also instrumental in bringing this collection to life. Thomas Price undertook arduous corrections of the text, which was copyedited by Katie Pfalzgraff, Matt Knutson, and Ann Hackett. Alex Dimeff was the graphic designer for the layout of the book and Kevin Stone designed the cover. Chelsey Shannon edited the introductions and spent hours verifying Tom's text at Amistad.

Were it not for the aforementioned people, this book could not have been assembled. Fortunately, Tom's friends and cultural colleagues understood the importance of preserving Tom's letters, taped interviews, notebooks, photographs, and library, as well as other memorabilia and paraphernalia, in addition to Tom's published and unpublished literary work.

For a variety of reasons, much of the historical record of black American life and culture has been either lost or under-documented. This neglect of the preservation, curation, and study of black cultural work is systemic on a national level, and particularly pernicious in the South. Not only are black Americans barred from the full history of our accomplishments; in far too many cases, we are led to believe that we've made no significant contributions to the country in general, or American art and culture in particular. Especially in the Deep South, where the majority of blacks live, the history, life events, thoughts and feelings of black creatives are seldom afforded the attention they deserve. *New Orleans Griot* is thus a rectifying cultural testimony that we are proud to present to the world.